Current Trends in European Second Language Acquisition Research

Multilingual Matters

Age in Second Language Acquisition
  BIRGIT HARLEY
Bilingualism and the Individual
  A. HOLMEN, E. HANSEN, J. GIMBEL and J. JØRGENSEN (eds)
Bilingualism in Society and School
  J. JØRGENSEN, E. HANSEN, A. HOLMEN and J. GIMBEL (eds)
Bilingualism and Special Education
  JIM CUMMINS
Bilingualism: Basic Principles
  HUGO BAETENS BEARDSMORE
Code-Mixing and Code Choice
  JOHN GIBBONS
Cultural Studies in Foreign Language Education
  MICHAEL BYRAM
The Education of Linguistic and Cultural Minorities in the OECD Countries
  STACY CHURCHILL
Introspection in Second Language Research
  C. FAERCH and G. KASPER (eds)
Key Issues in Bilingualism and Bilingual Education
  COLIN BAKER
Language Acquisition: The Age Factor
  D. M. SINGLETON
Language in a Black Community
  VIV EDWARDS
Language and Education in Multilingual Settings
  BERNARD SPOLSKY (ed.)
Learner Language and Language Learning
  C. FAERCH, K. HAASTRUP and R. PHILLIPSON
Methods in Dialectology
  ALAN R. THOMAS (ed.)
Minority Education: From Shame to Struggle
  T. SKUTNABB-KANGAS and J. CUMMINS (eds)
Minority Education and Ethnic Survival
  MICHAEL BYRAM
Modelling and Assessing Second Language Acquisition
  K. HYLTENSTAM and M. PIENEMANN (eds)
Oral Language Across the Curriculum
  DAVID CORSON
Raising Children Bilingually: The Pre-School Years
  LENORE ARNBERG
The Role of the First Language in Second Language Learning
  HÅKAN RINGBOM
Schooling in a Plural Canada
  JOHN R. MALLEA
Variation in Second Language Acquisition
  SUSAN GASS, CAROLYN MADDEN, DENNIS PRESTON and LARRY SELINKER
  (eds)

Please contact us for the latest book information:
Multilingual Matters, Bank House, 8a Hill Road,
Clevedon, Avon BS21 7HH, England.

MULTILINGUAL MATTERS 51
Series Editor: Derrick Sharp

Current Trends in European Second Language Acquisition Research

Edited by
Hans W. Dechert

MULTILINGUAL MATTERS LTD
Clevedon · Philadelphia

Library of Congress Cataloging-in-Publication Data
Current trends in European second language acquisition research /
edited by Hans W. Dechert.
p. cm.—(Multilingual matters : 51)
Papers originating from a workshop held July 27–28 1985 at
Georgetown University in conjunction with the 1985 LSA/TESOL Summer
Institute.
  Includes bibliographies and indexes.
  1. Second language acquisition—Congresses. 2. Language and
languages—Study and teaching—Europe—Congresses. I. Dechert,
Hans W. (Hans-Wilhelm) II. LSA/TESOL Institute (1985 : Georgetown
University) III. Linguistic Society of America. IV. Teachers of
English to Speakers of Other Languages. V. Series: Multilingual
matters (Series) : 51.
P118.2.C87 1989
428'.007—dc19   88-25207

British Library Cataloguing in Publication Data
Current trends in European second language
  acquisition research—(Multilingual
  matters; 51)
  1. Foreign language skills. Acquisition.
Research.
  I. Dechert, Hans W.
  401'.9

  ISBN 1-85359-024-X
  ISBN 1-85359-023-1 Pbk

Multilingual Matters Ltd

Bank House, 8a Hill Road   &   1900 Frost Road, Suite 101
Clevedon, Avon BS21 7HH   Bristol, PA 19007
England   U.S.A.

Index compiled by Meg Davies (Society of Indexers)
Typeset by Photo·Graphics, Honiton, Devon
Printed and bound in Great Britain by WBC Print, Bristol

Contents

Preface

This volume is the result of the common efforts of many more people involved in SLA research than those whose contributions it collects.

In a letter of May 25th 1984 Deborah Tannen, the Director of the 1985 LSA/TESOL Summer Institute asked me whether I'd like to organise 'some sort of a symposium linking linguistics to teaching ESL . . .' on the occasion of the 1985 Summer Institute. My immediate answer was that this seemed to be a challenging suggestion. Yet I was careful enough not to agree immediately as I realised that organising such a workshop in a year's time would create many problems among which the task of raising funds was not the easiest one. During the following months I contacted many individuals as well as institutions and asked them for their assistance. All in all, there was an overwhelmingly positive reaction to the idea of the Georgetown Workshop so that I finally came to the conclusion that I might as well say 'yes'! In a letter of August 22nd 1984 Professor Tannen officially invited me to organise 'a special workshop on the topic "Current Trends in European Second Language Acquisition Research" to take place July 27th and 28th in conjunction with the 1985 Institute of the Linguistic Society of America and the Teachers of English to Speakers of Other Languages, to be held jointly on the campus of Georgetown University the summer of 1985.' She further stated in the same letter 'I believe there is a great need to bring to the awareness of the American and International linguistics and TESOL communities, the important work being done by European researchers in this field.'

'European Second Language Acquisition Research', the second part of the Workshop's topic and this volume's title is, of course, an overextension. I am fully aware of it. There is not such a thing as a unified SLA research tradition in Europe. Even if there was, the many constraints imposed on the Workshop — personal, organisational, temporal, and last but not least financial ones, only permitted me to ask some scholars from some countries to present and discuss some of their ideas. All of us at the Workshop realised that we could not claim to give more than a glimpse into the enormous richness and variety in European SLA research. Actually, the experience that there exists such a diversified research tradition in Europe of which we were just a part is perhaps one of the most intriguing results of our meeting. All this is meant with the phrase 'Current Trends', the first part of the topic of the Workshop and the title of the following pages. To be sure, because of the organisational restrictions and difficulties alluded to above various European cultures and languages, and thus research traditions, are overrepresented in this volume; others are underrepresented, or not represented at all. There is, for instance, a severely felt lack of contributions dealing with Eastern European research. Nevertheless, the decision to meet at Georgetown and discuss our research activities with the participants of the Summer Institute in spite of these limitations has proved to be an extremely rewarding one. To my knowledge it has been the first Workshop of that sort and of that size ever to take place in the United States.

Some of the articles collected in this volume are identical or almost identical with the papers read at the Workshop. Most of them, however, represent modified versions written afterwards in light of the discussions during the Workshop.

For me collecting, reading, and editing them has been an exciting experience, firstly because of the remarkable variety of methodologies approaching the problem of SLA, and secondly because of the conceptual and cultural differences surfacing through them. Editing such a collection in the course of time has proved to be a rather complicated task. This is to say that many portions of this volume have undergone various stages of modification during the last two years. I have been fortunate enough to have had my graduate student assistants Silke Baier, Bärbel Treichel, and Brigitte Schwarz patiently reading and rereading the various versions during the 'growth' of the final manuscript, thus sharing with me their knowledge in APA standards. This procedure could only be practised with the kind help of M. Burba, B. Carl-Mast, and C. Kuchta, the secretaries in the Department of English and Romance Languages and Literatures of the University of Kassel.

I surely hope that my intention to preserve each contribution's 'flair', its particular shade of culture and wealth of thought has been realised in spite of the need to standardise it. With the exception of the two native speakers of English among us, all articles were written by learners of English as a second or foreign language. I hope that the many linguistic compromises to be found on the following pages may be acceptable for native English readers. Unfortunately this procedure has taken lots of time.

First of all I would like to thank all contributors to this volume for their patience. Secondly I wish to thank the officials of Georgetown University for giving us the opportunity to meet at this inspiring campus and participate in the various activities of the 1985 LSA/TESOL Summer Institute. In this context I am particularly grateful to Deborah Tannen for suggesting the original idea of the Workshop, and to her colleagues and the staff in the Department of Linguistics of Georgetown University who have all made our stay a very pleasant and successful one. Among them, Heidi Byrnes deserves a special word of thanks for the never-ending assistance she offered to us before and during the Workshop. John Hammer from the Linguistic Society of America did his best to activate his connections and overcome our problems in the planning and financing of the Workshop.

This Workshop would not have been possible without the grants made available to the participants from the Federal Republic of Germany by the German Research Council (Deutsche Forschungsgemeinschaft), the financial grants provided to other participants by the European Cultural Foundation in Amsterdam, and the assistance given by various national sponsors and European universities.

I finally wish to thank Multilingual Matters, our publisher, for the close cooperation and professional diligence in bringing out this volume.

Hans W. Dechert
Kassel, March 1988

Introduction

It is the object of this volume, as it has been the goal of the Georgetown Workshop, to bring to the awareness of its readers examples of the work being done in European SLA research.

When I addressed my colleagues in various European research groups and asked them to participate in the Workshop it was my primary intention that they might represent a large variety of different, even controversial, research traditions. They were asked to report on their ongoing research without being given any thematic constraints. The structuring of the Workshop was done after the individual proposals and abstracts of the papers to be read had been submitted. Eventually not all scholars who had expressed their consent to participate were able to do so. There was, in other words, a certain lack of consistency in the final thematic structure of the Workshop due to these cancellations. This is reflected in the structure of this volume which follows exactly the sequence of presentations at the Workshop. Yet it seems to me, however fragmentary it may appear, that after all this volume does represent a rich selection of topics and methodologies which are characteristic of current trends in European SLA research.

It was my second intention to introduce our audience at the Workshop as well as the readers of this volume to various established SLA research projects. For this reason the participants were asked to elaborate on these projects in their presentations. A list of these projects which are referred to on the following pages is given in the index section. It stands for a rich research tradition which, to my knowledge, has not been described in detail, nor even been fully perceived in the international SLA literature.

SLA may currently be said to be by no means adequately understood, or described, or modelled, either in Europe or anywhere else. After decades of intensive research we still do not have satisfactory answers to many important questions, even elementary ones, such as the role of the first language in SLA. SLA is, as the various implicit or explicit controversies

1

on the following pages disclose, a controversial issue. This is even more so when it comes to the problem to what ends and in what way second languages should be taught. Is, for instance, the answer to that problem really as simple as the proponents of a communication oriented approach have made us believe for many years? Or is it not evident that metalinguistic awareness develops parallel to learners' linguistic progress? Why then should not metacognition have an essential function in SLA as well?

This volume brings together research findings in restricted areas of SLA. None of the following articles would claim to cover more than a small segment of information relevant to the overall topic SLA: the acquisition of a particular second language; the acquisition process of a particular learner or group of learners; the interaction of two or more particular languages, similar or distant; the acquisition within a particular linguistic and cultural environment; the acquisition of particular linguistic phenomena or non-verbal behavioremes; the acquisition at a particular developmental stage of the total learning process; the acquisition on particular levels of cognition and description; the exemplification of a particular research approach or methodology, and so forth. The tremendous variety of such individual approaches discussed on the following pages suggests that SLA is not, and must not be seen as, a simple homogeneous process which may be easily assessed with one method or modelled in terms of one theory.

To sum up, the articles collected in this volume represent the research efforts of various European scholars and groups of scholars who have approached the complex phenomenon of acquiring different second languages from different perspectives and at different levels in the light of different paradigms. It is my hope that the articles will contribute to the international discussion across languages, research traditions, and cultural constraints. For centuries Europe has been a place of continuous contact and interaction of languages and cultures. It is an excellent field for the study of SLA.

Part One, *Theory and Methodology in Second Language Acquisition Research*, comprises four contributions by two Scandinavian and two German researchers. They elaborate on the notions of *lexicon* (Dietrich), *typological markedness* (Hyltenstam), *automaticity* (Lehtonen), and *competition* (Dechert) as basic theoretical concepts in the discussion of L2 production, and reaction time data.

Rainer Dietrich discusses in his article *Nouns and Verbs in the Learner's Lexicon* the order of acquiring nouns and verbs in first and second language acquisition and raises the issue of a theoretical explanation for such order in terms of children's as well as adults' cognitive development. The data collected within the framework of the European Science Foundation project comprise the oral reproduction of a film by three early adult learners of German, two Italians and a Turk. R. Dietrich presents the first results of his pilot analysis of these data, the early individual repertoire of his informants, the proportion of different categories, and the individual rate of growth in the subjects' lexicon.

These results demonstrate that beginning adult L2 learners, like children, in their reproduction of a film pick up more nominal referential items than predicative ones. The use of verbs increases in later stages of L2 acquisition. The noun–verb ratio in early adults' narrative reproduction may be interpreted as a reflection of more fundamental properties of complex verbal behaviour.

Kenneth Hyltenstam in his article *Typological Markedness as a Research Tool in the Study of Second Language Acquisition* bases his arguments on the concept of linguistic markedness, which has been employed in various SLA studies in order to assess what L2 features are acquired at what stage of development or what L2 features are easy or difficult to acquire. K. Hyltenstam argues (a) that the notion of typological markedness is valuable in the hypothesis formation phase of SLA research, (b) that it cannot be considered a satisfactory explanatory concept, and (c) that, however, SLA data contribute to a general theory of markedness and, generally speaking, to a theory of language. He expands his theoretical discussion of markedness through empirical data taken from two studies on the use of different aspects of Swedish (a) in the treatment of pronominal copies in Swedish relative clauses by adult learners of Swedish with a Finnish, Greek, Persian, and Spanish L1-background, and (b) in the treatment of voicing in stops by child and adult learners of Swedish with Finnish as their primary language.

Jaakko Lehtonen proposes reaction time measurement as a valuable empirical research instrument in his article *Foreign Language Acquisition and the Development of Automaticity*. He sets out with a discussion of the development of second language procedural knowledge in the light of two experiments (a) one with Finnish university students at the University of Jyväskylä learning English, or German, or Swedish, and (b) with German university students at the University of Kassel learning English, or French, or Spanish. He focuses his analysis of the data on the development and degree of automaticity as found through the measurement of differences in the Reaction Time (RT) latencies of his subjects, tested in various linguistic decision tasks on the acceptability of visually presented correct/incorrect L2 sentences.

Automatised second language perception and production processes are typical of competent linguistic behaviour. According to Andersen, there may be five stages in the development of such automaticity: unconscious incompetence, conscious incompetence, conscious competence, unconscious competence. This fourth stage seems to be the final goal of the ideal second language learner, whereas the fifth stage, conscious supercompetence, might only characterise peak performance and knowledge. Decision times are likely to indicate the degrees of automaticity; the faster the reaction time, the higher the level of automaticity. RT-measurement promises to provide an extremely valuable tool in SLA research methodology.

Hans Dechert in his article *Competing Plans in Second Language Processing* presents five cases of blending to be taken as indications of an underlying competition of plans. Competition is held to characterise the human information processing system in general. Second language processing, in other words, is seen as being determined by general system characteristics which may be found in other types of system output as well. Examples of such system characteristics are the high flexibility at the periphery and a potential lack of central control under task stress conditions. In an introductory passage the famous case of the collision of two jet planes on the Island of Tenerife in 1977 is interpreted as a striking behavioural example of the competition of plans in the decision processes of one of the pilots. The following linguistic samples are all taken from the Kassel corpus of second language production data. The first one reveals a case of blending of an advanced learner of English in the oral production of an L2 frozen binomial. The second linguistic example on the sentence level is taken from a narrative oral production of a native speaker of English. Blends as indications of competition are found in the oral productions of native and non-native speakers. The third sample is a case of written production of an advanced adult German learner of English on the collocation level. Blends, thus, are found in oral as well as written language productions. In the concluding portion an intentional blend found in an article from the *Wall Street Journal* gives an example of blending for stylistic and argumentative reasons. Blends occur unintentionally as well as intentionally. For a psycho-linguistics of language processing blends give immediate access to the mechanisms of information processing which is very likely to be a parallel, distributed, and competitive system.

The Second Part, *Children's First and Second Language Acquisition*, contains articles by an English, Italian, German, and French author. In all four reports the informants' second language acquisition is related to their first language development. They all deal, one way or the other, with

projects on the teaching of second languages in tutored pre-school and
school contexts.

Peter Skehan's contribution to the topic SLA, *The Relationship Between
Native and Foreign Language Learning Ability: Educational and Linguistic
Factors*, stands in an empirical research tradition that has called particular
attention to language learning ability of the learner and the individual
differences or learner types which are responsible for variation in language
achievement. His own project which is a follow-up study of the well-known
Bristol Language Project by Gordon Wells is situated in the tradition of
foreign language aptitude measuring. It attempts to relate three sets of
variables (a) the measure of first language acquisition, (b) the measure of
foreign language acquisition, and (c) the measure of foreign language
achievement. Each of these variables and the respective tests are described
in detail.

Since P. Skehan's report is closely related with the Bristol Project, an
extensive review of the methodology (the test instruments) and its results
follows. A preliminary outline of the first results of his own study concerning
(a) the first language–foreign language aptitude relationship, (b) the foreign
language aptitude–foreign language achievement correlations, and (c) the
first language development–foreign language achievement correlations is
then presented, summarised and discussed.

As far as foreign language achievement is concerned, these results
suggest that first language individual differences are uncorrelated with
variations in foreign language performance. The other striking result of the
study is that learning a foreign language in school settings is likely to be
successful when the student is able to cope with literacy and to make sense
of the typical verbal classroom activities (question answering, drills,
dialogues).

Renzo Titone takes up a special case in SLA research that has been
an issue of debate in Europe for more than twenty years, *Early Bilingual
Reading: Retrospects and Prospects*. The question of the feasibility of teaching
reading in two languages simultaneously at pre-school age and the study of
factors underlying the processes of early bilingual reading has attracted the
particular interest of students of child bilingualism and SLA. Early bilingual
literacy may have positive effects upon the intellectual growth of children.

In retrospect Titone gives an extensive account of the literature on
early bilingual reading before he outlines in detail The Early Bilingual
Reading Experimental Project, its aims, its methodology, and its evaluation
instruments. This large-scale project with the author's standard materials,

The Early Bilingual Reading Kit, has been under way for several years in bilingual/multilingual (French/Italian; German/Italian) parts of Italy, and in the Basque country (Basque/Castilian).

From a methodological point of view, Werner Hüllen suggests, *Investigations Into Classroom Discourse* provide valid access to the study of SLA, as classroom discourse is more controlled and patterned than natural discourse and may be easily segmented into relatively unequivocal units. Language learning in the classroom is only a special case of communication. It must, however, be looked at in its own right. Hüllen's analyses attempt to explain classroom performance data as symptoms of processes aiming at successful communication.

In the second part of his article, Hüllen describes the results of three experiments which he and his associates have presented. The objective of the first study, devoted to learning sequences for syntactic and semantic rules, was the analysis of classroom discourse in which students were asked to remember and repeat passages from a textbook. The investigators then compared the model text with the learners' utterances. The deviations which were found were categorised like this: (a) learners preferred simpler structures; (b) learners preferred simpler words; (c) learners tended to cut down the model text into miniature texts without using proper connectors. The learners' performance was obviously based on a semantic nucleus. The second study on the speech planning of teachers investigated the use of impromptu elements (such as *yes, right, OK*, or non-verbal elements such as smiling) by teachers and students. In the sequence of teacher–student discourse in the classroom: elicitation–response–evaluation, the last sub-unit, evaluation, which also leads to the following unit, proved to be of particular interest. Impromptu elements and the intrusion of source elements in this sub-unit indicate a lack of control. L1 interference depends on the strain of the moment.

The third study aimed at the identification and quantification of the rhetorical distribution of speech acts between teacher and learner in classroom discourse. Learners' speech is uniform compared with teachers' speech and with their own everyday discourse. It is mainly up to the teacher to instigate initiative, elicitative, commenting, and evaluative speech acts.

Typical of the formal approach of teaching English to French learners in a school setting, which Danielle Bailly reports upon in her contribution *The Linguistics of Enunciative Operations and Second Language Learning* are (a) the grammatical progression and (b) an explicit conceptualisation phase. They both aim at making the learner fully aware of the functioning of language operations of location and determination. This remarkably unconventional approach is based on the Theory of Enunciative Operations (TEO) of the French linguist Antoine Culioli.

D. Bailly devotes the first introductory part of her article to the basic assumptions of TEO. She then reports on a 15-year-long teaching experiment based on TEO. Its results indicate that L2 learning in formal settings depends on two determining factors: tutoring strategies inspired by TEO linguistics positively influence learners acquiring their L2. A metalinguistic approach of language teaching that concentrates on generalisable language operations, and on the learner's interlanguage as related to these operations, influences interlanguage development itself. On the other hand, it must not be overlooked that general cognitive and linguistic mechanisms may interfere with this positive influence. In a following section of her article the author exemplifies her theoretical statements with three extracts from classroom discourse. These extracts are to illustrate the potential cognitive activities which are initiated through a TEO based teaching method. In conclusion D. Bailly develops a follow-up research design and a number of hypotheses to be tested.

Part Three of the volume takes up an issue which, among others, has been one of the central topics in the European Science Foundation Project *Reference in Second Language Acquisition*. The authors have been associated with this project for years. C. Noyau has been the coordinator of the Paris team, and D. Véronique of the Aix-en-Provence team.

Colette Noyau's study *The Development of Means for Temporality in the Unguided Acquisition of L2: Cross-Linguistic Perspectives* deals with the early informal acquisition of linguistic expressions of temporality in French as found in the oral narratives and conversations of three adult Spanish-speaking refugees (a Colombian male and two Chilean female informants) in Paris, covering a period of 18 months. The results for the language pair Spanish SL–French TL are compared with each other and with other similar language pairs from the corpus of the ESF project in order to identify recurrent stages of development among the informants across SLs and TLs.

The study proposes a three-stage procedure: (a) the description of individual learner language systems at different stages of acquisition, (b) the reconstruction of the psycholinguistic processes responsible for them, and (c) the theoretical explanation of these processes under study. Samples of the informants' speech data are presented, analysed, and discussed. The various lexico-syntactic and morphological means for temporality as well as the developmental trends in the learner data are analysed. These chapters are followed by a discussion of the influence of the conceptual structure, of the particular discursive needs, and of the source language on the organisation of discourse.

The results of the study are finally summarised: the problem of the early acquisition of TL means that conceptual domain (such as temporality) is multiple. Adult learners may rely on their knowledge of the world and thus be able to communicate with a limited TL repertoire. A concept-oriented cross-linguistic approach to the study of SLA enables us to understand at a deeper level the conceptual categories responsible for certain L2 utterances.

The aim of Daniel Véronique's article *Reference and Discourse Structure in the Learning of French by Adult Moroccans* is to investigate the extent to which the acquisition and the use of L2 expressions of reference to person, time, and space in the early stage of development of an Arabic speaking male adult learning French are discourse dependent, and conversely, how far such referential activities contribute to his discourse organisation. D. Véronique's data confirm his assumption that referential values for lexical items are contextually bound and are independent of the target system's semantic and pragmatic values of the determiners that occur in the learner system.

The author elaborates the theoretical framework for his study and reviews the relevant literature on the acquisition of reference and discourse structure in French in general. He then summarises previous work on the problem of the acquisition of reference by Moroccans, in particular, including other findings on the subject of this present article, one out of four Arabic learners of French in the European Science Foundation Project. There are features of reference and of discourse organisation that remain stable across the three oral reproductions of the same Charlie Chaplin film over the whole period of two years. The three most remarkable changes across these three versions are (a) a gradual disappearance of zero anaphora as pronominal marking on VP becomes more constant, (b) an extension of the non-personal pronominal paradigm, and (c) a change in the organisation of the narrative from monofunctional markers to more plurifunctional markers. There seems to be only minor interaction with the subject's L1. There is considerable convergence with other findings about the same subject and other subjects with a similar background.

The final Part, *Cross-linguistic Interaction in Second Language Ac-quisition*, addresses an old question in SLA research which has only recently found new interest. The three articles, based on research done in Finland, The Netherlands, and Germany, explore the mutual procedural dependence of languages and cultures in the acquisition of L2 from different angles and under different labels (*transfer*: Ringbom; *input from within*: Sharwood-Smith; *contact*: Oksaar). The cover term *cross-linguistic interaction* is meant to denote this new research trend in Europe.

Håkan Ringbom, whose work during the past ten years has to a large extent been devoted to the study of cross-linguistic interaction between Finnish, Swedish, and English among the Finnish- and Swedish-speaking population of Finland acquiring English attempts to draw an insight in the complexity of linguistic interaction. After a short discussion of the notion of transfer in SLA research he refers to a representative set of data concerning listening and reading comprehension, spelling, and the use of articles and prepositions of native and non-native learners of English with different L1 background. The analysis of these data refutes the naive expectation that Swedish-speaking Finns would do better in any test of English than an equivalent group of Finns speaking Finnish, a distant language. In fact, there are striking differences in the learners' trial to make use of their primary linguistic knowledge when comprehending or producing L2 utterances, or learning isolated items versus complex relationships between items, or being beginning or advanced learners.

What this contribution makes perfectly clear is that transfer between languages in the learner does take place. However, only an intensive study of the various levels, areas and mechanisms of that interaction in various languages will prevent us from premature conclusions about cross-linguistic influence, as a simplistic contrastive analysis may suggest.

Michael Sharwood Smith in his paper describes the theoretical and institutional framework of the SLA research being done in the Department of English, University of Utrecht, The Netherlands. Part of this research is undertaken to meet the needs of faculty and students through an assessment of cross-linguistic influence in the light of the competence-control distinction.

Sharwood Smith discusses the notions of cross-linguistic influence as well as transfer and interference which have a fundamental role in the project. A learner who has L2 competence will use his or her L1 in order to communicate in cases of insufficient control over his L2. Cross-linguistic influence in this case is the result of a control strategy. Cross-linguistic influence at the competence level, on the contrary, may be seen as input-from-within. Data concerning (a) the adverbial placement, (b) sentential complementation, and (c) proposition stranding of Dutch, Finnish, French, German, Polish, and Spanish learners of English illustrate this line of argumentation.

Quite in accordance with H. Ringbom's statements, Sharwood Smith concludes his paper with the assertion that cross-linguistic interaction is a highly complex phenomenon. What is needed, therefore, are more research and a more powerful explanatory theory.

The concluding contribution of Part Four, *Language Contact and Culture Contact: Towards an Integrative Approach in Second Language Acquisition Research* by Els Oksaar, based on her two long-term research projects at the University of Hamburg, seeks to expand the object of SLA research: since a particular language is embedded in a particular culture, an approach that integrates language and culture as well as language contact and language acquisition is necessary. Language is (a) accompanied by paralinguistic elements whose role differs between different cultural systems. Language is (b) connected with non-verbal and extraverbal signals. An integrative approach starts from the principle of the part–whole relationship in language and culture.

Sociocultural behaviour is systematised in the cultureme model. Culturemes are enacted through behavioremes which may be verbal, paralinguistic and/or non-verbal, and/or extraverbal. Verbal, non-verbal and extraverbal behavioremes vary considerably from culture to culture. Deviations from culturally determined norms may lead to misunderstand-ings in intra- and interlinguistic contact situations and create linguistic and situational interference. On the basis of the existing situational norms a speaker/hearer is expected to behave in a certain way according to the sociocultural group he or she belongs to. Second language acquisition must be considered as an integral part of a larger entity — a culture. We need an integrative approach in SLA research that investigates linguistic and cultural phenomena, an approach in which the individual is seen in contact with the new language and the new culture.

Part 1
Theory and Methodology in Second Language Acquisition Research

1 Nouns and Verbs in the Learner's Lexicon

RAINER DIETRICH

In her contribution to Kuczaj's volume on *Language, Cognition and Culture* (1982) Gentner presents a collection of observations on child language development which, apart from a lot of differences in detail, have one structural feature in common: that is, that nouns are learned before verbs. Evidence is given for both production and comprehension and for languages as different as Turkish, English, German, Japanese, Mandarin Chinese, and Kaluli. It is, of course, clear that *noun* and *verb* in this context do not refer to distributionally defined surface categories. What is meant by them is the dichotomy 'between object reference and predication; whether the predication is of states, actions, relationships or attributes is a secondary question. The corresponding syntactic contrast is between the category of nouns and the composite predicate category composed of verbs, prepositions, adjectives and adverbs' (Gentner, 1982: 302).

One may ask what the reasons for this are. Why do children obviously prefer nominal over verbal material when they start to learn a language? Gentner's explanation goes back to the psychology of perception and her fundamental reasoning is as follows: as a part of the perceptual world objects are composed of perceptive bits which are more salient, more concrete, more stable and, which is the most relevant fact, more cohesive in terms of spatial properties than processes, properties and relations. As a consequence of this, concepts of objects are more cohesive, too, than those of predicates, the perceptual elements of which are 'more sparsely distributed through the perceptual field' (Gentner, 1982: 324).

The fact that the concepts of objects have these perception-based properties of saliency, stability, and cohesiveness then makes it easier for the child to match this part of his or her knowledge with the stream of linguistic input. And therefore nouns are learned before verbs, although the linguistic properties of the material involved, such as relative frequency, morphological complexity, or word order phenomena would not necessarily cause us to expect it. So far then, there is unambiguous, universal and convincing evidence that in the very early stages of language acquisition the child makes selections from among the linguistic input he or she is exposed to, and first picks up the nominal, referential material instead of verbs, adjectives, adverbs, and prepositions. There is, secondly, a perception-based psychological theory to account for these observations, which claims that nouns are easier for the child to take in because of the perceptual constancy of objects and the corresponding concepts in the child's mind. Although this theory sounds plausible and reasonable, it is in fact no more than a theoretical consideration and allows for alternative hypotheses as well, such as linguistic and sociolinguistic ones.

The simultaneous development of cognitive and linguistic capacities has particular relevance in the psychological theory of nominal dominance. A control of the influence of the perceptual and cognitive structures and processes would be possible if there were subjects facing the same language acquisition problem without the additional complication of cognitive development. If there were an adult person with completely developed conceptual knowledge of the world, and that person had to acquire a new language without formal teaching but just like a child simply by exposure to the natural language environment, that would make it possible to control the influence of perception and cognition versus alternative factors. And such a situation is given in millions of cases in the second language acquisition of adult immigrants. What then would one expect to occur in natural second language acquisition of adults? Let us first recollect from Gentner's argumentation the main processes performed by the child's mind which seem to oversimplify the case:

1. Perception of the real world, which presents to the child a natural partition favouring things and objects over processes, states, properties, and relations.
2. The formation of concepts along the lines of the perceptual world.
3. The linguistic coding, that is (a) breaking down the stream of utterances and (b) bringing into correspondence with each other conceptual and linguistic elements.

What now, when an adult person faces a second language and begins to acquire that language in a natural untutored way, that is, by using it in communicative interaction? There are differences in many if not all parameters between the child's mental and linguistic abilities and that of an adult learner of language two.

— The adult person — to begin at the end — has built up a rich and detailed lexicon as part of his or her first language.

— He or she has developed a system of concepts containing items which represent the world of objects as well as other ones which refer to processes, relations, and the other predicative categories.

— He or she is familiar with the fact that there are concrete, salient, and spatially related perceptive bits in the world which together form an object, and more abstract and sparsely distributed perceptive bits which in different ways of conflation and combination constitute a process, a state, or a relation. In short: he or she is trained to perceive the world around him or her in terms of his or her conceptual knowledge which is more or less determined by his or her language. How would one expect, then, the adult second language learner to process the lexical material of the foreign language? Since there is no longer the problem of making sense of the perceptual world, no need for simultaneous concept formation along with the semantic learning, one would expect the growth of the L2-lexicon to be determined by the communicative needs of the learner, the linguistic parameters of L2, and the structure of the learner's L1-background. If all this determined the strategy of acquiring the vocabulary of the second language one would expect the L2-lexicon to comprise nouns as well as verbs, auxiliaries, and prepositions from the onset, and, for reasons of input frequency in German, the definite and indefinite articles. And one would predict cross-linguistic differences, when people with different L1-backgrounds learn the same foreign language. Whether this reasoning is adequate or not is one of the topics of the European research project on second language acquisition of adult immigrants sponsored by the European Science Foundation in Strasbourg. Before we look at the observations available so far, some more background information on the project as a whole should be presented for better understanding.[1]

As far as second language studies are concerned, there are at least four aspects of this project which, to our knowledge, go beyond previous related research. Firstly, the number of languages — both source and target — which are simultaneously studied; secondly, the attempt to carry out a coordinated longitudinal study (over a period of $2\frac{1}{2}$ years) in these different language environments; thirdly, the range and type of linguistic phenomena whose acquisition is investigated; and finally, the attempt to relate these multiple skills to each other and to various nonlinguistic factors which may determine their acquisition. The project is a comparative study in five European countries: France, Germany, Great Britain, the Netherlands, and Sweden with the corresponding target languages French, German, English, Dutch, and Swedish. Six source languages are taken into account: Arabic, Finnish, Italian, Punjabi, Spanish, and Turkish. The project will run over six years with a staff of about 30 researchers.

The project has three ojectives:

1. An investigation of the psychological and social factors that can be shown to determine the structure and tempo of language acquisition.
2. A description of the structural and temporal properties of the language acquisition process, that is, establishing what communicative devices are available to adults at the onset of acquisition, what devices specific to the target language are acquired, in what order, and at what rate relative to each other.
3. An investigation of adult immigrants' use of the TL, which involves a description both of an informant's language system at a given time and of how this system is put to use in everyday interaction.

As mentioned above, the TLs are French, German, English, Dutch, and Swedish. They were chosen because they are the most important languages for immigrant workers (ranging from German with about 5.5 million potential learners to Dutch with more than half a million). For each target language two source languages were selected. The selection was essentially based on two criteria. First, those languages with the largest number of native speakers (in a given target country) should be given priority. Second, it should be possible to make linguistically interesting comparisons; this means that paired comparisons should be made of the acquisition of one target language by speakers of source languages with very different structures and of the acquisition of two TLs by speakers with the same SL. Over a period of $2\frac{1}{2}$ years, data were collected from both initial learners and — in some countries — from resident learners. Obviously, there is no ideal way to obtain all relevant data; so, a whole range of techniques was used which may be roughly subdivided into two groups: weakly prestructured free conversation and stronger prestructured planned encounters with experimental elicitation of particular second language performances. Whilst it is true that language acquisition proceeds on many different levels, it is obviously beyond the scope of this project — or any project — to study all linguistic aspects of a learner's acquisition and relate them to the explanatory factors. Four broad topics of investigation have therefore been chosen: (a) understanding, misunderstanding, breakdown of communication, (b) thematic structure of utterances, (c) reference to person, space, and time, (d) processes in the developing lexicon.

These are first results of a pilot analysis of the early L2 lexical repertoire of three initial learners. The study draws on data from a retelling of the content of a film. The informants are shown a short film clip ($2\frac{1}{2}$ minutes). It is an old silent film which shows a sequence of mishaps centred around a farewell scene at a railway station. The people involved are a young man (Harold Lloyd), his fiancée, and her parents, a woman with a baby in a wicker basket, the station master, and a group of travellers. Salient objects are the train the young man wants to catch; his suitcase; the wicker basket with the baby in it; and a horse-drawn carriage. There is, in addition, a series of events, movements, processes, and actions performed by and happening to the various persons and objects respectively. Thus, the film is suited to eliciting various kinds of references, attributes, and predications. The informant sees the film three times and then tells what happened first in German and then in his or her first language. The experiment was run three times in intervals of seven to ten months. So, we have three comparable sets of data over a period of about two years.

Table 1 shows some of the first results: the size of the individual lexical repertoires (lemma); the proportions of the different categories; and the differences between the first and second performance (t1 versus t2), that is, the individual growth rate of two Italians (Angelina, Tino), a Turkish learner (Ilhami) and, for reasons of comparison, of a German native speaker (Stefan).

At a first glance no clear-cut development or profile is shown by these figures; neither is there any observable nominal or verbal dominance in the repertoires used in the different retellings. There are developmental processes common to all the learners, and there are differences.

— All three of the learners made some progress in terms of the absolute size of the repertoire available to them at t1 versus t2.

TABLE 1. *Size of lexicons of subjects*

| | Angelina | | Tino | | Ilhami | | Stefan |
	t1	t2	t1	t2	t1	t2	
Items	27	33	28	47	35	68	185
% Nouns	40.7	45.5	28.6	23.4	34.3	23.5	25.1
% Pronouns	11.1	9.1	7.1	10.6	5.7	4.4	10.6
% Verbs	18.5	24.2	28.6	29.8	17.1	32.4	23.1
% Adjectives	3.7	6.1	–	2.1	5.7	4.4	4
% Adverbs	–	–	17.6	12.8	14.3	19.1	20
% Prepositions	14.8	9.1	7.1	6.4	5.7	5.9	11.3

— All the learners have command of items in all relevant categories from the onset with only one exception; Angelina does not use adverbs, although there was a strong stimulus in the film as is confirmed by Stefan's reaction to it. What about the verb–noun ratio, then?

Table 2 shows the numbers resulting from both performances; a value of 1 indicates equal proportions of verbs and nouns, a value below 1 indicates more nouns than verbs, a value above 1 more verbs than nouns. As the table shows, the verb–noun ratio of the German native speaker is 0.98. The learner informants, however, seem to exhibit different individual developments. Angelina's repertoire shows a strong preponderance of nouns with a slight increase of verbs. Tino starts at an almost target-like-ratio of 1, running into an overproduction of verbs at time t2, whereas Ilhami, after a start with a nominal language, also seems to counterbalance by an increase in using verbs.

TABLE 2. *Comparison of the verb-noun-ratio between t1 and t2*

	t1		t2
Angelina	0.45		0.53
Tino	1		1.27
Ilhami	0.5		1.39
Stefan		0.98	

A more detailed investigation of the individual developments, and especially the different growth rates of the three second language learners, might shed some light on the intricate situation. Table 3 presents a much more regular pattern, indeed.

Three different growth rates per subject are calculated: the overall growth rate of the repertoire as a whole and, besides this, the isolated values of the development in the verbal and nominal categories. As can easily be seen, a clear and distinct developmental pattern results from these values. Angelina with an overall growth rate of 22.2% is the slowest learner; the increase of Tino's repertoire amounts to 67.8%, and Ilhami is by far the fastest learner. The new words, however, are not equally distributed over the verbal and nominal categories. The nominal category seems to be independent of the general development; its expansion is steady and uniform for all of the three subjects. The development of the verbal repertoire, however, is completely different, but nevertheless regular according to the principle: the better the learner the higher the increase of the verbal lexicon.

TABLE 3. *Growth rates per subject*

	Items at t1	Items at t2	% growth	% growth of N	% growth of V
Angelina	27	33	22.2	36.4	60
Tino	28	47	67.8	37.5	75
Ilhami	35	68	94.2	33.3	233.3

An appropriate interpretation of these findings has to take into consideration that the values and ratios listed in the tables above are based on observations of a developing process focusing on early phases but obviously not on the earliest ones in all cases. Since knowledge of the very first phases could not be obtained by direct observation it can only be inferred from the evidence available so far. And the result of a theoretical backtracking is the fact that the very early lexicon of the adult learner, like that of the child, is a mainly nominal one. The more or less rapid development of the verbal category is a subsequent process. The overall picture, then, is the same as in first language acquisition. At the very beginning, the adult learner, like the child, picks up more referential items than predicative ones. The correctness of these theoretical assumptions is confirmed by additional analyses of a much broader data base, namely that of the cross-sectional study of the former Heidelberg Project. A sample of 3500 utterances from conversations with 40 Italian and Spanish immigrant workers was divided into two subgroups: utterances containing a verb (V) and utterances without a verb. Mean length of utterances (MLU) was calculated for both subgroups. Figure 1 shows the resulting distribution.[2] MLU is widely taken as a valid measure of relative linguistic maturity — at least as far as the early phases of acquisition and low range MLU-values are concerned. On the basis of these experiences Figure 1 presents additional convincing evidence that verbal elements mostly appear in later phases of the acquisition process than nouns.

We then might ask whether adults proceed the same way for the same reasons as children are known to do. The answer is Yes and No.

— No, because adults are no longer struggling with perceptual bits of relations and processes sparsely spread over the field of perception. Adults are familiar with perceptions of relations, processes, and states.

— No, because — as opposed to children — adults have established verbal concepts against which they can match the stream of L2-input and, thus, pick up verbal material as well as referential expressions of the second

Length of utterances

sentence type = proposition

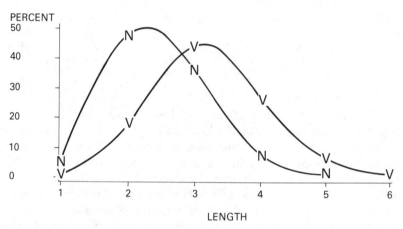

FIGURE 1. *Mean length of utterances in a cross-sectional study of the Heidelberg project*

language they are exposed to. Why, then, do adults, like children, take the referential approach to language? Imagine you were asked to tell a story like the plot of the Harold Lloyd film and you had the choice either to do the job without using a single noun or without a verb. If you try out both ways, you will realise that with a purely nominal version enough of the narrative skeleton of the story can be built up, enough at least to guarantee a minimum of comprehension.

> A guy. Harold Lloyd. Station.
> Station. Girl friend. Harold Lloyd.
> Mother. Girl friend. Father. Girl friend.
> A black lady. Station.
> Black lady. Baby.
> Baby. Floor. Suitcase. Harold Lloyd.
> Station officer. Signal. Train.
> . . .

Contrasted with this, a purely verbal text would be for instance:

Come. Has to leave.
Say 'Good bye.'
Kiss.
Come. Put down.
Take. Run.
. . .

Why can a narration be produced with nouns but not purely with verbs? There seem to exist general macrostructural rules for different kinds of complex verbal actions like narratives, orders, argumentation, and so forth. As far as narratives are concerned, some of the general requirements might be:

— First build up the stage, introduce persons, indicate place and time.

— Relate the events one after the other in indicative mode.

— Make explicitly clear when the actor changes.

— . . .

These global patterns are different for different types of complex actions. As the example above shows, there are complex actions the foreground information of which can be given by a skeleton of nominal referential expressions. Among these are narratives, orders, and commands. There are, on the other hand, patterns in which more verb-like information is required to process the foreground information, for instance the description of the rules for playing chess. The relevant information, in this case, consists of movements, relations, information as to what to do under certain constellations. The referential information is mainly supplied by the global pattern.

Considering the processes of language acquisition again, the noun–verb ratio in early adult learners' language could be a reflection of these fundamental structural properties of complex verbal actions. Angelina, then, does not manage more than the kernel information of the narration, which is reference to persons and objects. Supplementary information can in most cases be inferred from the global rules of that pattern and from the semantics of the particular nouns. Tino and Ilhami, the more advanced learners with a larger lexicon and more verbal material, can do more than only give the pure skeleton of what has happened. They refer to background information and even perform evaluations.

Besides other phenomena, the categorical features of lexical repertoires in early language acquisition strengthen the assumptions of global patterns of complex verbal actions. A learner, having only limited command of the language, automatically aims first to develop the most crucial and important parts of the lexical material of the new language. And for the first verbal activities of adult immigrants these are the nouns.

Notes to Chapter 1

1. For full description of the project compare Perdue, C., 1984, *Second Language Acquisition by Adult Immigrants: A Field Manual*. Rowley, MA: Newbury House.
2. These statistics were programmed, run and printed by Wolfram Steckner.

Reference

GENTNER, D., 1982, Why nouns are learned before verbs: linguistic relativity versus natural partitioning. In S. A. Kuczaj (ed.), *Language Development: Language Cognition and Culture*. Hillsdale, NJ: Erlbaum, 301–34.

2 Typological Markedness as a Research Tool in the Study of Second Language Acquisition

KENNETH HYLTENSTAM

Background

Research into second language acquisition has provided a growing body of observations that point to regularities in developmental sequencing, in patterns of transfer, and in the communicative use of a second language. A number of fruitful attempts have been made to reveal general principles that would predict structural regularities for various L1/L2 combinations in different settings. Discovering such principles is, of course, one central aim for a theory of second language acquisition.

The approach taken in the studies that will be presented here has its background in a development in linguistic research during the last fifteen years that involves a new cross-fertilisation of different research branches that had been investigated more or less in isolation from each other for some time. There are numerous examples of such cross-fertilisation, for example between sociolinguistic research and historical linguistics (e.g. Weinreich, Labov, & Herzog, 1968), between these two areas and pidgin and creole studies (Traugott, 1977), between pidgin and creole studies and studies of language acquisition, in particular second language acquisition (e.g. Schumann, 1978), and so forth. Not least interesting is the recent drawing together of typological research on the one hand and formal syntax on the other (Hawkins, 1983).

This tendency to relate research from one area of linguistic application to another was of course brought about by the observation that extensive similarities in structural regularities seemed to exist in the various branches.

Thus, a central task was to describe these similarities in greater detail. The more general and pervasive the similarities, the more probable the existence of common underlying principles, central to the theory of language.

As a framework in this search for similarities in linguistic structuring, *the cross-linguistic perspective* has helped researchers identify what is general and what is particular, for example in first (Slobin, 1982; Berman, 1984) and second language acquisition (e.g. Johansson, 1973), both fields where the cross-linguistic aspect has played an important role. This is where *language typology* and concepts used in this field such as language universals and markedness are potentially applicable. For example, language typology helps us pose questions on possible interactions of L1 and L2 in a given learning situation in that the properties of the two languages can be framed in a universal perspective. Questions such as what is unique for the particular languages, how corresponding structures differ in markedness, and so forth, can be specified.

A specific impetus for the studies I will present here was the fact that the language typology approach had developed as a framework for second language acquisition research in Sweden as early as the 1970s. For example, phonological second language acquisition research was carried out within a typological framework by Faith Ann Johansson in the early 1970s (Johansson, 1973), and syntactic and semantic studies by Björn Hammarberg and Åke Viberg in the middle and late 1970s (see, for example, Hammarberg & Viberg, 1977; Viberg, 1983). This research development in Sweden can, among other reasons, be seen as a consequence of the pedagogical needs of a linguistically heavily heterogeneous immigrant population. Among a population of less than 500,000 persons (i.e. the number of foreign citizens in Sweden), some 140 languages are represented.

Now, how can the field of language typology more precisely be useful for research into second language acquisition? Most important, in my view, is the role the regularities found in language typology play as a basis for hypotheses in the descriptive phase of second language acquisition data. The typological regularities give ideas on what to look out for. Further, at an initial explanatory level, we can investigate whether principles such as proposed hierarchies and markedness conditions have any predictive value for phenomena such as developmental sequences and transfer.

Before I go into the presentation of the present studies, I would just like to mention, in order to avoid confusion, that the notions of language universals and markedness will be used in a strictly typological sense here. The same notions are also used with different assumptions in recent derivatives of generative grammar, a framework which is now gaining increased application in second language acquisition research (see e.g. White, 1983; Sharwood Smith, 1983; Mazurkewich, 1985).

The studies

The two second language acquisition studies I will present here were designed to assess structural areas where typological patterning seemed to be reasonably reliably described. One concerned the pattern of retention/ deletion of pronominal copies in relative clauses, the other the voice distinction in stops. Both areas had been discussed earlier in second language acquisition research (see Schachter, 1974; Ioup & Kruse, 1977; Gass, 1979; Eckman, 1977, for relative clauses, and Eckman, 1977, also for voicing in stops). Both areas had also been identified as problematic for second language learners of Swedish with certain L1s. The presentation of the studies will necessarily be brief and inconclusive here. For further details concerning the study of pronominal copies in relative clauses, see Hyltenstam (1984), and concerning the study of the voice distinction in stops, Hyltenstam & Magnusson (1983).

Pronominal copies in relative clauses

With regard to the phenomenon of pronominal copies in relative clauses, languages differ both with respect to whether they use this strategy or not, and, if they do, to what extent. English and Swedish are examples of languages that do not use this device, at least not in simple relative clauses. If they did, examples such as the following, which I have taken from Schachter (1974), would have been grammatical under coreference conditions between the pronoun and the head noun of the relative clause.

Subject: the boy that *he* came
Direct object: the boy that John hit *him*
Indirect object: the boy that I sent a letter to *him*
Object of preposition: the boy that I sat near *him*
Possessive noun phrase: the boy that *his* father died
Object of comparison: the boy that John is taller than *him*

The typological distribution of the use of pronominal copies has been found to reflect the so called NP Accessibility Hierarchy (Keenan & Comrie, 1977). This generalisation states that there is a universal hierarchy of positions, that is, grammatical functions, out of which an NP may be relativised. This hierarchy is, in fact, reflected in the order in which the examples above are given. We thus have

SU > DO > IO > OBL > GEN > OCOMP

(where SU = subject, DO = direct object, IO = indirect object, OBL = oblique object, in English and Swedish, object of preposition, GEN = genitive, OCOMP = object of comparison). The distribution of pronominal copies is thus in accord with this hierarchy, as seen in Table 1.

TABLE 1. *Typological patterns for retention (+) or deletion (−) of pronominal copies in relative clauses*

SU	DO	IO	OBL	GEN	OCOMP	
−	−	−	−	−	−	most marked
−	−	−	−	−	+	
−	−	−	−	+	+	
−	−	−	+	+	+	
−	−	+	+	+	+	
−	+	+	+	+	+	
+	+	+	+	+	+	least marked

Typological markedness conditions can be formulated both for the grammatical functions as such and for the use of pronominal copies on the basis of implicational statements, which can be derived from the patterning in this table. The implicational statements are as follows: if a particular grammatical function in the hierarchy is relativisable in any given language, then all positions higher in the hierarchy must also be relativisable in that language. Parallel formulations can be given for the deletion of pronominal copies in relative clauses: if a pronominal copy is deleted in a particular position in the hierarchy, it must also be deleted in all positions higher in the hierarchy. If we define the typologically implying term as more marked than the implied term, we get the markedness conditions as stated in Table 1.

In the present study, the choice of L1's to be represented among the learners was made on the grounds that both marked and unmarked languages should be included. To find appropriate languages, the descriptions given in Keenan & Comrie (1977) were followed. Thus, the decision was made to include Finnish, Greek, Persian, and Spanish. The patterns of pronominal copies in these languages and Swedish, according to Keenan and Comrie, are those seen in Table 2.

TABLE 2. *Retention (+) and deletion (−) of pronominal copies in Swedish, Finnish, Spanish, Greek, and Persian relative clauses*

SU	DO	IO	OBL	GEN	OCOMP	
−	−	−	−	−	−	Swedish
−	−	−	−	−		Finnish
−	−	−	−	−		Spanish
−	−	+?	+?	+	+	Greek
−	(+)	+	+	+	+	Persian

( ) = optional
? = inconclusive data

The questions, now, that were of particular interest to me were the following:

1. Do learners whose L1 contains marked forms produce unmarked structures even when they are acquiring a language with similarly marked forms?
2. Is the universal hierarchy for deletion of pronominal copies retained in the learners' interlanguage? If, for example, a learner initially uses pronominal copies and then learns to suppress them, are they then first suppressed in the higher positions in the hierarchy?

The subjects in this study were 45 adult learners of Swedish, 12 from each language group except for the Finnish group where there were only 9. All the subjects attended Swedish language courses and were at a fairly advanced level; at the time of investigation they had received 350–600 hours of instruction.

The elicitation material consisted of a set of eight pictures for each relativisable function. The set for the object function exemplifies the procedure (cf. Appendix). In each set there were two pictures of women, two of men, two of girls, and two of boys, and for each of them two predicates could be used. The eight pictures were numbered 1–8, and it was the subject's task to orally identify the person on each numbered picture. The question asked was 'Who is number x?' and the answer expected would be 'The man who sings', for example. Within each set, five responses were elicited in a row, then, in a last cycle, one further response was elicited from each of the eight sets of pictures. The rationale behind this pictorial task, of course, was to have the subjects unambiguously identify referents among a set of minimally differing objects, a task which rather naturally elicits relative clauses.

The results can be seen from Table 3–6, where all responses of a subject on a particular grammatical function have been collapsed. This procedure was justified since there was little variation within a given relativised function for all subjects. For a display of the raw data, see Hyltenstam (1984: 48f).

TABLE 3. *Implicational scale showing pronominal retention for Persian learners of Swedish. Scaling according to the NP Accessibility Hierarchy. Scalability 93.1*

Subj nr	SU	DO	IO	OBL	GEN	OCOMP
21	−	−	−	−	−	−
32	−	−	−	−	+	+
17	−	⊕	⊕	−	+	⊖
18	−	⊕	⊕	−	+	+
7	−	−	+	+	+	+
16	−	−	+	+	+	+
6	−	−	+	+	+	+
34	−	+	+	+	+	+
30	−	+	+	+	+	+
28	−	+	+	+	+	+
29	−	+	+	+	+	+
15	−	+	+	+	+	+

TABLE 4. *Implicational scale showing pronominal retention for Greek learners of Swedish. Scaling according to the NP Accessibility Hierarchy. Scalability 97.1 (if 0 = −) or 98.7 (if 0 = +)*

Subj nr	SU	DO	IO	OBL	GEN	OCOMP
20	−	−	−	−	−	−
41	−	−	−	−	+	⊖
14	−	−	−	−	+	0
43	−	−	−	−	+	+
12	−	−	−	−	+	+
13	−	−	+	+	+	+
40	−	−	+	+	+	+
27	−	+	+	+	+	+
42	−	+	+	+	+	+
22	−	+	+	+	+	+
11	−	+	+	+	+	+
10	−	+	+	+	+	+

TABLE 5. *Implicational scale showing pronominal retention for Spanish learners of Swedish. Scaling according to the NP Accessibility Hierarchy. Scalability 90.3*

Subj nr	SU	DO	IO	OBL	GEN	OCOMP
2	−	−	−	−	−	−
31	−	−	−	−	⊕	−
37	−	−	−	−	⊕	−
33	−	−	−	−	⊕	−
3	−	−	−	−	−	+
8	−	−	−	−	+	+
5	−	−	⊕	−	+	⊖
4	−	−	⊕	−	+	+
9	−	−	⊕	−	+	+
19	−	−	+	+	+	+
24	−	+	+	+	+	+
35	−	+	+	+	+	+

TABLE 6. *Implicational scale showing pronominal retention for Finnish learners of Swedish. Scaling according to the NP Accessibility Hierarchy. Scalability 85.2–92.6 depending on whether 0 = + or −*

Subj nr	SU	DO	IO	OBL	GEN	OCOMP
48	−	−	−	−	0	−
52	−	−	−	−	0	−
44	−	−	−	−	⊕	−
47	−	−	−	−	⊕	−
51	−	−	−	−	⊕	−
45	−	−	−	0	⊕	−
50	−	−	−	−	0	+
46	−	−	−	−	+	+
49	−	−	−	−	+	+

As we can see, pronominal copies are used in all groups of learners, even by those who do not have them in their first language. The pattern seems to be dependent also on first language structure, however, as there are more copies in the Swedish of those learners whose L1 uses this strategy more frequently. It is, for example not probable that Finnish speakers would use pronominal copies high in the hierarchy even in earlier phases of acquisition. It is, however, possible that the correct generalisation is that learners use pronominal copies in higher positions in their interlanguage than in their native languages; note, for example, the Greek learners who do not use pronominal copies in DO position in their L1 according to our norm description from Keenan and Comrie (1977), whereas in the interlanguage of some of the Greek speakers, this is a fairly common solution. The Spanish group would seem to be particularly interesting for question 1 above, since in spite of the fact that Spanish, according to our description, does not use pronominal copies, such a device is employed to a considerable extent in their Swedish interlanguage. A closer look at descriptions of Spanish reveals, however, that the Keenan and Comrie description seems to hold true for standard varieties of Spanish, but that there are colloquial varieties, especially in certain regions of the Spanish speaking community, where pronominal copies are indeed employed. Unfortunately, the study reported here did not check for how the actual learners of the investigation would express the required utterances in their L1, but L1 structure may be part of the explanation for the pattern in the Swedish interlanguage of the Spanish speaking group.

The result of the Finnish group is thus the most crucial evidence in this study, that our question 1 can be given an affirmative answer: although pronominal copies do not occur in Finnish, the learners' L1, nor in Swedish, their L2, we find a small number of occurrences in their interlanguage. The number of occurrences is, as we can see, extremely small but in the wider theoretical framework of this investigation, the mere existence of the category is of significance.

With regard to the second question, that is, whether the hierarchy is reflected in the interlanguages of the learners, a glance at Tables 3–6 gives some indication that there might be a fairly good mapping here.

Deviations from the implicational patterns are indicated by circled entries. Scalability figures show that the subjects adhere to the typologically valid patterns to a high degree. Parenthetically, we actually get a better fit for our second language acquisition data, if we invert the order between OCOMP and GEN on the one hand and between IO and OBL on the other in the hierarchy.

Interestingly, the same result for the positions OCOMP and GEN was obtained in an acceptability study among first language learners (Hawkins & Keenan, 1974), suggesting that a psychologically valid hierarchy might be slightly different from the typological one (for further discussion of this point, cf. Hyltenstam, 1984).

In a replication of my 1984 study with the same elicitation instrument, Pavesi (1986) achieved parallel results to those that have just been described.

Her subjects were adolescent and adult Italian learners of English in both formal and informal settings. Both languages involved in Pavesi's study, as L1 and L2 respectively, were languages with marked forms in the area of pronominal retention/deletion. In spite of the fact that none of the languages retain pronominal copies in relative clauses, the interlanguage of these learners contained numerous instances of such elements. In fact, the learners of this study produced more relative clauses with than without pronominal copies and adhered to the same implicational pattern as the subjects of my own study, that is, to the accessibility hierarchy. Moreover, the inversion of OCOMP and GEN and IO and OBL respectively gave higher scalability figures also in this study.

The results of this replication provides even stronger support for the contention that even in cases where both L1 and L2 contain marked forms, the learner can come up with the typologically corresponding unmarked form. Further, in the process of oppressing the unmarked form in favour of the marked one, the learner adheres to patterns that have been identified for natural languages on a typological basis. At present, however, the generality of these results for other structural areas remains to be investigated.

The Voice Distinction in Stops

The study of the acquisition of the voice distinction in Swedish stops involved also a comparison between first and second language acquisition data, but here, we will consider only the L2 data. The study was carried out in co-operation with Eva Magnusson, a phonetician and speech therapist at the University of Lund.

Typological markedness conditions for voicing in stops can be formulated at two levels. At a more general level, it is commonly accepted since Jakobson's formulation in 1941 that voiced stops imply their voiceless counterparts. For a qualification of this statement, see Hyltenstam & Magnusson (1983). This means that if a language has voiced stops, it necessarily also has voiceless stops. Therefore, voiced stops are considered more marked than voiceless stops. At a more specific level, there seems to be a regular difference in contextual distribution of the distinction according to Dinnsen & Eckman (1975). According to this proposal, the existence of a voice distinction in word final position implies the maintenance of the same distinction in medial position, which in turn implies the maintenance in word initial position. We thus have the pattern given in Table 7, where examples of languages with the different distributions are given. (The case of Finnish is not totally clear-cut, since this language has a marginal distinction between /t/ and /d/. Finnish /d/ is not given a phonemic status in all descriptions due to the fact that it is marginal in the phonological system.

It is, for example, restricted to morphological context in that it occurs only in certain inflectional forms, and in many varieties of Finnish, it does not occur at all.)

TABLE 7. *Typological patterns for voicing in stops*

Initial	Medial	Final		
+	+	+	e.g. Swedish	most marked
+	+	−	e.g. German	
+	−	−	e.g. Corsican	
−	−	−	e.g. Finnish	least marked

On the basis of the patterning in Table 7, it can be stated that it is more marked to maintain the voice distinction in word final position than in medial position where it in turn is more marked than in initial position. It is the least marked case not to maintain the distinction at all.

Now, one of the questions asked in this study was the following:

In the acquisition of the voice distinction in stops in a second language setting, are the markedness conditions as formulated on the basis of typological facts reflected in the learner's output during the period of acquisition, that is, would the learner be more advanced in the acquisition of the voice distinction in the less marked contexts?

The second language learners of this study were child and adult native speakers of Finnish. They were chosen for the study on the criterion that they had still not completely mastered the voice distinction in Swedish, but exhibited variable use of voicing in Swedish voiced stops, indicating that the acquisitional process had started. There were ten adults and six children, 4 to 6 years of age. The data were elicited with the help of pictures illustrating words which contain voiced and voiceless stops, and every effort was made to cover all possible structural contexts of the stops. The data were analysed auditorily in two steps. In the first step it was decided whether the manifestation fell within the normally accepted variation or not for voiced stops in the various contexts. In the second step, a narrow transcription of all manifestations was undertaken. Here, only the result from the first analytical step will be presented. For a more detailed presentation of the results, see Hyltenstam & Magnusson (1983: 7–15).

The results are shown in Table 8.

TABLE 8. *Proportions of acceptably produced voiced stops in word-initial, -medial, and -final position*

		'_V	V_V	V_
/b/	children	44	40	10
	adults	68	38	33
/d/	children	92	56	55
	adults	89	87	86
/g/	children	64	60	30
	adults	59	56	45

Very briefly, as can be seen in the Table, the voiced stops are produced acceptably more often in initial position than in medial position, where they are in turn more acceptable than in final position. Thus, it seems that we can answer our question for this study in the affirmative: a parallel does exist between the typological data and our second language acquisition data in this phonological area.

Conclusions

Even though these two studies are far from conclusive, especially considering the small number of subjects involved and the fact that they are cross-sectional rather than longitudinal, the results do point to the usefulness of typological data and notions such as markedness for second language acquisition research. As mentioned in the introductory part of this paper, I believe the usefulness is particularly salient in the descriptive phase of research. Thus, I do not see typological markedness as an explanatory concept for structural regularities in second language acquisition data, where I would rather look for explanations at a processing level. In phonology, for example, the physiological constraints in production and perception provide an obvious frame of explanation. As regards the pragmatic and semantic levels of language, more central and cognitive aspects of language processing must be taken into consideration. Phenomena such as reference and deep case relations, which are both involved in the deciphering of the relativised function in relative clauses, might be dealt with in this way. To take the example of pronominal copies in relative clauses, one explanation that suggests itself for the fact that pronominal copies are used in some relativised functions but not in others, and more extensively by language learners than by native speakers, is that they make the referential conditions of the relative clause clearer and the semantic relationships between the verb and its arguments more transparent. In short, the pronominal copies make the deep relations of the relative clause show up at the surface more clearly, and this is an obvious way of making it easier to process. If it is the case, as seems reasonable, that the NP Accessibility Hierarchy has a psychological validity in the sense that relative clauses with functions low in the hierarchy are more difficult to process, then the use of pronominal copies can be seen as a means to reduce the processing load where it is largest.

Finally, as is obvious from the discussion of results in this article language typology seems to be a useful basis for making predictions on second language acquisition patterning, if due consideration is given to how the structures of the languages involved in the learning situation (L1 and L2) pattern within a typological framework.

Appendix

References

BERMAN, R.A., 1984, Cross-linguistic first language perspectives on second language acquisition research. In R.W. ANDERSEN (ed.), *Second Languages: A Cross-linguistic Perspective*. Rowley, MA: Newbury House, 13–36.

DINNSEN, D.A. & ECKMAN, F., 1975, A functional explanation of some phonological typologies. In R. GROSSMAN, J. SAN & T. VANCE (eds), *Functionalism*. Chicago: Chicago Linguistic Society, 126–139.

ECKMAN, F., 1977, Markedness and the contrastive analysis hypothesis. *Language Learning 27*, 315–330.

GASS, S., 1979, Language transfer and universal grammatical relations. *Language Learning 29*, 327–344.

HAMMARBERG, B. & VIBERG, Å., 1977, The place-holder constraint, language typology, and the teaching of Swedish to immigrants. *Studia Linguistica 31*, 106–163.

HAWKINS, J.A., 1983, *Word Order Universals*. New York: Academic Press.

HAWKINS, S. & KEENAN, E.L., 1974, *The psychological validity of the accessibility hierarchy*. Paper presented at the Summer Meeting of the Linguistic Society of America.

HYLTENSTAM, K., 1984, The use of typological markedness conditions as predictors in second language acquisition: The case of pronominal copies in relative clauses. In R.W. ANDERSEN (ed), *Second Languages: A Cross-linguistic Perspective*. Rowley, MA: Newbury House, 39–58.

HYLTENSTAM, K. & MAGNUSSON, E., 1983, Typological markedness, contextual variation, and the acquisition of the voice contrast in stops by first and second language learners of Swedish. In T.K. BHATIA & W. RITCHIE (eds), Progression in second language acquisition (Special Issue), *Indian Journal of Applied Linguistics 9*, 1–18.

IOUP, G. & KRUSE, A., 1977, Interference versus structural complexity in second language acquisition: Language universals as a basis for natural sequencing. In H.D. BROWN, C.A. YORIO & R.H. CRYMES (eds), *On TESOL '77: Teaching and Learning English as a Second Language*. Washington, DC: TESOL.

JAKOBSON, R., 1941, *Kindersprache, Aphasie und allgemeine Lautgesetze*. Uppsala: Almqvist & Wiksell.

JOHANSSON, F.A., 1973, *Immigrant Swedish Phonology: A Study in Multiple Contact Analysis*. Lund: CWK Gleerup.

KEENAN, E.L. & COMRIE, B., 1977, Noun phrase accessibility and universal grammar. *Linguistic Inquiry 8*, 63–99.

MAZURKEWICH, I., 1985, Syntactic markedness and language acquisition. *Studies in Second Language Acquisition 7*, 15–36.

PAVESI, M., 1986, Markedness, discoursal modes, and relative clause formation in a formal and an informal context. *Studies in Second Language Acquisition 8*, 38–55.

SCHACHTER, J., 1974, An error in error analysis. *Language Learning 24*, 145–151.

SCHUMANN, J.H., 1978, *The Pidginization Process: A Model for Second Language Acquisition*. Rowley, MA: Newbury House.

SHARWOOD SMITH, M., 1983, Crosslinguistic aspects of second language acquisition. *Applied Linguistics 4*, 192–199.

SLOBIN, D., 1982, Universal and particular in the acquisition of language. In L.R.

GLEITMAN & E. WANNER (eds), *Language Acquisition: The State of the Art.* Cambridge: Cambridge University Press, 128–170.

TRAUGOTT, E. CLOSS, 1977, Natural semantax: its role in the study of second language acquisition. In S.P. CORDER & E. ROULET (eds), *The Notions of Simplification, Interlanguages, and Pidgins and their Relation to Second Language Pedagogy.* Neuchâtel: Faculté des Lettres, 132–162.

VIBERG, Å., 1983, The verbs of perception: a typological study. In B. BUTTERWORTH, B. COMRIE & Ö. DAHL (eds), Explanations for language universals [special issue]. *Linguistics 21* (1). Berlin: Mouton, 123–162.

WEINREICH, U., LABOV, V. & HERZOG, M.I., 1968, Empirical foundations for a theory of language change. In W.P. LEHMANN & Y. MALKIEL (eds), *Directions for Historical Linguistics.* Austin, TX: University of Texas Press, 95–188.

WHITE, L., 1983, Markedness and parameter setting: Some implications for a theory of adult second language learning. *McGill Working Papers in Linguistics 1*, 1–21.

3 Foreign Language Acquisition and the Development of Automaticity

JAAKKO LEHTONEN

The bias of the present paper is to discuss some aspects in the development of foreign language (FL) procedural knowledge in terms of the results of tests with Finnish students of English, German, and Swedish at the University of Jyväskylä and with German students of English, French, and Spanish at the University of Kassel in West Germany (for the concept of procedural knowledge in FL processing, see Dechert & Raupach, 1985). The focus in this discussion is on the assessment of the development and the degree of automaticity on the basis of the differences in the reaction time (RT) latencies of the informants in various linguistic decision tasks. The German data were collected in cooperation with the *KAPPA* psycholinguistic research group of the University of Kassel.

Investigation into the cognitive processes underlying language perception and production is the ultimate task of psycholinguistics. Today it is also one of the focuses of research in the *Jyväskylä Cross-Language Project*, which is more than ten years old. In the contrastive framework this kind of emphasis means analysing the learner's language processing modes or strategies as compared to the processes in his or her native language behaviour and to the processes of the native speakers of the target language. To quote Hans Dechert (1983: 122), 'contrastive psycholinguistics, less interested in the products of first and second languages than Contrastive Linguistics is, seeks to investigate the underlying processes of perception and production. What we should be looking at . . . is not so much the different linguistic systems the learner is struggling against, but the one information processing system he or she has and the procedures he or she uses to deal with his or her linguistic in- and output.'

In the perception and production of speech the processes of the identification of various linguistic structures and the retrieval of words from memory must take place in real time. If the processes are too slow, the communicative consequences are fatal both to the speaker and to the listener. As a speaker, a slow processor becomes disfluent, and his or her speech is characterised by frequent and long hesitation pauses and other disfluencies. As a listener, he or she loses the track easily and is unable to generate relevant responses in interaction. Both are typical characteristics of a foreign language speaker or listener (see e.g. Lehtonen, 1979). In addition to the most obvious general explanation of these phenomena, that is, too low a level of all kinds of knowledge relating to the foreign language, there are two features of his or her procedural knowledge resulting in a delay in the rate of processing which serve as a partial explanation for the disfluencies of his or her FL processing: (a) the FL speaker may not have developed a network of semantic, lexical, grammatical, textual, and pragmatic associations which would facilitate the processing and/or (b) the processes have not been automatised and are therefore time-consuming. They also require a large amount of system capacity, and distract the system from entering a higher level of processing.

Shiffrin & Dumais (1980) distinguish between two qualitatively different forms of cognitive processing: controlled and automatic. Controlled processing requires attention and decreases the system capacity which is available for other processing. Automatic processing does not necessarily demand processing resources, which means that there is capacity in the system for higher-level processing. Everyday examples of automatised sequences are, for instance, driving a car, playing the piano, typing, and reading aloud, which all involve aspects of rather complex behaviour.

According to McLaughlin, Rossman & McLeod (1983), the distinction between controlled and automatic processes is related to the degree to which the skills in question have been routinised and established in long term memory: if the skills are well-mastered and permanent, information processing can be said to be automatic. It is worth noticing — having the foreign language learning situation in mind — that retraining to adopt a new automatic sequence can be arduous and more difficult than the initial learning process. This suggests that if there is any procedural transfer from the native language processing mode during the process of foreign language acquisition, an inhibitory effect could be expected to take place in acquisition as concerns processes which are automatised in the mother tongue but must be modified to fit the target language system.

There are several instrumental methods which can be applied for the purposes of psycholinguistic experimentation. Likewise, the possibilities of controlling the testing procedure as a whole are unlimited. The present article concentrates on the application of reaction time measurements to the analysis of automatic and controlled transfer in processing from the native language and of the development of automaticity in the foreign language speaker's language processing system. The ways there are to learn about the human information processing system are rather restricted: we can analyse its printouts, that is, spoken and written texts, produced in various contexts; we can try to discover its weak points by listing errors that it makes, or we can feed into the machine various problems which are simple enough and see how accurately and how fast it succeeds in solving them. This is what is attempted with the reaction time experiments.

It will be hypothesised for the purposes of the present article that reaction times reflect the degree of automaticity: the faster the reaction is the higher the level of automaticity in decision making. This kind of interpretation of RT data implies that there are two modes of retrieval, or two access modes to linguistic knowledge in the central nervous system: automatic and controlled. Some tasks consume more cognitive resources and involve slower processing; these are called controlled processes. Automatic processes again utilise a relatively permanent set of associative connections and proceed at a faster rate. Both controlled and automatic processes can in principle be either conscious or not (McLaughlin, Rossman & McLeod, 1983). Since most automatic processes occur with great speed, they are mostly hidden and are unattainable by conscious perception and introspection. McLaughlin, Rossman & McLeod (1983) emphasise the conceptual distinction between automaticity and consciousness: the distinction between automatic and controlled processing is not based on conscious and subconscious awareness but, instead, relates to the degree to which the skills in question have been routinised and established in long term memory. This also implies that a process requires training to be automatic.

The poorer performance of bilinguals in their second language is, according to Edith Mägiste (1984), due to their failure to achieve the same level of automatic familiarity with words of the second language as monolingual subjects achieve. Similarly, Favreau and Segalowitz (1983) conclude in their study of bilingual Canadians that the less skilled readers showed less automaticity (or inhibitionless facilitation) in their second language than the more skilled readers did or they themselves did in their first language.

The experiment

The starting hypothesis is simple in that reactions to familiar and automatised structures are faster and more accurate, while decisions concerning the acceptability of less familiar constructs are slower and less accurate. The linguistic tasks in the present experiments include correct/incorrect decisions of sentences which do, or do not, contain an apparent grammatical error. It will be hypothesised that such acceptability tests touch upon the production mechanism in two ways: (a) if the listener/reader accepts the pattern, it implies that he or she accepts the same construct also in his or her own speech; and (b) a fast rate of reaction indicates a high degree of availability of the data for the processing mechanism and a high level of automaticity in the decision process (for further discussion, see Lehtonen & Sajavaara, 1985).

It is known from experience that the reaction time to a simple yes/no stimulus (e.g. light on/light off) is about one fifth of a second. This time includes the identification of the stimulus, its categorical recognition, the selection and planning of the response and the motor activity. If the task is more complex, if the informant has to choose between two or more alternatives, the reaction times tend to grow longer. In simple word/non word decision tasks and in lexical naming tasks, typical reaction times of native informants vary around 600 milliseconds. In acceptability tasks with short sentences in a foreign language the times needed for the decision may vary from one second to several seconds (Lehtonen & Sajavaara, 1985). The interpretation of reaction times to linguistic stimuli is often problematic, because there is no straightforward relationship between reaction times and the complexity of the task in terms of the linguistic complexity of the stimulus. Linguistic complexity or the complexity of the stimulus according to a given grammatical theory is not necessarily isomorphic with the procedural complexity of the task in question. The interpretation of the results of contrastive or interlanguage RT-tests is somewhat easier, because a comparison of the foreign language speaker's and the native's reactions as such serves as data for the establishment of the degree of similarity between the foreign language speaker's and the native's processes.

Table 1 summarises some of the most recent tests carried out by the Jyväskylä Cross-Language Project. In these tests a total number of 91 English sentences and a varying number of corresponding Finnish, Swedish, and German sentences were presented tachistoscopically to a group of 20 Finnish university students of English at the University of Jyväskylä, Finland. In addition, the English and German sentences were presented to a group of German students of English at the University of Kassel, Federal Republic of Germany. The task was to decide, as fast as possible, whether the sentence seen on the screen was correct or not, or whether the translation of the sentence which was seen in one of the subtests on the screen below the English sentence was correct or not. The informants reacted by pushing one of two buttons before them. In both language groups half of the students had completed their term abroad or had stayed for a period of six months or more in an English-speaking country. Ten of the Finnish students had German, and five Swedish as their minor subject. Most of the German subjects had French or Spanish as their minor subjects at university.

TABLE 1. *Mean decision times with speakers of Finnish, German, and English to various acceptability decision tasks*

	sentences					translation	
	1	*2*	*3*	*4*		*5*	
speakers of	*English*	*Finnish*	*German*	*Swedish*	*E/Fi*	*E/Ge*	*E/Sw*
Finnish (N=20)	2870	2426	3379	3082	3446	3962	3784
German (N=20)	2178	–	1785	–	–	2306	–
English (N=15)	1998	–	–	–	–	–	–

Figures in column 1 stand for the reaction times of Finnish, German and English informants to an acceptability decision of visually presented sentences in English (1), column 2 in Finnish, 3 in German and 4 in Swedish. Column 5 represents reactions in tasks in which the subjects were asked to decide whether the translation of an English sentence was correct or not. The difference of the means between the mother tongue reactions and the two foreign language decision tasks are statistically strongly significant, both in the Finnish and in the German group. In each subtest, the stimuli were presented in a randomised order. Various distractor sentences were used to prevent conscious monitoring of any features in the test sentences. The syntactic and lexical structure of the sentences was as simple as possible. Sentence length varied slightly but each sentence took only one line in the tachistoscopic projection. The linguistic problems embedded in the sentences were selected from the error analysis data collected by the Jyväskylä Cross-Language Project. Accordingly, most of the erroneous stimuli were similar to typical errors made by Finnish students of English, German, and Swedish.

The test pattern was originally constructed for the assessment of the influence of the native language as well as of any other foreign language on the processing of a given target language. The hypothesis was that English, which is the first foreign language taught to the great majority of Finnish comprehensive school children, might interfere in the learning of Swedish, German and other foreign languages.

A few words may suffice to illustrate this aspect in the data: in general, there was some evidence in the data which suggests the existence of some L3-transfer in the decision tasks. For instance, in the translation task one of the fastest reactions by Finns was the decision on the German translation of the sentence *He was given a book* = *Er wurde ein Buch gegeben.*[1] The majority of the Finns (12 out of 20) accepted this incorrect German sentence, which was, of course, rejected by the native Germans, the decision time being the fastest of all English–German sentence pairs. A similar piece of evidence for L3-transfer at a rather automatised level of processing is the Finns' reaction to a 'false friend' in German and Swedish sentences: 17 out of 20 Finnish informants accepted very fast (the rate was the 7th out of 23 sentences) the erroneous German translation of *They rushed to the station* = *Sie raschten zum Bahnhof* (pro *Sie eilten zum Bahnhof*). Similarly 18 out of 20 accepted the Swedish nonsense-translation *Lisa rasade till parken* (Sw. *rasa* 'to rage') of the English sentence *Lisa rushed to the park* with an average RT of 3630 milliseconds. It is interesting to see that the great majority of the Finns also accepted the erroneous words *raschen* and *rasa* in isolated German and Swedish sentences respectively with a corresponding speed and unanimity: German *Er raschte zur Bank* 16/20 'right' in 3060 msec, and Swedish *Hon rasade till Stockman* 17/20 'right' in 2780 milliseconds. It is somewhat confusing that at the same time the same informants apparently knew the right word, which is indicated by the fact that 17/20 of them also accepted the correct Swedish sentence *Pelle rusade in i huset* 'Pelle rushed into the house' very fast (2675 msec). Similarly, about half of the Finnish students accepted the isolated erroneous sentence *Ich wurde ein Buch gegeben*, although after a long decision time (3805 msec) but 10 out of 20 also accepted the correct sentence *Mir wurde ein Auto gegeben* 'I was given a car'.

In each group of Table 1 the tasks in a foreign language required more time than the decisions in the mother tongue. This is in accordance with earlier findings from several different tasks in which the RT's of the Finnish students of English and German to the native and target language stimuli were recorded (see e.g. Lehtonen & Sajavaara, 1985); in all test types the students' reactions to foreign language stimuli had been slower than those of the native speakers and slower than their reactions to stimuli in their mother tongue. This has been interpreted as an indication of a lack of automaticity in the FL procedures.

The difference between the mean reaction times of the Finnish group and the German group in Table 1 is surprisingly high. The Germans are faster in their mother tongue decisions, but the difference between the two groups' two English language tasks is still higher. Several tentative explanations are possible. The physical test environments were different, but this should have rather benefited the Finnish group, which was tested in a proper testing studio. Otherwise the conditions were identical: similar instructions, the same exposition time (2 sec), and the same picture size on the screen. A more probable explanation for the Finns' longer reaction times can be found in a different focus of attention among the Finnish and German FL students. The Finnish students had learned at school to monitor the formal correctness of the utterances both in their mother tongue and in foreign languages. This focus on errors and grammatical correctness at the cost of fluency of delivery and communicative skills may have been further reinforced by Finnish university education. The German students may have been taught more interactive skills and they may have been encouraged to communicate even if their utterances are not always formally perfect. This hypothesis is supported by the preliminary findings that the Germans seem to make more errors in their reactions to the unanimously correct or false sentences in their native language than Finns do. But there is one more explanation which is theoretically obvious but hard to verify: the typological interrelationship of the languages. Germans may be faster in English because of the structural similarity of these two related languages. The Finns' reactions to tasks in any Germanic language are slower because they cannot transfer the procedural schemata of their mother tongue to the processing of languages which are totally unrelated to their native language (cf. Ringbom, 1979, 1985).

Phenomena in foreign-language processing, however, depend on several other factors in addition to the differences and similarities between the source and target languages. These are, among other things, cultural patterns, motivational factors, the amount of language contacts, and the mode of language exposition. The last factor, that is, whether the knowledge of the foreign language has been acquired primarily in naturalistic interaction with native speakers in various social situations or whether most of it has been acquired in formal classroom situations, appears to be especially important for the development of native-like automaticity. The Finnish informants had been taught English (or German) for the most part through traditional teacher-centred methods. Because Finland is almost entirely monolingual and there is practically no immigration from other countries, Finns, except those living in the narrow bilingual coastal area, had only been minimally exposed to real life communicative FL situations.

Although the variation in reaction times between individuals has not yet been analysed in detail, some preliminary remarks are possible here. The mean reaction times of individual informants of the two language groups to each subtest are given in graphic form in Figure 1 and Figure 2. In each figure, the informants have been arranged in the order of the rate of the reactions in the native tongue tasks. The running number of those students who had completed their term abroad is italicised. Preliminary inspection of the reaction times seems to suggest that the stay of six months in an English speaking country did not speed up the reaction rates in either language group. This finding contradicts earlier results which showed a significant quickening of the Finns' reactions to English idioms and collocations in the residence group. It is also worth noticing in Figure 1 and Figure 2 that Finns and Germans seem to experience the difficulty of the translation task in a different way: the translation task required more time than individual sentences for all Finns except no. 12, but in the German group there are nine informants who performed the translation task faster than the English sentence task.

Automatic processing has been said to free cognitive capacity for higher level tasks such as integration of information and inferencing. It is possible to hypothesise that in the case of isolated sentences or sentence pairs such as those included in the tests reported above, automatic processing proceeds independently at several levels simultaneously. One of these levels could be one of acceptability, which involves decisions on the acceptability and non-acceptability of utterances. It could be possible to hypothesise the existence of an acceptability-detection automaton, which automatically weighs the 'familiarity value' of the incoming sentence in the case of the natives' reactions to unambiguous sentences. According to this hypothesis both the rejection of erroneous stimuli and the acceptance of correct sentences are fast and automatic, if the stimulus exceeds the thresholds. But if the familiarity/unfamiliarity falls below the threshold value, or if the sentence deviates from what is plausible, a monitoring or searching process is triggered which results in lengthened reactions in the case of native speakers. This hypothesis explains, for instance, the native Germans' and the Finnish students' reactions to German sentences in one of our earlier tests (Lehtonen & Sajavaara, 1985). The majority of the Finnish students accepted very fast the erroneous sentence *Hast du viele Photos genommen which was construed on the basis of the Finnish collocation ottaa valokuvia 'to take photos', because of the transfer from their mother tongue, while the natives needed almost the same time as the Finns to reject it. Apparently this sentence did not exceed the rejection threshold but triggered a search for such contexts in which the sentence could be possible.

The theory of grammatical decision-making can be integrated into the general model of signal detection, which explains the slower responses found in the tests on the basis of the concept of stimulus familiarity. According to this concept, items that fall below the threshold of unfamiliarity or above the threshold of familiarity are responded to very quickly, because they require no search of memory. But items which fall between the two thresholds are responded to only after a relatively time-consuming memory search (cf. Lachman & Butterfield, 1979). In tests like those reported above, the sentences which fall unanimously below the level of acceptability or plausibility, and are therefore rejected, and the sentences which correspond to the general patterns of expectations, and are accordingly accepted, elicit a markedly faster reaction in the native speakers than those that fall between two thresholds (cf. Lehtonen & Sajavaara, 1983). The foreign language students, on the other hand, because of their small amount of knowledge in the new language, may not have developed such a network of associations which would function like an 'acceptability automaton'. Consequently, they need more time for their decision-making.

There are several different theories which could be adapted to the analysis and description of automaticity in the language processing of the foreign language learner. Logan (1985) presents a view of automaticity which is different from that of the representatives of the automatic-controlled dichotomy theory. He refers to an interesting aspect of automaticity, skill and control: normally, skilled, that is, more automatised, performance is better controlled than less skilled performance; skilled performers are usually able to control their performance better than unskilled performers, even though their performance is likely to be more automatic. Accordingly, he suggests that the contrast between automaticity and control may be an artifact, and that the general belief that automaticity and control are opposites may be mistaken or, at least, overstated. According to Logan, psychologists often characterise phenomena as dichotomies. In this way, automaticity in the literature is contrasted, if not with control, with some binary opposite such as strategic processing or conscious processing. Logan also criticises the standard theory of automaticity, which describes automatisation as a reduction of the resources needed to perform a task. According to Logan, skilled performers carry out their tasks differently from beginners; this means that automatisation is rather a shift in the kinds of resources used than a mere reduction of the resources.

It seems obvious that the development of native-like automaticity is crucial in the process of foreign language acquisition. Future research questions to be answered include, among others, the following: what is the role of native language automaticity in the process of FL acquisition? Is

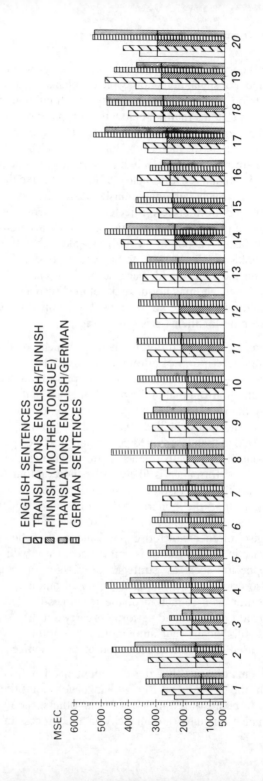

The Finnish informants' reaction times to various linguistic decision tasks

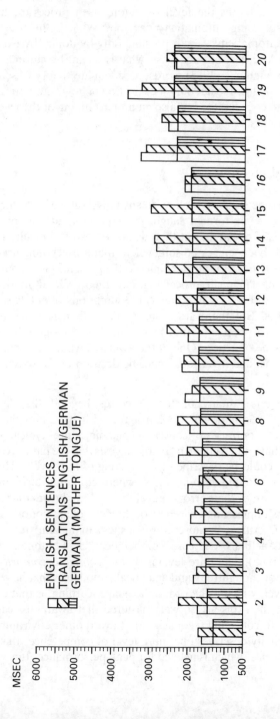

The German informants' reaction times to various linguistic decision tasks

there any transfer at the level of automatised processes, and how does language processing automaticity develop? What is the role of practice in producing automaticity — is it possible only by doing, by experiencing and exercising? And, last but not least, what is meant by automaticity after all? Yet, in McLaughlin's (1983) words, an adequate theory of second language learning should include not only specification of how automatic and controlled processes are coordinated but also an understanding of the role and function of consciousness.

General discussion

There is no reason to believe in any universal theory of the development of automaticity in foreign language acquisition at the present state of psycholinguistic research, but there is no need to favour ultimate pessimism either. It has been suggested somewhere that a psycholinguist is like a blind Indian trying to describe an elephant. At the present state of our experimental knowledge of language processing our theories and models necessarily contain black boxes or hypothetical assumptions about various structures and processes. But there are more windows than just one through which one can try to peep into the boxes and learn about their structure and prospective line of action. One of the available windows is the measurement of the times needed in various linguistic decision tasks, which was discussed above.

But even if many of the processes beyond the development of automaticity are unknown, we can agree with the claim that automatised processes (as contrary to conscious planning) are typical of competent linguistic behaviour. Andersen (1986) suggests that the path to communication competence could be described as consisting of five levels. The lowest level is that of *unconscious incompetence*, where communicators make mistakes but are unaware of their errors. Level two is that of *conscious incompetence*, which means unpleasant awareness of the poor quality of one's performance (this stage is critical because consciousness of incompetence may add to anxiety and actually decrease competence; cf. Lehtonen, Sajavaara, & Manninen, 1985). The third level is that of *conscious competence*, since the communicator thoughtfully and analytically modifies what he or she is doing. The next level, which is the goal of language learning, is that of *unconscious competence*: the skills are so well mastered that awareness can be directed to listening, to collecting feedback, and toward other environmental stimuli. Andersen finally describes one more level of competence, that of conscious *supercompetence*, which is needed for peak performance. It is worth noticing that in this theory unconsciousness appears at both the lowest and the highest level of communicative competence. In these terms, competence refers to skills which are mastered automatically, saving resources for higher level processing.

Both the linguist and the language teacher sometimes underestimate the complexity of the control mechanisms which underlie competent or successful language behaviour: a competent performer has to control his or her personal goals, he or she has to organise diverse perceptions into a coherent plan of action, he or she has to adapt his or her behaviour to situational needs, he or she has to predict and explain the other's communicative behaviour, he or she has to control both verbal and non-verbal cues of the other's behaviour, he or she has to control the turn-taking procedures, fill pauses, react to interruptions and, at the same time, seek appropriate words and utterances in his or her memory, plan his or her own speech, and decode that of his or her interlocutor. And most of this is supposed to proceed subconsciously in an automatised manner. One obvious problem in the attempts to assess the degree of automaticity is that the processes or procedures (or maybe scripts and schemata) which automatise are not equal to the entire performance but represent individual aspects or partial subroutines. Consequently, decision times can be recorded with a conclusion that the faster time is a consequence of a higher level of automaticity, but we do not know which one of the procedures was automatised and resulted in the faster behaviour and in which way.

Notes to Chapter 3

1. Ungrammatical otherwise erroneous sentences are marked with an asterisk.

References

ANDERSEN, P.A., 1986, Consciousness, cognition, and communication. *Western Journal of Speech Communication 50* (1), 87–101.

DECHERT, H.W., 1983, A plea for contrastive psycholinguistics. In K. SAJAVAARA (ed.), *Cross-language Analysis and Second Language Acquisition 1*, Jyväskylä: University of Jyväskylä, 115–123.

DECHERT, H.W. & RAUPACH, M., 1985, Hypothesen zur Zweitsprachenproduktion. In R. EPPENEDER (ed.), *Lernersprache: Thesen zum Erwerb einer Fremdsprache*. München: Goethe Institut, 219–288.

FAVREAU, M. & SEGALOWITZ, N.S., 1983, Automatic and controlled processes in the first- and second-language reading of fluent bilinguals. *Memory and Cognition 11* (6), 563–574.

LACHMAN, R. & BUTTERFIELD, E.C., 1979, *Cognitive Psychology and Information Processing: An Introduction*. Hillsdale, NJ: Erlbaum.

LEHTONEN, J., 1979, Speech rate and pauses in the English of Finns, Swedish-speaking Finns, and Swedes. In R. PALMBERG (ed.), *Perception and Production of English: Papers in Interlanguage*. Åbo: Åbo Akademi, 35–51.

LEHTONEN, J. & SAJAVAARA, K., 1983, Acceptability and ambiguity in native and second language message processing. In H. RINGBOM (ed.), *Psycholinguistics and Foreign Language Learning*. Publications of the Research Institute of Åbo Akademi Foundation. Åbo: Åbo Akademi, 101–125.

— 1985, *Psycholinguistic Testing of Transfer in Foreign-language Speech Processing* (Series B, paper no. 117). Trier: University of Trier.

LEHTONEN, J., SAJAVAARA, K. & MANNINEN, S., 1985, Communication apprehension and attitudes toward a foreign language. *Scandinavian Working Papers in Bilingualism 5*, 53–62.

LOGAN, G.D., 1985, Skill and automaticity: Relations, implications, and future directions. *Canadian Journal of Psychology 39* (2), 367–386.

MÄGISTE, E., 1984, Stroop task and dichotic translation: The development of inference patterns in bilinguals. *Journal of Experimental Psychology 10* (2), 304–315.

MCLAUGHLIN, B., ROSSMAN, T. & MCLEOD, B., 1983, Second language learning: An information-processing perspective. *Language Learning 33* (2), 135–158.

RINGBOM, H., 1979, The English of Finns, Swedes, and Swedish Finns: Some concluding remarks. In R. PALMBERG (ed.), *Perception and Production of English: Papers on Interlanguage*. Åbo: Åbo Akademi, 77–85.

— 1985, The influence of Swedish on the English of Finnish learners. In H. RINGBOM (ed.), *Foreign Language Learning and Bilingualism*. Åbo: Åbo Akademi, 39–71.

SAJAVAARA, K. & LEHTONEN, J., 1986, The mother tongue and the foreign language in interaction. In D. KASTOVSKY & A. SZWEDEK (eds), *Linguistics Across Historical and Geographical Boundaries. In Honour of Jacek Fisiak: Vol. 2. Descriptive, Contrastive, and Applied Linguistics*. Berlin: Mouton de Gruyter, 1443–1455.

SHIFFRIN, R.M. & DUMAIS, S.T., 1980, The development of automatism. In J.R. ANDERSON (ed.), *Cognitive Skills and their Acquisition*. Hillsdale, NJ: Erlbaum, 111–140.

4 Competing Plans in Second Language Processing

HANS W. DECHERT

On March 27th 1977, due to the explosion of a terrorist's bomb in the terminal at Las Palmas on the island of Gran Canaria, two airplanes, among others, were diverted to Los Rodeos Airport close to Santa Cruz on the nearby island of Tenerife. The weather on this particular day was foggy. Runway visibility was worsening during the afternoon. There were other circumstances which contributed to the dramatic course of events[1]: the inadequate technical equipment at Los Rodeos (the centre lights on the runway did not function, two out of the three radio frequencies for the transmission of messages between the tower and the cockpits had been out of order during the preceding six months, there was no ground radar to trace taxiing planes); the narrow width of the slipways; the Spanish accent of the tower personnel; the heavy congestion of the airfield and — as a consequence — the high task stress on the three air traffic controllers in the tower and on the crews, especially the pilots and copilots. At 5:06 p.m., after several hours of refuelling and waiting, a Boeing 747, flight number KLM 4805, on a charter flight from Amsterdam to Las Palmas, with 234 passengers and a crew of 14 on board, began to taxi along the runway and to gain speed in order to take off, without having received final takeoff clearance from air traffic control. It collided with another Boeing 747, flight number Pan Am 1736, on a charter flight from Los Angeles and New York to Las Palmas, taxiing down the runway and waiting for information from the tower, carrying 373 passengers and a crew of 16. After striking the American plane, KLM 4805 crashed to the ground and exploded immediately. Not a single person escaped. Five hundred and seventy-seven passengers and crewmembers were killed in this fatal accident, the most serious one that had happened in the history of aviation.

What were the real causes of this accident? Why did the captain of KLM 4805 take off without being given final takeoff clearance? Besides the listing of a number of immediate answers to these questions the Air Line

Pilots Association Study Group Report gave particular regard to the fact
that the captain of KLM 4805 was the head of his airline's Flight Training
Department and had spent most of his time during the preceding six years
in instructing and training pilots according to a highly condensed and
standardised training programme. The report describes this function as
follows:

> The task of a training instructor is to compress the maximum amount
> of training into the available simulator or airplane time. In order
> to accomplish this, he may *delete* [italics added] normally *realistic
> Air Traffic Control procedures and delays* [italics added] when
> training and checking a crew. There are no Air Traffic Control
> constraints in the simulator and only minimal constraints to the
> operation of the training aircraft. In the simulator, the instructor
> acts as the *controller* [italics added], always responding affirmatively
> to the trainee pilot's requests for expedited handling during
> emergencies. The instructor generally issues Air Traffic Control and
> takeoff clearance to the crew just prior to the final items of pre-
> takeoff checklist. There is never a need for the crew to hold
> the simulator in position awaiting takeoff clearance. (Reason &
> Mycielska, 1982: 216.)

What the Study Group Report quite obviously suggests is the possibility
that the Dutch captain's attempt to solve an unusually complicated real task
was seriously impeded by his many years' experience as a training instructor.
There may have been, in other words, competition

(a) between the nature and complexity of the real task and the nature
    and complexity of the simulated tasks;
(b) between the immediate action to be taken to solve the real task
    and the simulated actions practised in the simulated tasks;
(c) between an attitude that anticipates immediate affirmative evidence
    and response and an attitude that takes into consideration
    disconfirming evidence and response;
(d) between the real role of captain of the airplane and the simulated
    role of controller in the training programme, that is, between the
    status and authority attributed to the role of captain in the real
    task and the status and authority attributed to the role of controller
    in the simulated task;
(e) between the real role of captain of the airplane and the real role
    of Air Traffic Control, that is, between the status and authority
    attributed to the role of captain in the real task and the status and

authority attributed to the role of Air Traffic Control in the real task;

(f) between the simulated role of controller in the training programme and the real role of Air Traffic Control, that is, between the status and authority attributed to the role of controller in the simulated task and the status and authority attributed to the role of Air Traffic Control in the real task.

This competition must have eventually ended up in a blend in which a clear distinction between roles and actions to be taken to solve the real task were blurred: the Air Traffic Control's real clearance which was not at all meant to function as the final takeoff clearance — although the term *takeoff* was mentioned — and the anticipated final takeoff clearance — which was never given by Air Traffic Control — were mixed up. The KLM captain acted as if final takeoff clearance had been given.

What has this got to do with the topic of this chapter 'Competing Plans in Second Language Processing'?

Any theory of human action (and of language processing) must consider that quite frequently plans for action and sequences of plans for action run out of control and combine to form unintended and unforeseen behaviour and language. Usually we hardly notice such blends. Sometimes they have disastrous consequences as in the case of the Tenerife crash.

Blends are the result of a competition of two (perhaps more) plans which cannot be solved within the system. Although such competition may lead to erroneous behaviour and language, our ability to plan and reason in terms of more than one solution to the task we are confronted with is most likely the very source of the dynamics, flexibility, and adaptability of the human action system. This is the basic idea behind Baar's competing plans hypothesis (1980a, 1980b; cf. also Dechert, 1983c; Reason, 1984). This hypothesis corresponds with quite a different line of research concerning the integration of competing information in the production of novel reconstructed memories. The phenomenon of compromise memories, so far mainly studied in the recollection for colours (Bornstein, 1976; Hall & Loftus, 1984; Loftus, 1977), further exemplifies an apparently general tendency of the human information processing system: the integration of competing items of information. In Loftus' experiment subjects, who had been shown a number of slides with an automobile accident involving a green car, and later, on purpose given the wrong information *blue car*, selected a bluegreen hue which obviously represented a compromise, or a blend between the two competing items of information (Loftus, 1977).

Sample 1

The following text was produced by an advanced German learner of English.[2] It is taken from a large corpus of oral reproductions of an American Indian narrative 'The Lonesome Opossum' (Levitas, Vivelo & Vivelo, 1974: 12).[3]

TEXT 1 *Episodes 3 and 4 of the non-native reproduction of the Opossum story*

AFTER THAT (0.18) um (3.74) SHE (0.29) TOOK HER BABY (0.24)/
AND (0.51) uh (0.98) WENT ALONG WITH THE BABY THROUGH THE FOREST (0.44)//
THERE THEY MET (1.02) um (2.01) AN (9.49) WOLF (1.33)/
oh I forgot something/[chuckles]
um BEFORE (0.46) THE (0.12) BABY (0.19) WAS (0.16) FEEDED WITH (0.09) um (1.38) A (0.1) RATTLESNAKE IN THIS HOUSE (0.5)/
AND (0.12) THE OPOSSUM WAS (0.32) VERY ANGRY ABOUT THAT (1.69)//
AND LATER ON [chuckles] (0.14) WHEN THEY WENT ALONG IN THE FOREST (0.2)/
um THE OPOSSUM GAVE HER BABY (0.72) A FAWN TO EAT (0.98)//
THIS (0.44) met (0.64) m (0.1) m ja MET (2.2) uh WAS DISCOVERED BY THE WOLF (0.06) AND (0.1) THE WOLF WANTED TO HAVE SOME OF THE MEAT (0.52)//
BUT THE OPOSSUM SAID (0.22) THAT THEY (0.12) DON'T HAVE (0.08) ANY (1.3)//
s (0.26) uh BUT BECAUSE (0.1) THE WOLF HAD (0.26) A BORROW with it (0.18) WITH IT/
uh THE OPOSSUM (0.3) GOT AFRAID (0.23)/
AND THEY WENT UP (0.16) A TREE WITH THE BABY (0.09)//
THERE THE BABY DIED (1.74)/

Line 22 is of particular interest. The blend BORROW stands for the irreversible binomial

BOW AND ARROW
BO   RROW

No attempt is made to correct the blend and we do not even know if the subject was aware of it. It is a fine example of competitive planning.

There is, first of all, a higher level processing problem the student must solve: the establishment of coherence concerning the gender to be attributed to WOLF. This subprocess is indicated by the repetition of WITH IT. Gender attribution is a special problem characteristic of German learners of English since there is a fixed system of grammatical gender in their L1 of which they know that it cannot be transferred into English where gender attribution, especially with animals in narratives, is much more open. This problem produces task stress.

The binomial *Bow and Arrow* is irreversible in English just as is the German equivalent *Pfeil und Bogen*.

As Peters (1983: 57–59) has shown, the acquisition of this binomial by American children is a very complicated one and takes a comparatively long time. Binomials in general, and frozen binomials in particular, represent a special case of syntagmatic formulaic units of language processing. They are highly proceduralised in primary speech production. From a contrastive point of view, the reversal of order across languages is very likely to create particular processing problems.

As has been widely discussed in the literature on binomials, it is not only the semantic constraints, but also the syllabic and rhythmic gestalt which determine their production and reception within and across languages, according to a representation model of language processing (Slowiaczek, 1981).

The binomial

German	Pfeil und Bogen
	`× × ´× ×
English	Bow and Arrow

Bo(r)   row

is characterised by

(a) the reversed order of elements;
(b) the same syllabic and rhythmic gestalt of the whole unit in German and English: `× × ´× ×;
(c) the phonological and etymological similarity of one element in German and English

| German | Bogen | (bo:gǝn) | from OHG | 'bogo |
| English | bow | (bou) | from OE | 'boga |

(d) and the possibility of a vowel blend between German and English

German   o:
English   ou   blend ɔ in 'bɔrou

(e) the phonological and etymological dissimilarity of the other element in German and English

German   Pfeil
English   arrow

(f) the existence of a semantically totally dissimilar but rhythmically and phonologically partly similar word in English *borrow*, consisting of (i) a *first* syllable *bo(r)*, bearing the main stress, as in the equivalent syllable of the second element *Bogen* in the German binomial; (ii) a vowel in this first syllable resulting from a vowel blend ɔ from German *o:* and English *ou*; and (iii) a *second* syllable *-row*, taken over from the second syllable of the equivalent English word *arrow*, the phonologically and etymologically dissimilar second element of the English binomial whose first syllable is bearing the main stress.

All these factors are responsible for the interaction of an L1 and L2 induced plan, their competition and final blending, in addition to the task stress exerted by the pronominalisation problem. It is this kind of indirect interaction (*interference*) of languages which deserves particular attention in L2 processing research.

Sample 2

In the oral reproduction of a cartoon 'Wishing Well', taken from the elicitation material Goldman-Eisler (1961: 162–174) used in her experiments, one of our exchange students, a girl from England, produced the following text:[4]

TEXT 2 *Native reproduction of the Wishing Well story*

A MAN AND A WOMAN ARE WALKING UP TO A WISHING WELL (1.0) //
A::N (2.5) THE WOMAN IS SMILING (0.26) /
BUT they (1.64) THE MAN IS NOT SMILING (0.62) /
PERHAPS HE KNOWS THAT THE WOMAN IS GOING TO: (1.80) um (0.36) ASK HER SOME MONEY TO PUT IN THE WISHING WELL (5.0) //
THE WOMAN (0.62) HAS GOT THE they MONEY (0.76) /

AND SHE IS THROWING IT INTO THE WISHING WELL (0.96) /
THE MAN DOESN'T LOOK VERY INTERESTED (3.18) //
A::N (6.67) THEY ARE NOW WALKING AWAY FROM THE WELL (1.14) /
THE WOMAN IS SMILING (2.86) /
A::N (2.98) AGAIN THE MAN (1.98) ISN'T SMILING (12.18) /
A:ND IN THIS PICTURE THE MAN (0.46) IS NOT WEARING A BEARD (0.66) //
SO THE WOMAN (0.72) MUST HAVE WISHED (1.36) a::n THAT HIS BEARD WOULD DISAPPEAR (0.7) //
THE MAN DOESN'T LOOK VERY HAPPY ABOUT THIS //[5]

The passage THE WOMAN IS GOING TO ASK HER SOME MONEY is of particular interest for us. It is a blend of the two underlying sentences:

| The woman is going to ask | | him (for) | | some money |
The woman is going to ask	(for)	her		money

THE WOMAN IS GOING TO ASK HER SOME MONEY

What she intends to say is perfectly clear:

> He knows that the woman is going to ask him for some money to put it in the wishing well.

This idea may be directly inferred from the 'knowing' facial expression of the husband in the cartoon. That's why he is not smiling! There is no indication in the cartoon, however, that the lady may not have the money she wants to put in the well and that she must ask him for that money. She rather carries a purse with her which makes clear that it is her money that is being used. There is, in other words, every justification for the development of the second plan (and final statement) in which her money is talked about. The first plan is the student's invention. Her knowledge of the world where women ask for money is added to the cartoon and the man's smiling is perceived and interpreted according to the money-claiming-wife-script she has in her mind. There is a collision of scripts which explains the blend in this particular portion, such as the comparatively long pauses preceding and following this passage are indications of the high task stress.

Blends occur in first *and* second language processing. They must not be taken as a particular indication of a limited linguistic competence, but rather as a special limitation — or characteristic, if you will — of the human information processing system in general.

Sample 3

In a hitherto unpublished paper 'Collocational Blends of Advanced Second Language Learners',[6] P. Lennon, an English colleague of mine in the Kassel research group, and I have been dealing with the competition of plans in written language. After we had come across an astonishingly large number of collocational blends in the final examination essays of two highly competent students, the same topic was given to seven other advanced students for experimental reasons:

Topic

1. The British police have been advised by an Oxford University study group to base the amount of fines for motoring offences on how much the offender earns, rather than having a fixed fine for a particular offence.
2. This raises the moral issue of whether the punishment should fit the crime or the offender.
3. With reference to motoring offences in particular, but also to crime and punishment more generally, discuss this issue.
4. What do you see as the advantages and disadvantages of the Oxford study group's suggestion both with respect to motoring offences, and in terms of its possible application to other offences?

Task analysis

As one may imagine and as the post hoc analyses in the study disclosed, this topic and the way it was phrased produced many problems for all students: Above all this topic is quite complex. It may be analysed as follows:

Sentence 1.   Presentation of discussion material: statement of the Oxford University Study Group's advice to the British police.

Sentence 2.   Inference by the question setter — presentation of more discussion material: moral issue of whether punishment in general should fit the crime or the offender.

Sentence 3.   Formulation of task proper — instruction to the writer to discuss the issue of whether the punishment should fit the crime or the offender, specifically with reference to motor offences; and, generally, with reference to crime and punishment.

Sentence 4.   Additional information on how to approach the task: discussion of the advantages and disadvantages of the study group's advice, given in the first sentence.

Blends

Let me discuss one of the many collocational blends which were found in the data:

'To me there is a difference whether somebody steals a poor old lady DM 50.- or . . . goes to a big store and takes anything which is worth DM 50.-'

This statement is, of course, a mixture of the two English expressions

(For me, . . .) *there is* a difference *between* + NP *and* + NP

as in the sentence

For me there is a difference between the financial situation of a poor old lady and Ø (the financial situation of) a big department store.

and

(To me, . . .) *it makes* a difference *whether* NP + VP *or* NP + VP

as in the sentence

To me it makes a difference whether DM 50.- are stolen from a poor old lady or an object of the same value is stolen from a big department store.

Out of the large variety of equivalent German collocational phrases to express the same idea some may be easily blended as well; for this reason, we cannot say whether the English blend was influenced by an interaction with the subject's L1.

It is important to note, however, that a purely formal analysis of the linguistic structure of the English blend does not fully reveal the underlying competition of plans. The larger contextual environment must be taken into consideration. This may be done by looking at the function of the blended statement in question and by expanding it:

Statement

'To me there is a difference whether somebody steals a poor old lady DM 50.- or . . . goes to a big store and takes anything which is worth DM 50.-'

Function

Quite in accordance with the message of the two preceding statements:

(a) 'Then we have to see that there are *different* offences concerning danger' and
(b) 'There is a difference whether a person drives 100 km/h through a city or somebody parked his car wrong.' (which, of course, is another blend).

This statement, according to the instruction given to the writer, attempts to give an example for other than motoring offences, after the perspective has shifted from the particular category of motoring offences to a more general notion of offences, exemplified by robbery.

Expansion

Whatever a legal system which does not sufficiently discriminate between single individual cases may demand, I — the writer of this essay — strongly argue that there are differences as to the effects offences bring about for potential victims. One and the same offence, such as stealing DM 50.- or an object of the same value, committed twice does have an entirely different effect. The theft of a tiny insignificant item worth DM 50.- from a display of tens of thousands of other such items in a big department store ('anything') is only a minor insignificant delict if one considers the actual damage being done to the extremely wealthy owners or shareholders who are not affected personally anyhow, especially if one is aware that thefts are covered by an insurance. For a poor old lady, quite contrary to that, the sudden unexpected loss of DM 50.- may have disastrous financial and psychological consequences. Any legal system which takes no notice of such differences between different victims with different social status, income, and chance of recovery is extremely unjust. It does make a difference that there are differences.

It is the conceptual ambiguity of the statement and the essay's central notion *difference*, which is responsible for the competition and blending of the two collocational expressions.

Collocational blends on the sentence level are by no means restricted to second language production. 'Overlappings' have been found in the productions of native speakers of English as well and have been discussed in the composition research literature just recently (Daiute, 1984).

Conclusion

In the June 21st 1985 edition of *The Wall Street Journal* there appeared an article with the headline 'Jimmy Reagan'. This article was a critical comment

on President Reagan's press conference on June 18th 1985 in which he gave
a very careful consideration of the steps to be taken to free the American
hostages held in custody by the Lebanese Amal.

> President Reagan's press conference Tuesday must have made
> Jimmy Carter feel good, but it's hard to find another saving grace.
> If the position staked out by Mr. Reagan is to be taken at face
> value, he has just issued engraved invitations to terrorists throughout
> the world.

And at the end of the article's final paragraph:

> Of course, the US cannot 'pinpoint' the villain. So under the President's
> rhetoric, it cannot move to assert American interests. This was
> President Carter's logic in Iran. It was not President Reagan's logic in
> Grenada. The president won the public's support for action instead of
> inaction; in the TWA case it seems there is much support in the
> country for taking action rather than doing nothing. Whether the
> President's rhetoric on Tuesday is to be taken as his final word of
> course remains to be seen.

The implied meaning of the blend 'Jimmy Reagan' in the context of the
dramatic events in the Lebanon in the June of 1985 is perfectly clear to the
reader even before he starts reading the text: he is reminded of an analogy
between President Carter's hesitant behaviour during the Tehran hostage
crisis and President Reagan's supposed inactivity as seemingly revealed by
the statements made during the press conference. The critical implications
of that analogy are additionally enforced by the fact that Ronald Reagan's
criticism of President Carter's handling the Tehran crisis during his 1980
election campaign considerably contributed to his victory. 'His campaign
contempt for Carter's failure to win an early release of the US hostages
held in Iran ("They shouldn't have been there six days, let alone six
months") was thrown back at him at such moments' (*Time*, July 1st 1985:
15). The blend of names in 'Jimmy Reagan' is used to comment critically
on President Reagan's statements during the press conference in terms of
his own successful criticism of President Carter in an analogical situation,
or to put it in another more general way, this blend serves as a rhetorical
means of analogical reasoning.

Blends in the somewhat broader sense of a cover term which I have
been using throughout this article is a preferred pattern of rhetoric and of
word formation in English. In an article in *American Speech* (1974)

M. Bryant lists 306 examples from modern American English. There is also a vast literature on the various synchronic and diachronic aspects of blends. Since blends, as our example indicates, are easily formed and understood, they may easily serve to fill in a semantic slot for which two plans compete whose final dissolution is intended to be achieved by the hearer or reader. Blending occurs on various linguistic levels, the word, the phrase, and the sentence level, in spoken as well as in written language, unintentionally as well as intentionally for stylistic, rhetoric or even advertising reasons. Blends are based on an inherent analogy between two semantic dimensions which they connect. In language production they may be subsumed to what is generally considered an error. For psycholinguistics they provide immediate access to the inner workings of production, especially when they go along with other indications of planning and editing, such as temporal variables, and so forth.

In such a perspective they are traces of the contact and the interaction of various cultures, cognitive systems and languages. Such a contact and interaction within a hearer or speaker or within a speech community may be judged as a potential danger for the singularity and purity of the dominant language and culture. It may also be seen, vice versa, as a potential source of enrichment and depth. The same is true in particular with the phenomenon of competition of plans and of blending. There are numerous examples of either way of interpreting language contact and interaction in Europe.

Notes to Chapter 4

1. This account of the fatal course of events follows closely the detailed record given in Reason & Mycielska, 1982: 210–217. The analysis of the possible main cause for these events differs considerably from the one suggested by these authors.
2. Compare Dechert, 1984: 162–164.
3. This is the original text of the Indian narrative which was presented to the subject before the oral reproduction. The two episodes in question are italicised:
   She came to a house. Somebody was there and she asked if they had seen anybody going by, carrying a baby. The person in the house said 'Yes.' The opossum went in the direction they indicated and on the road she met two people and asked them the same question. Then she had been to two places and met two people, and sang her 'lonesome song' twice. After a while she came to another place. In that place the baby had been hidden. There were four or five houses, some occupied and some empty. The opossum asked her question and somebody pointed to a house saying, 'They got the baby in there.' *She went over, opened the door and found the baby inside. Somebody had killed a rattlesnake, cooked it, and given it to the baby to eat. The mother was angry and told them to take it away. She took the baby and started home. She killed a little fawn, ate some of the meat, and gave some to the baby. They stayed there a while. That*

made three times she sang the song. A wolf came to that place and smelled the meat. The opossum lied and said she had no meat, but the wolf smelled the meat. The wolf got a bow and arrow. Then the opossum was afraid she would be killed. She went up a big tree, took the baby with her and stayed up in the top of the tree. The baby died up there in the tree. That was the fourth time she sang the song. The old opossum came down and walked away. She found a skunk who was her friend and went home with the skunk. They lay down together and sang. They sang another 'lonesome song' and then they both died.

4. Dechert, 1983a: 92; Key to symbols used in the transcriptions

(2.66)	Pause (2 66/100 sec.).
uh	Filled Pause.
THE WELL	Capital Letters: Intended Ideal Version.
the	Small Letters: False Start, Parenthetical Remark etc.
	Unit Boundary Lines:
/	Rise – Fall.
	Intonation Contour + Pause: Episodic Unit.
	Fall –Rise.
//	Falling Intonation Contour +Pause: Episode.

5. Compare Dechert, 1983b: 36–40.
6. This article 'Collocational blends of advanced second language learners: A preliminary analysis' is to appear in: Wieslaw Oleksy (ed), *Contrastive Pragmatics.* Amsterdam, The Netherlands: John Benjamins.

References

BAARS, B.J., 1980a, On eliciting predictable speech errors in the laboratory. In V.A. FROMKIN (ed.), *Errors in Linguistic Performance: Slips of the Tongue, Ear, Pen, and Hand.* New York: Academic Press, 307–318.
— 1980b, The competing plans hypothesis: An heuristic viewpoint on the causes of errors in speech. In H.W. DECHERT & M. RAUPACH (eds), *Temporal Variables in Speech: Studies in Honour of Frieda Goldman-Eisler.* Janua Linguarum Series Maior 86. The Hague: Mouton, 39–49.
BORNSTEIN, M.H., 1976, Name codes and color memory. *American Journal of Psychology 89,* 269–279.
BRYANT, M.M., 1974, Blends are increasing. *American Speech 49,* 163–184.
DAIUTE, C.A., 1984, Performance limits on writers. In R. BEACH & L.S. BRIDWELL (eds), *New Directions in Composition Research.* New York: The Guilford Press, 205–224.
DECHERT, H.W., 1983a, First and second language processing: similarities and differences. *Rassegna Italiana di Linguistica Applicata 15*(2/3), 77–93.
— 1983b, Some psycholinguistic considerations towards a theory of second language processing. In H. RINGBOM (ed), *Psycholinguistics and Foreign Language Learning: Papers from a Conference held in Stockholm and Åbo.* Åbo, Finland: Åbo Akademi, 30–46.
— 1983c, The competing-plans hypothesis (CPH) extended to second-language speech production. In R. DI PIETRO, W. FRAWLEY & A. WEDEL (eds), *The First*

Delaware Symposium on Language Studies: Selected Papers. Newark, DE: University of Delaware Press, 269–282.

— 1984, Individual variation in language. In H.W. DECHERT & M. RAUPACH (eds), *Second Language Productions*. Tübingen: Narr, 156–185.

GOLDMAN-EISLER, F., 1961, Hesitation and information in speech. In C. CHERRY (ed), *Information Theory*. London: Butterworths, 162–174.

HALL, D.F. & LOFTUS, E.F., 1984, The fate of memory: discoverable or doomed? In L.R. SQUIRE & N. BUTTERS (eds), *Neuropsychology of Memory*. New York: The Guilford Press, 25–32.

LEVITAS, G., VIVELO, F.R. & VIVELO, J.J. (eds), 1974, *American Indian Prose and Poetry: We Wait in the Darkness*. New York: Putnam's Sons and Capricorn Books.

LOFTUS, E.F., 1977, Shifting human color memory. *Memory and Cognition 5*, 696–699.

PETERS, A.M., 1983, *The Units of Language Acquisition*. Cambridge: Cambridge University Press.

REASON, J., 1984, The psychopathology of everyday slips: accidents happen when habit goes haywire. *The Sciences 24*(5), 45–49.

REASON, J. & MYCIELSKA, K., 1982, *Absent-minded? The Psychology of Mental Lapses and Everyday Errors*. Englewood Cliffs, NJ: Prentice-Hall.

SLOWIACZEK, M.L., 1981, *Prosodic Units as Language Processing Units*. Unpublished doctoral dissertation, University of Massachusetts.

Part 2
Children's First and Second Language Acquisition

5 Early Bilingual Reading: Retrospects and Prospects

RENZO TITONE

Theoretical perspectives: early bilingual reading (EBR) and the child's psychological development

Bilingual reading is related on the one hand to intellectual growth and on the other to basic education. It is therefore necessary to define some basic concepts connected with the three areas of primary concern, namely the mutual relationship between language and intelligence from a developmental point of view, the interdependence between bilingualism and reading, and the relationship between bilingual reading and basic education.

Early bilingualism and intelligence

Bilingualism is not a monolithic state of mind and behaviour but a kind of linguistic competence having varying degrees. Usually one language is dominant, at least in one area or level of communication. True bilingualism, or fully fluent, or balanced bilingualism implies a functionally sufficient command of two language systems with regard to phonological, grammatical, lexical, and pragmatic abilities. Only with respect to balanced bilinguals is it possible to consider the effects of bilingualism on cognitive growth.

Contrary to earlier indications more recent findings confirm that bilingual children appear to have a mental flexibility, a superiority in concept formation, and a more diversified set of mental abilities (Peal & Lambert, 1962; Bain & Yu, 1978; and other researchers).

More particularly it has been claimed that 'metalinguistic awareness is the primary variable mediating the positive effects of bilingualism on academic achievement. The argument, in summary form, is that fully fluent bilingualism results in increased metacognitive/metalinguistic abilities which,

67

in turn, facilitate reading acquisition which, in turn, leads to higher levels of academic achievement' (Tunmer & Myhill, 1984: 176). Metacognitive abilities imply the habitual capacity to reflect upon and manipulate thought processes, while metalinguistic consciousness implies the ability to reflect upon and manipulate language concepts and functions. The suggestion is that the process of conceptually separating two languages into functionally independent systems results both in an increase of metacognitive ability and in the strengthening of metalinguistic awareness. In support of this suggestion are several recent studies which seem to indicate that bilinguals do, in fact, enjoy superior metalinguistic, as well as metacognitive, functioning (e.g. studies by Ben-Zeev, 1977; Ianco-Worrall, 1972; Cummins, 1978; Feldman & Shen, 1971, quoted in Tunmer & Myhill, 1984: 177).

Early bilingualism and reading

There is sufficient evidence that reading acquisition depends to a very large extent on the development of both metacognitive and metalinguistic abilities. In other terms, the development of conscious control of perception and cognition on one hand and of the formal aspects of language on the other play a central role in learning to read. More specifically, it can be stated that efficient learning to read requires good phonological awareness (recognition and distinction of sounds or phonemes), distinct word awareness, sufficient form awareness (i.e. conscious control of grammatical forms and functions), and pragmatic awareness (or ability to use and appropriately select communication rules in pertinent situations).

Furthermore, 'the view that metalinguistic awareness is a prerequisite skill is not inconsistent with the possibility that reading *instruction* increases metalinguistic awareness, which would explain the sharp increases in metalinguistic abilities often observed among beginning readers' (Tunmer & Bowey, 1984: 167).

On the other hand, it remains true that balanced bilingualism enhances, in turn, metacognitive and metalinguistic development in very young children (4–8 years of age). The argument then could be phrased as follows: both bilingualism and reading are stimulated and fostered by the gradual acquisition of metacognitive and metalinguistic abilities; whereas bilingual reading is expected to enhance both linguistic competence and cognitive development to a very high degree and at a very precocious age level. A great many findings support the conclusion that learning to read as early as from the age of three results in greater intellectual flexibility, conscious cognitive control and richer linguistic competence as compared with illiterate peers (see Doman, 1975; Cohen, 1977). It is therefore safe to infer that early *bilingual* reading ability should have a strong impact upon the child's cognitive and linguistic growth.

Early bilingual growth: An objective of basic education

> It is more and more widely granted today that interethnic communication and world-mindedness are basic needs of the cosmopolitan citizen of the future. A defence of this statement will seem superfluous. The progress of human civilisation depends on producing a generation of peace-makers, peace-lovers, and peace-bearers. It is also unquestionable that democracy is built upon education for personal as well as international understanding and cooperation . . . . But it is essential, also, that the 'New Man' of civilised society will have to be a creative learner, endowed with an ability to decode cultural and moral messages from all the experiences of humankind. Now these axioms imply a rejection of monoculturalism and of its allied state, monolingualism, taken in its narrowest sense. They also demand that we take a new look at basic education. Education, understood as the formation of the human personality in its fundamental dimensions, will have to step beyond the mere teaching of the 'three R's'; it will have to reflect concern for the socialisation of the human infant, and his ethical orientation in the world of values. It will demand a basic capacity for communication and will seek to promote a sensitivity to the diversity of cultures and languages . . . . I believe that . . . bilingual education must seek to ensure personality formation and mental health, broad-mindedness in solving human problems, flexibility in strengthening intellectual powers, and meta-linguistic awareness. (Titone, 1984: 7–8)

Now reading is considered most rightly to be central in the instrumental system leading to general education. Therefore, no doubt bilingual reading can become the main source for all-round personality formation, intellectually, emotionally, and socially.

Among other authors, it is encouraging to find in Donaldson's book, *Children's Minds* (1978), the suggestion that a better introduction into formal activities such as reading will aid the child in grasping the formal or disembedded character of thinking which schooling demands. In Donaldson's view, reading in particular will contribute to language awareness. Much more so with bilingual reading, which, if carried out since very early childhood, will certainly lay the foundation of open-minded education at an age when prejudices are still unknown.

Retrospects: case studies of early bilingual readers

Theodore Andersson, in his captivating booklet *The Preschool Years* (1981) on family reading in two languages, starts off by quoting Burton White who expressed with emphasis his belief 'that the educational developments that take place in the year or so that begins when a child is about eight months old are *the most important and most in need of attention of any that occur in human life*' (1975: 129–130). It is particularly up to the point what Benjamin Bloom reports after extensive research, namely that 'put in terms of intelligence measured at age 17, from conception to age 4 the individual develops 50% of his mature intelligence . . . . This would suggest the very rapid growth of intelligence in the early years and the possible great influence of the early environment on this development' (1964: 68). All this amounts to underscoring the unique importance of early reading carried on while the child's brain shows a high degree of plasticity and undifferentiation.

The case for early reading

The movement in favour of early learning to read is becoming impressive and covering many different countries. The starting point was signalled by the marvellous experience initiated by Glenn Doman with his book *How to Teach Your Baby to Read* (1964), which recounted convincing principles and fascinating cases. According to Doman:

1. Tiny children *want* to learn to read.
2. Tiny children *can* learn to read.
3. Tiny children *are* learning to read.
4. Tiny children *should* learn to read. (1964: 9)

Facts proving the truth of Doman's assumptions are countless. Doman acquired valuable experience with early readers, which he set forth persuasively in his popular book, addressed to mothers. In it he declares: 'Children can read words when they are one year old, sentences when they are two, and whole books when they are three — and they love it' (1964: 1).

Following Doman many educators since the early sixties have tried out his method or similar ones and have reached wonderful results. Andersson (1981) quotes 23 instances of which at least five are not mere case studies but experimental investigations. Beside Doman's name, the names of Söderbergh, Jane Torrey, Goodman, Fries, Durkin, Terman,

Cohan, Fowler, Hughes, Lado, Callaway, Steinberg, Emery, Witte, Ledson, Smethurst, Perlish, Taft Watson, and so forth have become widely known as marking significant milestones in the history of the movement. Case studies have multiplied (Miño-Garcés, 1981). Besides these cases related to home influence, some investigations can be quoted, like the one conducted by the Denver Public Schools (1961–1962) and another reported on by Harvey Neil Perlish (1968) on the effectiveness of television reading programmes, or the CRAFT Project (Harris, Morrison, Serwer & Gold, 1968) on a comparison of academic achievement of early readers and non-early readers, or especially Durkin's first study (1966) on the achievement of early readers from first grade to the end of grade six. Her main conclusion was that 'over the years, the early readers in this research continued to show higher achievement in reading than the non-early-readers with whom they were matched' (p. 110).

Andersson's accounts of early reading are far from exhaustive. In Europe the movement has found followers. A rather detailed account by Schmalohr (1973) reviews several home case studies (Kratzmeier, 1967; Walter, 1967) and also institutional investigations carried on in kindergartens. Of particular interest is the experiment organised by Lückert (1967, 1968) with the cooperation of 240 families on two-year old children. Specific studies (by Schmalohr, 1969; Schüttler-Janikulla, 1969; Brem-Graeser, 1969; Rüdiger, 1970; Wilke-Denig, 1972) aimed at examining young children in school settings so as to ascertain the effects of early reading on intelligence, language development, socio-emotional growth, long-range reading ability. Results were by and large positive (see reviews in Schmalohr, 1971).

But one of the best experiments was carried out by Rachel Cohen in France (1977) and reported on in her book *L'Apprentissage Précoce de la Lecture*. One hundred and sixty-one children were tested; their ages ranged between 3;8 and 4;11. The use of a multiple test battery evidenced that young children of pre-school age can learn to read, and secondly that reading can help them to develop their ability to grasp and formulate basic concepts.

Finally, it can be added that since 1976 the Chair of Educational Psycholinguistics (University of Rome, Italy), headed by R. Titone, has assigned five experimental doctoral dissertations (partly published) dealing with early reading projects carried out in different kindergartens throughout Italy. Three conclusions have been drawn as a result of such investigations: (a) children can learn to read from the age of three; (b) their intellectual improvement can be seen as a result of proper reading instruction (in comparison with control groups of non-readers); (c) reading can be taught in kindergarten settings by well-trained teachers (Annessi, 1979).

The case for early reading in two languages or early bilingual literacy (EBL)

What kind of relationship can there be between pre-school reading and the bilingual child? Andersson, on opening chapter 3 of his book (1981: 31), rightly comments:

> If a monolingual child can get a headstart by learning to read before going to school, why can't a bilingual child get a double headstart by learning to read two languages before entering school? No one would deny the educational importance of skill in reading; nor would many deny the advantage of a knowledge of two spoken languages. The theoretical advantage of knowing how to read and write in two languages would seem to be self-evident, and yet biliteracy is rarely emphasised as an objective in our schools.

In order to examine more closely the psychological aspects and the educational outcomes of early bilingual reading, Andersson (1981: 32–45) presents three cases of pre-school biliteracy.

Mariana and Elena Past have learnt to read in both English and Spanish, the former beginning at age 1;5, the latter at about the same age. Word games with word cards were used following approximately what Doman (1964) suggests in his method. During her third and fourth month of reading Mariana was already skilled in reading sentences, and she was frequently reading independently. At age 3;8 she was reading English at the level of the average first grader in the second half of first grade. The same was revealed with regard to Spanish. At age 4;11 her entering a bilingual kindergarten did the rest.

Raquel and Aurelio Christian also learnt to read English and Spanish very early. At 18 months Raquel had already asked her parents the names of the letters as they bought her an alphabet book in Spanish. Aurelio took no interest in the alphabet until much later, but absorbed words by mere association. Neither child had much interest in reading books of any length until about five. Reading Spanish at home transferred to reading English when they entered school. Later progress in grade school was excellent for both children.

Yuha and Chinha Ok Ro Lee are Korean/English bilinguals and biliterates. Since Yuha's development in Korean was far in advance of her development in English, her father decided, in order to prepare her for kindergarten, to initiate her into reading in English, her weaker language. Yuha liked to watch television, especially 'Sesame Street', and learnt all of the letters of the English alphabet. Then her parents taught her to read systematically. She learnt how to read first in English, while the language of instruction and explanation was Korean. But later on, in one month, thanks to a special programme, Yuha learnt to read and write Korean just before she became a first grader. Lee observes that at the end of 1-month instruction Yuha's skills in reading and writing the Korean language were better than her corresponding English skills. Biliteracy is more than just knowledge of two languages; it implies behaving properly in two cultures. In fact, Lee writes about his daughter: 'She speaks and behaves like an American among Americans; she speaks and behaves like a Korean among Koreans. Early bilingual reading seems to have aided her for her bilingual and bicultural adjustment in the United States' (Lee, 1977: 143–144).

Andersson (1981) submits the following correct conclusions:

The experience of the children in the three bilingual families . . . suggests that, far from being a double burden, learning to read in two languages is a double joy, leading to a positive self-image. The term 'early' in the expressions 'early reading' or 'early reader' is seen to vary all the way from age six months, as with Kimio Steinberg, to nearly five years, as in the case of Yuha Lee, suggesting that this concept is, or at least can be, quite flexible.

One notes significant uniformities among the parent-teachers involved in the cases I have cited. They exert no pressure on the child; rather they try to sense what will interest the child. The parent-teacher's task seems to consist in reading the child's wishes and in inventing games to stimulate this interest. Successful parents seem to include their young child in their conversations and activities. Above all, early reading appears, as in the case of Yuha Lee, to be related to establishing a sense of personal and social values. Parents who read, study, and discuss interesting or important subjects in the presence of their children and who answer their children's questions create a close relationship with their children, a relationship which older children are quick to adopt with their younger siblings. (pp. 44–45)

Experiences and investigations on early bilingual reading are taking impetus now as is documented by research reports and the launching of the new *IPRA* (International Preschool Reading Association) *Newsletter*. Among more recent reports it is worth considering what Els Oksaar, University of Hamburg, has tried to check with her investigation on a group of bilingual children (1984). Of the 20 bilingual children (from middle and working classes) who grew up hearing and speaking German and Swedish, or German and English, or Swedish and Estonian, 13 (65%) could read and write both languages more or less fluently by the age of four to five years. In the control group of six monolingual German or Swedish speaking children, four (67%) demonstrated this ability.

She adds that of the 13 children in her project who learnt to read two languages before they were five years old, 10 children were not exposed to any one particular method, but rather a sort of methodological pluralism, in which the interaction between the child and mother or other reference person played a dominant role. The children were read aloud to in both languages very early, following the well known rule 'one language — one person'; they knew much of this by heart and, finally, wanted to read themselves.

Furthermore, she notes that in bilingual marriages the children usually learn to read first in the language of the mother, or in the family language. The fact that in learning to read the second language, they had no difficulties, and progressed even more quickly than in the first language, would seem to support the generally accepted statement that children actually only have to learn to read once, and that this skill can be transferred from one language to another.

The transfer effect from one language to the other is also confirmed by Hélène Businger (1984) when she writes about her bilingual child that 'his ability to visualise and memorise words was transferred to the second language and he succeeded in reading with [her] a short book in English entitled "Teddy Bears 1 to 10". So the experiment has had a very positive effect on his bilingualism. It has also encouraged him to become biliterate' (p. 8).

With regard to method it is worth recalling what Nguyên Ngoc Bích (1984) writes in concluding her report on the progress in reading of her Vietnamese-speaking child, Victor Quang. Bích (1984) remarks that

> The element of play is an integral part of the learning process of young children; one needs to start with vocabulary that is not only simple from the linguistic point of view but also is immediately recognised in the child's environment; comprehension and miscue analysis are all very important parts of teaching as one tries to structure the child's learning environment. And, of course, it is of primary importance that the child be allowed to test and use his creative power to develop new sentences and gain a sense of power, of ownership. Thus, far from being a passive process of decoding and understanding only what is there, the reading process should be seen and allowed to be the creative process it has always been. (p. 8)

Now the question is: can bilingual reading be taught in pre-elementary schools by teachers? And why not use early bilingual reading instruction as a means to aid disadvantaged children like migrants' children? The answer to such questions can be given only by institutional experiments to be carried on with larger samples of young subjects. It is this perspective that will now be illustrated.

Prospects: a research project on early bilingual literacy

I will try to summarise the main lines of a research project designed by the writer aimed at developing the experimental conditions for teaching early bilingual reading in institutional settings. The essential traits of this project have already been outlined in a previous essay (Titone, 1983).

The Early Bilingual Reading Experimental Project

Stepping from mere experience to scientific experimentation means defining more accurately objectives, materials, instruments, and evaluation measures.

It is advisable: (a) to clarify the basic issues connected with early bilingual reading (during the pre-school years), its psycho-educational aspects, its advantages and possible drawbacks; (b) to prepare a transition from mere occasional experience in family circles to true scientific experimentation in kindergarten and/or nursery schools; (c) to design and build appropriate teaching materials linked with child motivation and language abilities.

The present author has built special materials (a reading kit and guide book for parents and teachers) for teaching playfully to read in two languages simultaneously (viz. Italian/English; Italian/French; Italian/German; Italian/Spanish is being prepared; Castilian-Spanish/Basque is being tried out). A discussion of the experimental paradigm follows.

Aims of the Research

This research intends to check: (a) the possibility and effectiveness of simultaneous learning to read in two languages from the age of four years (in any case before six); (b) the correlation between early literacy and bilingual development; (c) the correlation between early biliteracy and cognitive development; (d) the correlation between early bilingual literacy and the overcoming of cognitive and linguistic disadvantages of lower-class or immigrants' children.

Research methodology

The experimental control of the above variables shall consist of the following procedures:

1. pre-testing verbal intelligence and ascertaining the non-existence of reading ability at the start;
2. the systematic use of appropriate reading materials prepared by R. Titone, namely the 'Early Bilingual Reading Kit' (Titone, 1977): the materials should be applied for at least one school year;
3. post-testing bilingual reading competence on the basis of the above material.

Special scoring scales are being produced in order to compare individual results. Subjects will be assessed with respect to age, sex, socio-economic level, learning motivation, IQ, rate of oral language development. Raw scores will be processed by Titone's research team. Teaching can be carried on also by parents if competent; but as a rule kindergarten teachers will do the teaching under supervision.

Standard materials are published by A. Armando Editore (Via della Gensola, 60–61, 00153 Roma, Italy). Each kit will serve for more than one child (two or three, no more).

Evaluation instruments

The following data and measures will be collected:

1. Intelligence pre-test: The Wechsler Intelligence Scale for Children at pre-school age or another equivalent verbal intelligence test can be used. To be administered before starting the experiment.
2. Bilingualism pre-test: for checking linguistic competence in L1 and L2 on the basis of visual or motor stimuli (picture test). Verbal responses in terms of short narratives will be evaluated as to:
   (a) phonological correctness;
   (b) grammatical correctness and completeness;
   (c) lexical richness (quantity and appropriate use of words);
   (d) verbal fluency.
Practically: One should check for:
   (a) number of pronunciation errors on the total of words;
   (b) number of errors on the total of sentences;
   (c) number of words and number of errors of meaning on the total of words;

(d) rhythm (fast, middle, slow) of utterances.
3. Pre-reading test: reading of one's own first and last names printed on the blackboard or on cardboard (in capital letters).
4. Reading post-test: based on the reading material of the last booklet presented in the kit; check speed, correctness, comprehension (total number of errors).
5. Bilingualism post-test: the same initial picture test; check number of words, sentences, descriptive details through comparison with initial results (pre-test).
6. Intelligence post-test: by means of the same initial test in an alternative form.
7. Questionnaire: to be submitted to both parents and teachers (see below).

Questionnaire on Early Bilingual Reading Experience

The questionnaire can be administered orally or in writing.
1. At what age did your child begin to speak?
2. When did he or she begin to find amusement in scribbling?
3. When did he or she show interest in writing or in written things, like: neon signs? advertising in television? posters? comics? words connected with pictures? . . .
(Please indicate age in general, if remembered, for each type of objects).
4. At what age did the first reading take place: in one language? in the other language?
5. What did he or she learn to read: in one language? in the other language?
6. Did he or she show fast or slow progress?
7. How often does he or she show the desire to read? — during the day? (number of times) — during the week? (number of times)
8. How long does his or her application to reading last? — less than 10 minutes? more than 30 minutes? . . .
9. Has he or she been undergoing an ebb and flow process in his or her reading interests? — In what period of age (and for how long) did he or she keep his or her reading interest alive? — In what period of age (and for how long) did he or she neglect or reject reading? . . .
10. What is his or her *present* degree of interest in reading? — high — middle — low . . .
11. Are you in favour of (or against) reading at pre-school age? Why? . . .

Teaching method

The general hints given here refer to Titone's Bilingual Reading Method as materialised in the reading kit published by A. Armando in Rome. However, keeping these indications in mind, other types of materials can be designed, especially if the two languages do not include Italian. The present hints concern the general teaching approach, some basic suggestions, and the use of the material.

One preliminary question: Is reading in two languages really easy? In order to answer this question we must first point out the activities which facilitate the child's learning to read in a single language:

1. Search and naming games for objects, animals, loved persons; games dealing with the inexhaustible curiosity towards an environment where surprise is continuous, where the unknown is a potential for personal conquest.
2. Global attainment of some realities and later tentative analyses: in the kitchen, tools; in the garden, plants; in the train, wheels; in dolls, legs, arms, head; and so forth.

   It is no different in the handling of bilingual reading: some basic activities come into play in enjoyable games which solicit spontaneous curiosity towards:

(a) the oral and written knowledge of words or sounds having to do with objects, animals, people of particular interest;
(b) the global perception of easy sentences dealing with the child's experience, that is, well defined, known objects of certain interest: one's own body, a toy, family members . . .

Objects which are not familiar or words which are not yet possessed in the oral form should be avoided, as should single letters totally isolated from the context of a phrase or sentence. The spoken and known must always precede the written.

Our method implies some preliminary suggestions such as the following:

1. Begin with a game or pleasant conversation.
2. Focus upon a word or a sentence in one of the two languages, writing it on a card or indicating it on the appropriate chart or in a booklet (see Titone's material); read it aloud and have the child repeat it.

   In the first phase one should not worry about having the child distinguish between the single letters. These will be discovered spontaneously by the child and one can, in any case, point them out later in the written or spoken word.

3. The main method of teaching a child a language is through play. Everything should appear like a game of discovery and invention in which words, and later on letters, serve to construct sentences, as if it were a question of placing one block upon the other, brick upon brick . . . . Many spontaneous games can come about through the child's initiative, others may be invented by the educator.

The games may be numerous and varied. Some may be of the following types: matching the cards with words and then later with sentences; rapid reading contests; finding the right card as in a game of cards; action cards, like in Montessori's 'command game'; sentences to construct — in this case cards with words or sentence pieces should be used: the child is asked to read, understand, link up the single cards in an order in such a way as to make up a sentence; when he or she has finished, he or she reads the whole constructed sentence aloud.

The material included in the box prepared by R. Titone (1977) is divided as follows:

1. The words *mommy* and *daddy* on two separate cards which have the word written in L1 on one side, and the word written in L2 on the opposite side.
2. Twenty words dealing with the child him- or herself, each on a separate card, in both languages.
3. Basic vocabulary relative to the immediate world of the child.
4. Essential vocabulary for the formation of sentences.
5. Vocabulary to be inserted in structured sentences.
6. Four booklets for progressively difficult reading, having a series of pictures, each of which is coupled with a sentence in both languages.
7. The alphabet in both languages, with references to words of immediate use.

The subdivision of the material corresponds to an exact grading of difficulty to be met with by the child.

As educators (parents and teachers) have found out, the child does not find it strange that objects and actions are not only said in two different languages, but are also written and read in two different languages. If, in fact, he or she lives in a bilingual environment he or she will be ready not only for hearing sounds, words, and sentences in two languages, but also for seeing books, magazines, comics and printed matter of all sorts in two languages as well.

Detailed instructions on how to go about in each phase are given in the guide accompanying the material (Titone, 1977). Basically the instructional method is grounded on the assumption that optimal learning takes place when there is harmony between:

Visual sensations (V)
Auditory sensations (A)
Tactile sensations (T).

The VAT language learning system emphasises the fundamental aspects and factors of an easy means of learning bilingual reading based on the use of:

(a) the visual (recognition of the forms of words),
(b) the auditory (association of sound and written word),
(c) the tactile (touching the cards on which the words are written)

as a pattern of meaning integrated by the direct and joyful experience of the child interacting with the adult.

One step at a time, one word at a time, one sentence at a time, one page at a time! The material is never shown all at once to the child, nor are the successive parts shown before the preceding step has been conquered.

Concluding remarks

Who are the targets of this early reading method?

At this moment the use of the 'Early Bilingual Reading Kit' by R. Titone is recommended and being used with children from the age of four living:

(a) in bilingual families;
(b) in bilingual or multilingual areas (in Italy, especially the French–Italian speaking area of Valle d' Aosta, the German–Italian area of Alto Adige/Bozen; in the Basque Country);
(c) in immigrants' children's homes or schools.

However, a few attempts are being made in bilingual or international kindergartens (Turin, Milan, Rome). Results are not yet available due to the short time elapsed since the beginning of the experiment, although the impressions gathered from parents and educators are so far favourable.

It is noteworthy that Titone's method and material has been adapted to an experimental project which is being carried on in the Basque Country with Basque–Castilian bilingual children (ages 4 to 6). The coordinator, Dr. Antton Kaifer Arana, has translated and adapted the 'Early Bilingual Reading Kit' into Castilian and Euskara and is using it to teach a large number of children reading in both languages at the same time. The project will achieve the result of strengthening command of L1, namely the Basque language, which has lost ground in recent times. The project is stimulating wide popular interest.

No doubt many problems are still open to discussion and research. But the writer believes that there is sufficient warrant for positive confirmation of the main hypotheses outlined at the beginning of this article. In particular, it is believed that great advantages will be achieved on behalf of the maintenance of bilingual competence in immigrant children in many countries. This expectation seems to be fulfilled by an attempt of applying the method to Italian immigrant children in some German-speaking areas of Switzerland as in Canada. Promises are substantial. This opportunity cannot be missed.

References

ANDERSSON, T., 1981, *A Guide to Family Reading in Two Languages. The Preschool Years*. Rosslyn, VA: National Clearinghouse for Bilingual Education.

ANNESSI, A.F., 1979, La lettura precoce, fattore positivo dello sviluppo cognitivo. *Rassegna Italiana di Linguistica Applicata 40* (1–2), 327–334.

BAIN, B.C. & YU, A., 1978, Toward an integration of Piaget and Vygotsky: A cross-cultural replication (France, Germany, Canada) concerning cognitive consequences of bilinguality. In M. PARADIS (ed.), *Aspects of Bilingualism*. Colombia, SC: Hornbeam Press.

BÍCH, NGUYÊN NGOC, 1984, Learning to read in bilingual setting, *IPRA Newsletter*, Winter.

BLOOM, B.S., 1964, *Stability and Change in Human Characteristics*. New York, NY: John Wiley & Sons.

BREM-GRAESER, L., 1969, Bericht über die Ergebnisse der Frühförderung in Münchner Kindergärten. *Schule und Psychologie 16*, 334–345.

BUSINGER, H., 1984, A case study in early reading, *IPRA Newsletter*, Summer/Fall.

COHEN, R., 1977, *L'apprentissage précoce de la lecture*. Paris: Presses Universitaires de France.

DOMAN, G., 1975, *How to Teach your Baby to Read*. New York, NY: Random House.

DONALDSON, M., 1978, *Children's Minds*. Glasgow: Collins.

DURKIN, D., 1966, *Children who Read Early: Two Longitudinal Studies*. New York, NY: Teachers College Press.

HARRIS, A.J., MORRISON, C., SERWER, B.L. & GOLD, L., 1968, *A Continuation of* the CRAFT PROJECT Comparing Reading Approaches with Disadvantaged Urban Negro Children in Primary Grades. New York, NY: Division of Teachers Educators.

KRATZMEIER, N., 1967, Kleinkindlesen. Schule und Psychologie, 14, 215–222.

LEE, O.R., 1977, Early Bilingual Reading as an Aid to Bilingual and Bicultural Adjustment for a Second Generation Korean Child in the U.S. Ph.D. dissertation. Washington, DC: Georgetown University Press.

LÜCKERT, H.R., 1967, Lesenlernen im Vorschulalter als Aktion der basalen Bildungsförderung. Schule und Psychologie 14, 297–312.

— 1968, Lesen – ein Spiel mit Bildern und Wörtern. Ravensburg: Maier.

MIÑO-GARCÉS, F., 1981, Early Reading Acquisition: Six Psycholinguistic Case Studies. Washington, DC: Georgetown University Press.

OKSAAR, E., 1984, Bilingual Reading and Writing in the Early Years. Paper presented at the Third International Congress for the Study of Child Language, Austin, TX, July 8–14.

PEAL, E. & LAMBERT, W.E., 1962, The relation of bilingualism to intelligence. Psychological Monographs: General Applied 76, whole no 546.

PERLISH, H.N., 1968, In W. SMETHURST, Teaching Young Children to Read. New York, NY: McGraw Hill.

RÜDIGER, D., 1970, Ansatz und erste Befunde einer experimentellen Längsschnitt-tudie zum Lesenlernen im Vorschulalter. Schule und Psychologie 17, 72–96.

SCHMALOHR, R., 1969, Psychologische Untersuchung zum Duisburger Frühleseversuch. Schule und Psychologie 16, 145–159.

— 1971, Psychologie des Erstlese- und Schreibunterrichts. München: Reinhardt.

SCHÜTTLER-JANIKULLA, K., 1969, Vorschulisches Lesenlernen und intellektuelle Leistungssteigerung, Schule und Psychologie 16, 169–179.

TITONE, R., 1977, A Guide to Bilingual Reading. Rome: Armando.

— 1983, Early bilingual reading: From experience to experiment. Rassegna Italiana di Linguistica Applicata 15, (1), 79–83.

— 1984, Early bilingual growth: An objective of basic education. The International Schools Journal 7, Spring, 7–16.

TUNMER, W.E. & BOWEY, J.A., 1984, Metalinguistic awareness and reading acquisition. In W.E. TUNMER, C. PRATT & M.L. HERRIMAN (eds), Metalinguistic Awareness in Children. Berlin: Springer Verlag, 144–168.

TUNMER, W.E. & MYHILL, M.E., 1984, Metalinguistic awareness and bilingualism. In W.E. TUNMER, C. PRATT & M.L. HERRIMAN (eds), Metalinguistic Awareness in Children. Berlin: Springer Verlag, 169–187.

WALTER, K.H., 1967, Sollen kleine Kinder lesen lernen? Kleine Kinder lesen, schreiben, rechnen. Duisburg: Goldmann.

WHITE, B., 1981, In T.ANDERSSON, A Guide to Family Reading in Two Languages. The Preschool Years. Rosslyn, VA: National Clearinghouse for Bilingual Education.

WILKE, J. & DENIG, F., 1971, Vorschulerziehung und Steigerung der Intelligenzlei-stung, Schule und Psychologie 19, 37–44.

6 The Relationship Between Native and Foreign Language Learning Ability: Educational and Linguistic Factors

PETER SKEHAN

General rationale: research into language learning ability

Most research into foreign language learning has emphasised instructional and methodological factors. In general this research, interesting though it is, has failed to find any clear indications that any particular method of foreign language instruction is superior to any other when global comparisons are made. The Pennsylvania Project (Smith, 1970), for example, did not find any clear advantage for cognitive-code learning over audiolingual methods. Similarly, the York study on the effectiveness of the language laboratory (Green, 1975) did not suggest any clear difference between children with access to a laboratory and those lacking such exposure. More recently, Davies & Beretta (1985), have reported results suggesting that a procedural syllabus, as implemented through the Bangalore Project, while slightly superior to traditional methods, is not superior in all domains of language learning.

In contrast, an alternative research tradition, that into characteristics of the language learner, although perhaps generating smaller quantities of research, has yielded more promising results in terms of being able to account for language learning success. Carroll (1965, 1982), for example, has consistently shown how important foreign language aptitude is for predictions of classroom foreign language learning success, while Reves (1983) has also attested to the importance of aptitude in an informal setting. Gardner (1986) has researched into differences in attitude and motivation,

83

and demonstrated their importance for school-based learning, revealing an affective dimension for prediction clearly distinct from the cognitive abilities that make up aptitude. Another area which has received attention in the last decade is that of learner strategies. Naiman, Fröhlich, Stern & Tedesco (1978) have provided interesting biographical data which helps to characterise highly successful language learners, while Wong Fillmore (1976, 1979) conducted a longitudinal study of a small group of young Spanish-speaking children learning English in the first years of school. She proposes that several cognitive and social strategies account for the degree of success that the children achieved.

These various studies have been very suggestive of the dimensions of individual differences that may account for variation in second and foreign language achievement. It is to be hoped that such research will grow in importance and that we shall see further studies which perhaps investigate the interrelationships between these different classes of individual difference variables. Equally interesting would be studies similar to that of Wesche (1982) who investigated aptitude methodology interactions, demonstrating that students identified as belonging to different 'learner types' did particularly well when paired with appropriate methodologies, and particularly poorly when they were mismatched in terms of instructional conditions. Such results are, of course, very significant for the methodology comparisons which were discussed at the beginning of this section since it may well have been that individual differences between subjects in (say) the Pennsylvania study, interacting with methodology, cancelled out or disguised actual treatment effects.

Against this background, the present project is situated in one of the main traditions of research into individual differences, that of foreign language aptitude. It attempts to relate three sets of variables:

1. Measures of first language acquisition
2. Measures of foreign language acquisition
3. Measures of foreign language achievement.

Each of these areas will now be described in more detail.

Individual differences in first language learning

Most first language research has emphasised universal processes of language acquisition. Investigators have attempted to uncover general features of language processing and developmental change, such as developmental order of certain morphemes, or the role of maternal speech in language development. However, there are some research studies which emphasise individual differences in first language acquisition and the variation that exists between learners, both in terms of rate of learning as well as in terms of route. The clearest and most comprehensive example of a study of rate of development forms a part of the Bristol Language Project (Wells 1981, 1985). The Bristol research has sought to determine the extent of the variation in first language development on a number of different dimensions. Indices of syntactic, semantic and functional language development, as well as the acquisition of pragmatic competence have been developed. In addition, considerable information has been assembled, from tape transcripts as well as interview data, on the relevant environmental factors which are associated with the variation in the rate of first language development. These indices show that there is massive variation in the rate at which features of one's first language are acquired. At the age of 42 months, for example, in terms of mean Morpheme Length of Utterance (MLU):

> We find that children scoring as high as two standard deviations (+2 SDs) above the mean have a score that is greater than the mean of the sample as a whole at the time of the last observation of the older children (18 months later), while those scoring as low as two SDs below the mean have a score equivalent to the mean observed for the sample as a whole as much as 15 months earlier. (Wells, 1985: 124)

Furthermore, there is evidence to link rate of language development, but not course of development, with features of speech addressed to the children (Barnes, Gutfreund, Satterley & Wells, 1983). In particular, the use of 'extending' responses by mothers, of direct requests for control, and of amount of adult speech are associated with a more rapid course of subsequent development.

Several investigators have also tried to uncover different *routes* of language development, and to link these to different styles and strategies of learning. Nelson (1973, 1981), for example, has proposed a referential/ expressive dichotomy, with children in the former category tending to name objects and acquire more extensive vocabularies early in life while those in the latter category are less noun-dependent in their early vocabulary growth, and more concerned with expressive uses of language. Bloom, Lightbown, & Hood (1975) have made a related distinction between 'substantive' (nominal) children who tend in early language development to use SVO sentence constructions and more nouns, and 'relational' (pronominal) children, who rely more on pronominal forms, pivot-open constructions, and imitations. Bloom *et al.* (1975) propose these as alternative routes to later language development. Peters (1983) has also made a similar distinction between a holistic/gestalt style, on the one hand, and a more analytical style, while Bretherton, McNew, Snyder & Bates (1983) suggest that varying degrees of analyticity underlie the various dichotomies proposed in the literature.

Individual differences in foreign language learning aptitude

There have also been studies of individual differences in foreign language aptitude. Here the underlying rationale is that there is a set of abilities uniquely related to success in foreign language learning which are separate from verbal intelligence, on the one hand, and previous achievement, on the other (Carroll, 1965, 1974). It is proposed that these abilities constitute general competences or learning capacities which enable some people to learn languages faster than others.

Carroll (1965, 1982) has proposed the following components for aptitude:

Inductive Language Learning Ability: 'the ability to infer or induce the rules governing a set of language materials, given samples of language materials that permit such inferences.'
Grammatical Sensitivity: 'the ability to recognise the grammatical functions of words (or other linguistic entities) in sentence structures.'
Phonemic Coding Ability: 'an ability to identify distinctive sounds, to form associations between those sounds and symbols representing them, and to retain these associations.'
Rote Learning Ability for Foreign Language Materials: 'the ability to learn associations between sounds and meanings rapidly and efficiently and to retain these associations.' (Carroll, 1982: 105)

Carroll has developed a test battery based on these postulated components of aptitude (Carroll & Sapon, 1957). Other investigators, drawing on similar aptitude theory, have also produced alternative aptitude batteries for use with different age groups or situations (Pimsleur, 1966; Green, 1975; Davies, 1971; Petersen & Al-Haik, 1976). Such batteries usually produce multiple correlations with foreign language achievement in the range 0.40 to 0.75, depending on the instructional conditions. Such batteries have also been used to assist in counselling of students (Pimsleur, 1968) as well as the basis for assigning students to more suitable teaching methodologies (Wesche, 1982).

Individual differences in foreign language achievement

It is widely and reliably established that there are considerable differences in foreign language achievement. These are sometimes related to differences in foreign language aptitude (Carroll, 1982), sometimes to affective factors (Gardner & Lambert, 1972), sometimes to learner strategies (Naiman, Fröhlich, Stern & Tedesco, 1978), sometimes to environmental factors such as opportunities for language use or instructional conditions (Long, 1982), and sometimes simply to time (Carroll, 1975). Although there is controversy as to what is measured by language proficiency tests, for example whether there is a unitary language competence (see e.g. Oller, 1983) or whether aspects of interaction (Morrow, 1979) and planning of speech (Brown & Yule, 1984) are properly examined by existing language tests, for present purposes the crucial factor is that there is no disagreement over the extent of the individual differences in foreign language achievement and proficiency. Consequently, the only requirement in this area is a good range of tests to assess achievement.

The Bristol Language Project

It has only been possible to investigate the three basic sets of variables (first language development, foreign language aptitude, and foreign language achievement) thanks to the existence of the Bristol Language Project and the help and encouragement of Professor Gordon Wells. Professor Wells generously agreed that a follow-up study of the children involved in the Bristol study could be undertaken and, prior to his departure from Bristol for the Ontario Institute for Studies in Education, helped to set up the present research,[1] funded in 1984–1985 by a grant from the British Economic and Social Research Council.

In view of this longitudinal aspect to the current research, a description of the Bristol Project is now necessary. The Bristol Project has been studying a total of 125 children, born in 1969–1970 or 1971–1972, by obtaining extensive tape recordings of the children's speech in natural situations (Wells, 1981, 1985). For each of the 125 children there are 10 recordings, at three-monthly intervals, each yielding about 30 minutes of conversation with an average of 150 utterances by the child and about as many by speakers to the child. The tape recordings have been analysed within the framework of a comprehensive coding scheme developed by the Bristol research team (Wells, 1972, 1975).

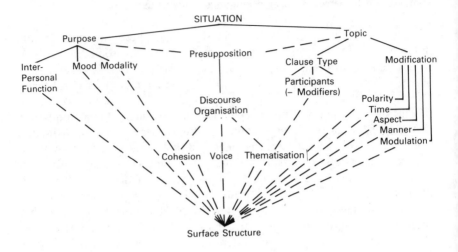

FIGURE 1. *The Bristol coding scheme.*

The coding scheme provides for analysis of the children's utterances in terms of interpersonal purpose, experiential content, appropriateness, and context of utterance occurrence. The relationship between these coding devices is shown in Figure 1 (drawn from Wells, 1972: 20). In addition, utterances are coded for syntactic structure and well-formedness. The coding scheme is clearly comprehensive, and influenced strongly by contemporary developments in linguistics, particularly those associated with Halliday (1970) and Fillmore (1968).

Subsequent phases of the Bristol Project have investigated the transition of a sub-group of the total population to school, and to the changed linguistic demands that this new environment has made, for example, subsequent language development, the beginning of reading, the relationship between earlier interaction patterns in the home and subsequent interaction patterns in school. In fact, there have been two follow-up studies involving 20 and 32 children (total = 52) from the original sample, with the most recent data collected by the Bristol team three years ago, when 32 of the younger children were extensively assessed at the age of 10+.

The current situation is that as of January 1985 the two age groups of children were twelve and a half to thirteen and a half, and fourteen and a half to fifteen and a half years old respectively. They are all embarked on a secondary school career and are studying or have studied a foreign language in typical classroom conditions.

The existence of such extensive first language data on such a large group of children, together with the potential for gathering data on their foreign language performance, is unique. No comparable study exists or has existed in the world, and it represents an opportunity to study the development of language ability that is unlikely to be repeated for some considerable time.

General description and research design

The fundamental aim of the present research project is to examine inter-relationships between three areas of language — first language development, foreign language aptitude, and foreign language achievement. In particular, the project ultimately aims to: (a) investigate whether greater *rate* of progress in first language development is associated with higher foreign language aptitude and also higher foreign language achievement; (b) examine whether *patterns* of first language development are related to *patterns* of foreign language aptitude; (c) explore first, whether foreign language achievement is dependent on capacities which may be a residue of first language learning ability, and whether foreign language aptitude can be regarded as an operational measure of this residual ability, or second, whether possible relationships between first language acquisition and foreign language aptitude are more connected to features of the environment in which the first language was learned.

The indices used to measure performance in each of the three key areas will now be described.

Indices of first language development

These indices were produced by the Bristol team, and were already available on computer files.[2] The main indices which were used were:

1. Global measures of rate of development, for example, MLU, Bristol Scale Level.[3]
2. Specific measures of rate of development, for example, range of language functions used; development of modification; complexity of noun phrases used.
3. Test-based measures of comprehension and vocabulary size.
4. Demographic/biographical indices of family circumstances, for

example, class of family background, parental occupations, and so forth.

5. Measures of the quantity and type of speech and literacy-based activities the children were exposed to.

The first two sets of measures were derived from the spontaneous language recorded in the home by the Bristol Research team. The two cohorts of children differed in terms of age at the time of data collection. Data was collected on the younger cohort at three-monthly intervals between the ages of 15 and 42 months, and on the older cohort between 39 months and 60 months. In other words, there was an overlap between the two cohorts for the data collection at 39 and 42 months to provide a basis for comparison. For some purposes the similarity of the cohorts enables them to be merged — for others it does not, but in any case the total age range of 15 to 60 months allows a fairly extended perspective on the course of language development.

The third set of measures was obtained from tests given to the children at around 39 months (both cohorts) and 57 and 66 months (older cohort only). The demographic measures were drawn from interview and background data, while the fifth set of measures were based partly on tape-recorded information and partly on interview data.

Indices of foreign language aptitude

Because of time constraints in terms of how much access was thought feasible with the children, a set of aptitude sub-tests was selected which would be easy to obtain and use, and also be relatively brief to administer, that is, could be completed in a two-hour testing session. In addition, the test battery so assembled was thought, in the time available for testing, to sample the sub-components of aptitude as comprehensively as was possible. The tests used[4] were:

AH2:　　　a verbal intelligence test
EMLAT1:　Hidden Words
EMLAT2:　Matching Words
York Language Aptitude Test
PLAB5:　　Sound Discrimination
PLAB6:　　Sound–Symbol Association

The AH2 was chosen as a 'marker' test for general verbal intelligence. The first test taken from the Elementary Modern Language Aptitude Test,

Hidden Words, requires the candidate to use a misspelled version of a word as a basis for guessing what the original word was. It is postulated that this is done on the basis of native language vocabulary and also phonemic coding ability. The second EMLAT test, Matching Words, requires the candidate to find the word (from five possibilities) in a second sentence which fulfils the same grammatical function as a particular word in a first sentence. The test attempts to measure Carroll's grammatical sensitivity factor (Carroll, 1982). The York test is 'of the pupil's ability to produce forms in an unknown language (Swedish) on the analogy of the forms presented' (Green, 1975: 72). In other words it is a test of inductive language learning ability. Finally the two Pimsleur tests assess auditory ability, with PLAB5 focusing on sound discrimination in context, and PLAB6 the candidate's ability to relate sound to symbol.

It was felt that this battery of tests provides measures of verbal intelligence, grammatical sensitivity, inductive language learning ability, and auditory ability/phonemic coding ability. As such they provide a reasonably wide sampling of the components of aptitude (Carroll, 1965, 1982; Skehan, 1980a). The major omission (through lack of time) is any consideration of memory ability, the other major factor that has been shown to be important in aptitude (Carroll, 1982; Skehan; 1980b, 1982, 1986).

Indices of foreign language achievement

As with the language aptitude measures it was necessary to find easily available assessment instruments. After an examination of a range of possible measures, it was decided to use the NFER/APU tests for both French and German.[5] Separate tests are available for Speaking, Listening, Writing, and Reading. The tests have the twin advantages that they have established high reliabilities, having been subjected to a considerable amount of item analysis and so forth and that they were designed for a situation comparable to the one being investigated, that is, use in a wide variety of schools with a wide variety of methodologies and textbooks. It was felt that such a battery of tests would be most able to cope with the problem of how not to disadvantage any particular school because of the methodology it had used. In addition there are several parallel versions of the NFER tests, thus allowing retesting to be done on a standard measuring base.

The NFER/APU tests are designed for use during the summer term of the second year of language study. They can be administered later than this and still discriminate effectively, indeed they are quite robust in terms of usability in third and fourth years of language instruction. However, they cannot be used earlier than the summer term of the second year. For this reason the children from the older cohort who are still studying French were tested during the spring term 1985, while the children from the second cohort studying French have been tested during the summer term, but these results have yet to be analysed.

Summary of phase one research design

The investigation is based on indices already available from the Bristol Language Project for (1), and the collection of test data for (2) and (3). The accumulation of such data is intended to answer questions on: (a) the relationship between individual differences in first language development and foreign language achievement, that is, whether fast developers in the mother tongue learn foreign languages more quickly: (b) the origin of foreign language aptitude, that is, whether such aptitude can be regarded as the residue of a first language learning ability; (c) the similarity of the dimensions of first language development, on the one hand, and foreign language aptitude and achievement, on the other; (d) the relative contributions of environmental influences, such as class of family background and the nature of the linguistic environment of the child to subsequent language development, versus individual make up concerned either with route or rate of development.

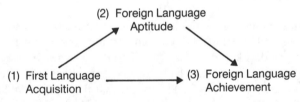

FIGURE 2. *The research design*

The results which follow are preliminary, and will be supplemented in the future by the accumulation of much more data. However, they do allow some discussion of each of the above questions.

Results

The situation at the time of writing is that the aptitude testing has been completed for both cohorts of traced children from the Bristol Project. The results used for the first language acquisition–foreign language aptitude correlations are therefore based on Ns of 53 and 50 respectively. Foreign language achievement test results, although now available, have only been analysed for the older cohort.[6] Indeed, because the older children are in the fourth year of secondary schooling, by which time it is possible to stop studying a foreign language, their number is considerably reduced (N = 23). The problems here do not simply involve reduced numbers, however. In addition, one has to take account of subject selection in that those who continue to study French may do so for a variety of reasons. Some schools may not allow French to be dropped. Other schools may only continue to offer French to those who are at least moderately successful at it. Alternatively, where pupil choice is concerned, this may implicate differential valuing of school subjects, or perhaps parental attitude. In all of these cases the reasons why some pupils pursue the study of French may also influence the pattern of relationship between the indices used. This, obviously, has implications for the generalisability of the results. It will be necessary, therefore, to wait for the achievement testing with the younger cohort, scheduled for the summer term, before any satisfactory conclusions can be drawn. However, for the moment, the available correlations will be reported, as they do at least provide some relevant information, even if it is incomplete.

First language–foreign language aptitude relationships

Table 1 summarises the relationships found for the older cohort. Several points need to be made about the information in this table.

First, structural indices of first language development tend to enter into higher correlation with subsequent aptitude than do the more semantic/pragmatic indices. MLUs 42; range of adjectives and determiners; range of nominal phrase complexity, for example, all have significant patterns of correlation with language analytic aspects of language aptitude. The Bristol Scale also has significant correlations, perhaps reflecting the fact that it is the more structural aspects of the scale which are differentiating between the children at the age levels concerned. However, the range of syntactic complexity measure, and MLUs 57 enter into very few significant correlations. The latter measure was not expected to continue to differentiate by the Bristol team as a source of important variation since it is simply based on length of utterance, an increasingly unreliable indicator of syntactic complexity. The poor performance of the range of syntactic complexity measure is, however, more difficult to understand, and its poor showing will have to await future explanation. One should also note with the more structural predictors that they show a lower level of relationship, in general,

TABLE 1. *First language–foreign language aptitude correlations*

	AH2	EMLAT 1	EMLAT 2	YORK	PLAB 5	PLAB 6
Family background	0.59**	0.37**	0.55**	0.56**	0.19	0.33**
Parental interest in lateracy	0.37**	0.34**	0.46**	0.36**	0.20	0.16
Ot child read to	0.55**	0.31*	0.46**	0.51**	0.20	0.16
Total parental education	0.48**	0.29*	0.48**	0.41**	0.08	0.29*
MLUs 42 mths.	0.31*	0.32*	0.52**	0.35**	0.12	0.39**
Comprehension 39 mths.	0.30*	0.34**	0.45**	0.34**	0.28*	0.48**
EPTV (Vocab. Test) 39 mths.	0.54**	0.45**	0.48**	0.50**	0.32*	0.28*
Range of language functions	0.00	0.05	0.09	−0.04	0.09	0.06
Range of sentence meanings	0.35**	0.30*	0.29*	0.09	0.19	0.04
Range of adjectives and determiners	0.43**	0.30*	0.44**	0.25*	0.00	0.31*
Range of modality, aspect+time markers	0.17	0.21	0.40**	0.24*	0.16	0.27*
MLUs 57 mths.	0.23	0.30*	0.15	0.05	−0.14	−0.03
Comprehension 57 mths.	0.36**	0.23	0.51**	0.43**	0.27*	0.27*
EPVT (Vocabulary) test) 66 mths.	0.33**	0.36**	0.21	0.37**	0.11	0.18
Range of syntactic complexity	0.15	0.2	0.28*	0.04	0.23	0.20
Range of nominal phrase complexity	0.36**	0.39**	0.43**	0.26*	0.19	0.31*
Bristol Scale 42 mths.	0.32*	0.26*	0.34**	0.29*	0.16	0.42**
Bristol Scale 57 mths.	0.33**	0.31*	0.38**	0.17	0.48**	0.11

N = 53:	Significance Levels	0.05 = 0.24
		0.01 = 0.33

with the more auditory aptitude tests, particularly those from Pimsleur's LAB.

Second, there are significant, and sometimes sizeable correlations between the comprehension[7]/vocabulary indices of first language development and some of the foreign language aptitude indices. This applies particularly to the vocabulary measure, and particularly at the earlier testing at 39 months.

Third, and undoubtedly related to the previous point, the biographical/ demographic variables enter into consistently significant correlations. This applies most clearly to the IQ score but is clear also for the EMLAT2 and York tests, suggesting that it is, once again, going to be difficult to disentangle environmental from other influences, and probably different environmental influences from one another.

Fourth, and finally, the more auditory-based aptitude tests are the least well predicted from the first language developmental indices. Although there are exceptions to this, for example, Bristol Scale 42 mths and PLAB6: 0.42, and Bristol Scale 57 mths and PLAB5: 0.48, the median correlations for the different aptitude measures are revealing. They are, in descending order: EMLAT2, 0.43: AH2, 0.35: York Test, 0.34: EMLAT1, 0.31: PLAB6, 0.27: PLAB5, 0.19. Interestingly, most of the higher correlations with the auditory aptitude tests are produced by comprehension/vocabulary indices of first language development, suggesting perhaps a distinct dimension for the development of both first language skills as well as foreign language aptitude.

Foreign language aptitude–foreign language achievement

Table 2 shows the relevant correlations. These correlations are the least innovative of the present study, duplicating much previous work. Even so it can be said that the correlations are unusually and uniformly highly relative to other comparable research (Carroll & Sapon, 1957; Davies, 1971; Green, 1975). This is probably for two reasons. First, the NFER tests are probably more reliable and valid than most achievement/proficiency tests that are used in studies of this sort. Second, the sampling procedures used

TABLE 2. *Language aptitude-foreign language achievement correlations*

	AH2	EMLAT 1	EMLAT 2	YORK	PLAB5	PLAB6
Listening	0.55	0.49	0.66	0.68	0.07	0.49
Speaking	0.59	0.55	0.66	0.68	0.10	0.33
Reading	0.58	0.73	0.67	0.65	0.16	0.50
Writing	0.68	0.64	0.69	0.74	0.17	0.48

N = 23: Significance Levels .05 = .41
.01 = .53

by the Bristol Language Project deliberately produced a wide range of children in terms of family background (although the non-random nature of the drop-out rate for the children still studying French may have counteracted this to some degree). Both these reasons — effective tests as well as heterogeneity of sampling — tend to provide the circumstances for high correlations to emerge. That they did so in the present case indicates that we have fertile ground on which to investigate the other relationships involved in the triangle of variables shown in Figure 1.

First language development–foreign language achievement

Table 3 shows the relevant correlations. Quite clearly, these correlations are generally lower than those shown in the other tables. The structural first language indices consistently fail to reach statistical significance, with most correlations below 0.20. Interestingly, it is one of the more semantic first language measures which leads to higher correlations, range of modality, aspect, and time markers, yet despite consistency (0.36/0.24/0.39/0.26), none of the correlations achieves significance.

The biographical/demographic variables, that is, family background, parental literacy, amount the child is read to, parental education, frequently enter into higher relationships. Family background, for example, generates correlations in excess of 0.40. However, the highest relationships shown in the table are, quite clearly, those between the comprehension/vocabulary measures taken relatively early in life (39–66 months) and foreign language achievement at age fourteen. Comprehension 39 months leads to correlations in the high 0.40s, as does Comprehension 57 months, while EPVT66 (Vocabulary Test) leads to correlations that average in the mid 0.50s, astonishingly high values when one considers the time intervals involved.

Summary of results

First, it should be repeated that these are preliminary results, and that the main series of comparisons, involving the younger cohort, will only be possible as results become available from the summer term's testing programme. However, these results are what are available at the time of writing. In terms of the basic sets of relationship that were investigated, one can say broadly speaking, that: (a) first language development and foreign language aptitude are significantly related at a moderate level; (b) foreign language aptitude and foreign language success are strongly related; (c) first

TABLE 3. *First language–foreign language achievement correlations*

	Listening	Speaking	Reading	Writing
Family background	0.43*	0.57*	0.47*	0.47*
Parental interest in literacy	0.23	0.35	0.38	0.24
Qt child read to	0.19	0.37	0.18	0.21
Total parental education	0.24	0.43*	0.34	0.32
MLUs 42 mths	0.19	0.20	0.18	0.13
Comprehension 39mths	0.57**	0.45*	0.48*	0.42*
EPTV (Vocab. Test) 39 mths	0.29	0.21	0.33	0.31
Range of language functions	−0.25	−0.17	−0.14	−0.20
Range of sentence meanings	−0.09	−0.22	−0.10	−0.20
Range of adjectives and determiners	−0.07	−0.22	−0.11	−0.08
Range of modality, aspect+time markers	0.36	0.24	0.39	0.26
MLUs 57 mths	−0.17	−0.13	−0.02	−0.08
Comprehension 57 mths	0.49*	0.49*	0.55**	0.46*
EPVT (Vocabulary test) 66 mths	0.67**	0.48*	0.57**	0.52*
Range of syntactic complexity	0.00	0.04	0.04	−0.05
Range of nominal phrase complexity	0.16	0.22	0.25	0.21
Bristol Scale 42mths	0.04	0.02	0.03	0.05
Bristol Scale 57mths	0.00	0.10	0.05	0.06

N = 23:   Significance Levels 0.05 = 0.41
                                0.01 = 0.53

language development and foreign language success do not seem to have a direct relationship to one another; (d) family background indices are related to language aptitude measures at a moderate level, and to achievement measures at a weak-to-moderate level; (e) comprehension and vocabulary indices obtained early in life are related to subsequent aptitude *and* achievement at a moderate/moderate-to-strong level.[8]

In addition, it is clear that the different sets of variables have different numbers of dimensions. The foreign language achievement measures look uni-dimensional, with a lowest intercorrelation of 0.86 (between listening and writing — the other correlations are shown in the grand correlation matrix given in Appendix B). Foreign language aptitude, however, looks to have two dimensions, involving grammatical ability and auditory ability. (The results of factor analyses which are soon to be conducted may result in a different structure appearing more satisfactory.) However, the most complex area seems to be that of first language development. There are the more structural indices, such as range of syntactic complexity and range of nominal group complexity; comprehension/vocabulary indices; linguistic environment indices; and biographical/family background indices. The different groups of predictors of FL achievement enter into different levels of relationship. In addition, it is likely that they interact with one another in complex ways. Certainly the complexity of the patterns of relationship will be a major focus in the proposed development of the present study, as it investigates individual indices further, and examines potential interactions between them.

Discussion

Several issues are worth discussing in relation to these results. First of all, there is the question of the origin of language aptitude. The results indicate relationships between aptitude and first language indices based on spontaneous data that are significant but moderate. In contrast, aptitude enters into stronger relationships with both biographical/background variables as well as with the test-based comprehension and vocabulary indices. To a certain extent, therefore, these results may be taken as evidence that more analytic components of aptitude (i.e. those measured by the EMLAT2 and York tests) are a residual ability of individual differences in first language learning ability. The MLUs–EMLAT2 correlation of 0.52, for example, the Range of Adjectives and Determiners–EMLAT2 value of 0.44, and the Range of Noun Phrase Complexity–EMLAT 2 figure of 0.43 all suggest that certain features of early syntax and complexity of language use are related to components of aptitude. Further work will attempt a finer-grained analysis of these first language developmental indices to try to isolate which of them relate to subsequent aptitude. Perhaps such analysis will be able to uncover reasons why some of the first language variables do not enter into clear relationships with aptitude, since, it has to be admitted, the results obtained are hardly uniform.

Even more important, the aptitude measures enter into even higher relationships with the background and test-based indices. In fact, the test-based indices and the background indices themselves often correlate quite highly at the age of 39 months (several correlations above 0.50: see Appendix B), although the level of relationship with the later test measures are distinctly lower. In any case, there is the possibility that the background indices and the test-based measures relate to some similar underlying dimension. Further work will be required on this issue. However, most crucially here, the linguistic developmental indices do not correlate very highly with the background/test measures, suggesting that the linguistic indices and background/test indices provide independent sources of prediction for subsequent language aptitude. Further regression analyses will clarify this issue. For the present, the evidence suggests that aptitude test scores are partly associated with early linguistic development and partly with background.

The second part of the triangle of relationships from Figure 2 that will be commented on here is that between the early measures and *foreign* language achievement. The first language indices enter into negligible relationships, while the family background and test-based measures enter into much higher relationships, often in excess of 0.50, and in one case (EPVT 66 months—Listening) as high as 0.67 (although here the small sample size counsels caution in interpretation).

On the face of it these results are depressing in terms of the original hypotheses since they suggest that first language individual differences are uncorrelated with variation in foreign language performance. The point needs to be made, however, that the dependent variable that is being used (test-based foreign language performance) might not be the ideal variable to examine in order to investigate the original hypothesis. It may well be that the issue here is the nature of conventional secondary school based language instruction, such that the type of tuition provided may not be especially communicative, or draw upon students' oral abilities, but instead emphasise a 'cover-the-textbook' approach.

In fact it is useful to broaden the discussion at this point and consider some other data from the Bristol Language Project. Subsequent phases of the study (see Wells, 1985) have followed sub-sets of the children as they entered the school system, and tracked their progress up to age of 10+. The results from this phase of the study (Wells, Homewood, & Offord, 1983; Wells, Barnes, & Wells, 1985) suggest that although during the 5–10 age range there are wide individual differences in oral language ability, these differences do not correlate with examination performance or with literacy-linked skills. Rather the child's *preparedness for literacy* on entry to school is the most significant predictor of how well the child will do in conventional school assessment. It seems as though the capacity to handle the symbolic, decontextualised aspects of language have, at least partially, a different set of determinants to those involved in oral language performance (Wells, 1985; Tizard & Hughes, 1984). Some children, and there is a social class linkage here, seem better able to handle this side of language use than others. This, of course, is highly significant since it is literacy-linked, examination-oriented aspects of performance that lead to educational success, and the fact that a particular learner may have very effective oral language skills may count for relatively little if these are not matched by similar abilities to deal with context-disembedded language (Donaldson, 1978).

The paradox of this analysis is that it is being applied to *foreign language learning*. It might be thought that while the above analysis might apply to other curriculum subjects, it would be irrelevant to the study of a foreign language, where it might be thought that the emphasis on skilled performance, creative language use, and the need to learn language by *using* language would produce a different set of conditions to that which operates elsewhere. The results available here are, however, more consistent with the view that learning a foreign language at school is just like learning any other subject. The results suggest that a considerable proportion of the success in language study relates to the ability to cope with literacy, and to the ability to make sense of the decontextualised ritual of display questions, pattern drills, and unbelievable dialogues characteristic of many classrooms. The successful student is able to cope with these characteristics, and one hopes, when the situation is appropriate, to transcend them. It would be nice to think that the move towards more communicative language teaching will reduce the reliance on skilled decontextualisers and instead allow learners' oral abilities to be exploited and built upon more effectively.

Notes to Chapter 6

1. This article, naturally, reflects the state of the art at the time of the Georgetown Workshop.
2. The author is grateful to Sally Barnes, School of Education, University of Bristol, for making this information available.
3. Please see Appendix A for more detailed descriptions of these indices.
4. The author would like to express his gratitude to Mary Gutfreund, Lucile Ducroquet, Brian Richards, and Zuzanna Crouch for their extensive work in carrying out the actual testing programme for the aptitude as well as the achievement data.
5. Thanks are due to Peter Dickson of the NFER Foreign Languages Section for his help in arranging for the use of these tests, together with instruction in their administration.
6. For this reason, that is consistency of comparison, the data reported in the following tables is for the older cohort throughout.

7. However, it must be said that the comprehension measure may not have been satisfactorily administered. Wells (1985: 39) expresses caution with respect to its validity, so interpretations of correlations between the comprehension score and other indices will have to be done circumspectly.

8. See Appendix A for more detailed descriptions of the indices.

Appendix A

Extended descriptions of variables used

Family background: The family background scale ranges in value from 6 to 18. Scores are based on the mother's and father's occupations (as based on the Registrar General's scale) and on mother's and father's education, based on a two-point scale developed by the Bristol team. The formula used is F.Occup. + M.Occup. + 2(F.Educ. + M.Educ.). Further details are provided in Wells (1985: 21–22).

Parental interest in literacy: During the interview conducted with each family, parents were asked about their own reading habits. A scale was derived based on the number of books owned by the parents and also the amount that each parent had read during the previous year. There were substantial differences between the families on this variable.

Quantity child was read to: Again from the family interview, data were gathered on the amount that mothers read to their children. A six-step scale was derived from these data.

Total parental education: For the parental education scales, finer discriminations were used than with the family background measure. An index was developed for each parent reflecting intermediate stages of education, such as straightforward school-leaving at various ages without any qualifications; CSE versus 'O' versus 'A' level; vocational training; professional qualifications; tertiary education.

MLUs 42 and 57 months: This index is based on previous work of Brown (1973), who proposed that the best single measure of development in first language is the mean length of utterance in morphemes. Brown suggested that increasing length is an index of developing control of the language system when one gives credit for greater morphemic complexity. The Bristol team used a variant of Brown's original measure in that they eliminated from calculations utterances which were classified as unstructured. In particular, they did not include in the corpus for scoring MLUs (where s = structured) utterances which were one word positive or negative idiomatic responses, for example, *yes, no*; idiomatic responses of greater length, for example, *come on, push off*; textual quotation, such as nursery rhymes or parts of advertisement jingles; routine functional formulae, for example, *hello, please*; and exclamations.

Comprehension 39 and 57 months: This test contained 63 items covering a wide range of sentence types, and involved the child in the 'acting-out' technique. Items were administered on a scale of increasing difficulty. However, it must be mentioned that Wells (1985: 39) says of this test: 'Unfortunately the effectiveness of the comprehension test as a measure of receptive language development was seriously compromised by a systematic failure to observe the instructions on the selections of items to be administered on each occasion'. The test scores are included in the present study because they enter into interesting relationships with the aptitude and achievement tests. Their complete interpretation, however, will have to be postponed until further information is available on the exact conditions of their administration.

EPVT (English picture vocabulary test) 39 and 66 months: This is a test of listening comprehension of individual vocabulary items.

Range of language functions: This is a cumulative score which counts the number of different functions of interpersonal purpose used by the child. It is also referred to in Wells (1985) as pragmatic range.

Range of sentence meanings: This measure is an indication of the range of relationships between participants encoded in the utterances used. It derives from scales described more fully in the Manual for the Coding of Child Speech developed by the Bristol team and reflects semantic meanings such as benefactive relationship, agent change of stage and so forth.

Range of adjectives and determiners: This index provides a measure of amount of noun phrase modification that is used.

Range of modality, aspect, and time markers: This index reflects the child's use of modifications of the proposition as a whole which go beyond the nuclear meaning of the clause. The index therefore is a measure of the child's attempts to indicate the probability of occurrence of the event in question; the temporal status of the event in question; and location in time of the event in question. Further details relevant to this index are to be found on pp. 77–78 of Wells (1985).

Range of syntactic complexity: This is an indication of the mean number of clause constituents per utterance, targeting on 34 structural elements. Additional credit is given in this score for every clause after the first.

Range of nominal phrase complexity: This is an indication of the range of possible elements in noun phrases and is based on the use of prepositions, modifiers, different types of headword, and simple and complex qualifiers.

Appendix B

Grand correlation matrix

	Fam Bkg	Par Lit	Qt Rd.	Par Ed.	MLU 42	Com 39	EPV 39	Fun	Sen mea	Adj Det	Rng Mod	MLU 57	Com 57	EPV 66
Family Backgr.	–	66	54	92	23	54	58	02	30	22	34	26	34	44
Par. Inter. Lit.		–	56	58	07	22	31	–06	26	22	34	16	27	26
Qt Chld. read to			–	37	09	04	35	–07	18	04	13	20	15	28
Total Par. Educ				–	27	52	51	01	27	16	36	35	30	30
MLUs42					–	30	24	39	16	29	38	04	38	–03
Comprehen. 39						–	58	17	35	30	40	22	53	37
EPVT (Vocab) 39							–	17	35	32	50	34	34	47
Range Functions								–	19	06	09	–04	01	–16
RangeSent. Mean.									–	42	48	46	39	19
RangeAdj. Deter.										–	30	39	38	–08
RangeModal. Etc.											–	40	35	24
MLUs 57												–	00	07
Comprehen. 57													–	35
EPVT (Vocab) 66														–

Continued overleaf

	Syn Com	Nom Com	BSc 42	BSc 57	AH2	EML 1	EML 2	Yrk	PLB 5	PLB 6	Lis	Spk	Rea	Wrt
Family Back.	13	33	14	25	59	37	55	56	19	33	43	57	47	47
Par. Inter. Lit.	11	28	03	04	37	34	46	36	20	16	23	35	38	24
Qt Chld. read to	09	38	-02	16	55	31	46	51	20	16	19	37	18	21
Tot. Par. Educ	11	28	10	26	48	29	48	41	08	29	24	43	34	32
MLUs42	42	34	45	59	31	32	52	35	12	39	19	20	18	13
Comprehen.39	30	33	42	32	30	34	45	34	28	48	57	45	48	42
EPVT (Vocab)39	27	31	33	30	54	45	48	50	32	28	29	21	33	31
Range Functions	26	-03	45	18	00	05	09	-04	09	06	-25	-17	-14	-20
RangeSent.Mean.	47	36	16	20	35	30	29	09	19	04	-09	-22	-10	-20
RangeAdj. Deter.	47	59	15	46	43	30	44	25	00	31	-07	-22	-10	-08
RangeModal.etc	50	28	13	22	17	21	40	24	16	27	36	24	39	26
MLUs 57	25	41	02	09	23	30	15	05	-14	-02	-17	-13	-02	-08
Comprehen.57	55	54	32	55	36	23	51	43	27	27	49	49	55	46
EPVT 66	16	07	11	03	33	36	21	37	11	18	67	48	57	52
RangeSyn.Compx.	—	47	43	55	15	20	28	04	23	20	00	04	03	-05
RangeNom.Compx.		—	31	49	36	39	43	26	19	31	16	22	25	21
Bristol Scale 42			—	54	32	26	34	29	16	42	-04	02	-03	-05
Bristol Scale 57				—	33	31	38	17	48	11	00	10	05	06
AH2					—	58	74	72	32	42	55	59	58	68
EMLAT1						—	55	36	27	30	49	55	73	64
EMLAT2							—	62	25	51	66	66	67	69
York								—	27	53	68	68	65	74
PLAB5									—	29	07	10	16	17
PLAB6										—	49	33	50	48
Listening											—	87	88	86
Speaking												—	89	91
Reading													—	96
Writing														—

References

BARNES, S.B., GUTFREUND, M., SATTERLY, D.J. & WELLS, C.G., 1983, Characteristics of adult speech which predict children's language development. *Journal of Child Language 10*, 65–84.

BERETTA, A. & DAVIES, A., 1985, Evaluation of the Bangalore Project. *English Language Teaching Journal 39* (2), 121–127.

BLOOM, L., LIGHTBOWN, P. & HOOD, L., 1975, Structure and variation in child language. *Monographs of the Society for Research in Child Development 40* (Serial No. 160).

BRETHERTON, I., MCNEW, S., SNYDER, L. & BATES, E., 1983, Individual differences at 20 months: analytic and holistic strategies in language acquisition. *Journal of Child Language 10*, 293–320.

BROWN, R., 1973, *A First Language: The Early Stages*. London: Allen and Unwin.

BROWN, G. & YULE, G., 1984, *Teaching the Spoken Language*. Cambridge: Cambridge University Press.

CARROLL, J.B., 1965, The prediction of success in intensive foreign language training. In R. GLASER (ed.), *Training, Research, and Education*. New York: Wiley, 87–136.

— 1974, The aptitude-achievement distinction: the case of foreign language aptitude and proficiency. In D.R. GREEN (ed.), *The Aptitude–Achievement Distinction*. Monterey, CA: McGraw Hill, 289–303.

— 1975, *The Teaching of French as a Foreign Language in Eight Countries*. Stockholm: Almquist and Wiksell.

— 1982, Twenty-five years of research on foreign language aptitude. In K.C. DILLER (ed), *Individual Differences and Universals in Language Learning Aptitude*. Rowley, MA: Newbury House, 83–118.

CARROLL, J.B. & SAPON, S.M., 1957, *Modern Language Aptitude Test*. New York: Psychological Corporation.

DAVIES, A., 1971, Language aptitude in the first year of the U.K. secondary school. *RELC Journal*, June 1971, 4–19.

DONALDSON, M., 1978, *Children's Minds*. London: Penguin.

FILLMORE, C.J., 1968, The case for case. In E. BACH & R.T. HARMS (eds), *Universals in Linguistic Theory*. New York: Holt, Rinehart, and Winston.

FILLMORE, L.W., 1976, The second time around: cognitive and social strategies in second language acquisition. Doctoral dissertation, Stanford University. (Published in 1979, Ann Arbor, MI: University Microfilms.)

— 1979, Individual differences in second language acquisition. In C.J. FILLMORE, W.S.Y. WANG & D. KEMPLER (eds), *Individual Differences in Language Ability and Language Behavior*. New York: Academic Press.

GARDNER, R.C., 1986, *Social Psychology and Second Language Learning: The Role of Attitudes and Motivation*. London: Edward Arnold.

GARDNER, R.C. & LAMBERT, W.E., 1972, *Attitudes and Motivation in Second Language Learning*. Rowley, MA: Newbury House.

GREEN, P.S., 1975, *The Language Laboratory in School: The York Study*. Edinburgh: Oliver and Boyd.

HALLIDAY, M.A.K., 1970, Language structure and language function. In J. LYONS (ed), *New Horizons in Linguistics*. Harmondsworth: Penguin, 140–165.

LONG, M.H., 1982, Does second language instruction make a difference? A review of research. *TESOL Quarterly 17* (3), 359–382.

MORROW, K., 1979, Communicative language testing: Revolution or evolution?

In C.J. Brumfit, & K. Johnson (eds), *The Communicative Approach to Language Teaching*. Oxford: Oxford University Press, 143–157.

Naiman, N., Fröhlich, M., Stern, H.H. & Tedesco A., 1978, *The Good Language Learner*. Toronto: Ontario Institute for Studies in Education.

Nelson, K., 1973, Structure and strategy in learning to talk. *Monographs of the Society for Research in Child Development 38*, (1–2).

— 1981, Individual differences in language development: implications for development and language. *Developmental Psychology 17*, 170–187.

Oller, J.W. (ed), 1983, *Issues in Language Testing Research*. Rowley, MA: Newbury House.

Peters, A., 1983, *The Units of Language Acquisition*. Cambridge: Cambridge University Press.

Petersen, C.R. & Al-Haid, A., 1976, The development of the Defense Language Battery (DLAB). *Educational and Psychological Measurement 36*, 369–380.

Pimsleur, P., 1966, *The Pimsleur Language Aptitude Battery*. New York: Harcourt Brace Jovanovich.

— 1968, Language aptitude testing. In A. Davies (ed.), *Language Testing Symposium: A Psycholinguistic Approach*. Oxford: Oxford University Press, 98–106.

Reves, P., 1983, What Makes a Good Language Learner? Unpublished doctoral dissertation. Hebrew University of Jerusalem.

Skehan, P., 1980a, Memory, language aptitude, and second language performance. *Polyglot 2* (3), 53–70.

— 1980b, Language aptitude: a review. *English Language Research Journal 1*, 85–101.

— 1982, Memory and motivation in language aptitude testing. Unpublished doctoral dissertation, University of London.

— 1986, Cluster analysis and the identification of learner types. In V.J. Cook (ed), *Experimental Approaches to Second Language Learning*. Oxford: Pergamon, 81–94.

Smith, P.D., 1970, *A Comparison of the Cognitive and Audiolingual Approaches to Foreign Language Instruction*. Philadelphia: Centre for Curriculum Development.

Tizard, B. & Hughes, M., 1984, *Young Children Learning*. London: Fontana.

Wells, C.G., 1975, *Coding Manual for the Description of Child Speech in Conversational Context* (rev. ed.). University of Bristol, School of Education.

— 1981, *Learning Through Interaction*. Cambridge: Cambridge University Press.

— 1985, *Language Development in the Pre-school Years*. Cambridge: Cambridge University Press.

Wells, C.G., Barnes, S.B. & Wells, J., 1985, *Linguistic Influences on Educational Attainment*. Final report to the Department of Education and Science, Home and School Influences on Educational Attainment Project. University of Bristol: Department of Education and Science, Elizabeth House, York Road, London.

Wells, C.G., Homewood, J. & Offord, D., 1983, *Home and School Influences on Educational Attainment*. Final Report to the Spencer Foundation. University of Bristol.

Wesche, M.B., 1982, Language aptitude measures in streaming, matching students with methods, and diagnoses of learning problems. In K.C. Diller (ed.), *Individual Differences and Universals in Language Learning Aptitude*. Rowley, MA: Newbury House, 119–154.

7 Investigations into Classroom Discourse

WERNER HÜLLEN

This article consists of two parts. The first contains some general assumptions that underlie investigations into classroom discourse that some collaborators and I have carried out. As the paper's length is rather limited, such assumptions can only be given as bare statements without doing much inducing or proving.

Further, in this first part, an attempt will be made at explaining why such investigations into classroom discourse may even be superior to the methods of natural language acquisition analysis outside the classroom. In this section a somewhat critical attitude towards some of the contemporary undertakings in this field will become visible. Again, owing to the limitations of length, no examples can be given.

The second part of the paper consists of reports about three projects that rest on the assumptions and follow the intentions just described.

I shall continually differentiate between *acquisition*, which is supposed to be natural, and *learning*, which is supposed to be formal or artificial. I want to stress that this is only a convenient simplification of terminology for a complex matter. It does not mean that in my opinion there is something like pure acquisition or pure learning as two independent types of interiorising a language. On the contrary, I believe that we never do the one without the other, though one of the two ways is always predominant in certain situations.

Three statements can be made upon the nature of teaching and learning (Hüllen, 1983):

1. There *is* a connection between teaching and learning; teaching triggers off the learning process though we do not know in which direction and to what extent. All experience points to the fact that the teaching concept and the learning result are only partly identical.

2. Learning is dependent on teaching (this is a consequence of the first statement), but teaching is itself also dependent on learning. Teaching methodology must be geared to the mechanism of learning in order to be effective.

3. There is undoubtedly a mental force for the processing of language data in man (this is again a consequence of the second statement), but we do not know much about its autonomy with reference to other faculties of the human mind and with reference to environmental factors. All experience points to the fact that there are *various* ways to learn a language according to varying circumstances but that such various ways have important elements in common. The mechanism of learning — mentioned above — shows itself rather as an amoeba: it is undoubtedly there, but its shape varies constantly and it is, thus, difficult to grasp.

For the analysis of foreign language learning in the classroom these experiences *exclude* two logically possible viewpoints: that the teacher can just do what he or she wants in the classroom because the learner *will follow* him or her anyway, and that the teacher can do nothing in the classroom besides providing input because the learner will *not follow* him or her anyway. Neither the teacher nor the learner are autonomous in what they do when teaching and learning is going on. Actually, no learner has presumably thought he or she is autonomous and, what is more important, no intelligent teacher has done so either. Scholars who think they must argue with teachers about this engage themselves in an issue of only rhetorical value. The whole business of foreign language teaching methodology only makes sense if we assume that learning a language is a process which *can* be influenced, but not *ad libitum*, and it is exactly the *limited* openness of learning to teach which has to be explored (Felix, 1982; Hüllen, 1984).

One way of doing this is by investigating discourse in the classroom with the help of discourse analysis (Sinclair & Coulthard, 1975; Stubbs, 1976). This means using a descriptive model which was originally set up to describe communication by competent speakers rather than by teachers and learners (Lörscher, 1983). However, the boundaries between communication and language learning are very difficult to draw. Any sort of learning is connected with finding new and appropriate expressions for meanings. If language competence is our ability to produce and to understand utterances which we have never produced or heard before, competence is indeed also our faculty to learn a language.

Foreign language learning then is, at least on an abstract level, a special and particularly dramatic case of what we always do when we combine meanings with the means to express them in particular circumstances. (It goes without saying that there is also a conventionalised form of linguistic performance where no learning in the sense mentioned above is involved.) This state of affairs allows us to approach foreign language learning in the classroom as a special kind of communication (Hüllen, 1976; Hüllen & Jung, 1979).

During the last two decades much progress has been made in the investigation of so-called natural language acquisition of the first and of any further language. The results of these investigations (Dechert & Raupach, 1980; Felix, 1982; Nicholas & Meisel, 1983; Wode, 1981), though sometimes contradictory and thus not generally accepted, cannot and need not be reported here. It has become customary (at least in the Federal Republic of Germany) to transfer findings about natural language acquisition to foreign language learning and to look at the latter as a special case of the former (Klein, 1984). The main topic of investigation in this context is that a fixed sequential order of learning (e.g. morphological items) said to be characteristic of language acquisition, is also supposed to show up in foreign language learning — or would do so if the teaching was better.

The attempt to analyse foreign language learning in the classroom with the help of insights into language acquisition is a legitimate one as long as we are aware of the fact that there are elements in the learning situation which never show up in the acquisition situation and which, thus, cannot be adequately analysed in this way. We cannot regard the context of classroom learning as some debased form of the context of language acquisition but must look at it in its own right. For that matter, the same holds true if we go in the opposite direction, that is, if we try to elucidate language acquisition from our insights into language learning. There is no inherent reason why we have to look into language acquisition first and/or into language learning second. What we do in this respect is not a matter of truth, but of usefulness for the analysis.

The method currently widely accepted for language acquisition research is analysing products of performance and explaining them as symptoms of processes in the mind. As such, processes of a higher intellectual order, to which language performance always belongs, are inevitably goal-oriented; such a goal must indeed be observed as a basis of our data analysis. It is communication which would be called 'successful' by a native speaker in a given situation. Our analysis, then, tries to explain products of performance as symptoms of processes which strive at establishing successful communication (Edmondson & House, 1981; Kasper, 1981).

This procedure which owes a lot to *gestalt* psychology without admitting it, leaves some doubt as to its reliance. *First*, it is essentially observer-oriented and not acquirer-oriented. It reconstructs a process in the mind from data by giving them sense according to the experience of the observer. Although the observer may be very particular in trying to find the speaker's communication goal, it is not at all clear whether he or she actually succeeds. The analyst may very well establish his or her own conception of sense in the data which deviates from the speaker's. *Second*, this procedure lacks a measurement for generalisation. It is not clear whether an utterance is to be looked upon as significant or not. The reason for this is that we usually work with decontextualised utterances which do not allow any conclusion on their position within the momentary state of competence of the acquirer. *Third*, there is no unanimity within language acquisition research on the unit of investigation. Is it a word, a syntagma, an utterance or an adjacency pair? As most data are elicited in dialogue, the question of the degree to which utterances of acquirers are predetermined by the elicitations of the researchers arises.

These three points of criticism show that we have not as much control over the method of our analytical work and the extent to which our method itself determines our findings as we wish. Classroom discourse, however, puts us in at least a slightly better position. It is more controlled and patterned than other discourse and can be broken down into relatively clear units of communication. The three problematical areas can be more easily (though, of course, not totally) overcome precisely because of these formal qualities. When analysing classroom discourse, the analyst is equally distant from learner and teacher, that is, from the two partners in communication, and can observe the interdependence of their utterances. As a unit of investigation the exchange between the two offers itself quite naturally. A measurement for generalisation can be found within the fairly narrow limits of classroom communication, since a goal of communicative acts can, as a rule, be clearly derived from the questions of the elicitative acts of the teacher.

Thus, there are good methodological reasons for analysing classroom discourse as the outward appearance of foreign language learning in its own right, or even for trying to elucidate natural language acquisition from it. Of course, we must keep in mind that what makes classroom discourse open to analysis is essentially an alienation from natural undirected forms of communication (Edmondson & House, 1981), so that there will be always the task of determining the differences between the one and the other. Discourse analysis gives us the tools to do this.

The three projects now to be described analyse details of the learner–teacher communication, but they do it within the general framework described above. They are thus meant to provide a few mosaic stones which, supplemented with many others, eventually may yield a picture.

Project 1 (Hüllen & Lörscher, 1979)

A stretch of classroom discourse was analysed in which the teacher, with the help of questions, tried to make the class repeat a text from their book in the particular way in which they remembered it. The objective of the investigation was to compare how far learner utterances deviated from the model text, which means that utterances which were identical with the model text could be ignored. The analytical tool was an adaptation of Sinclair and Coulthard's discourse model. Five hundred and eighty-two utterances (acts) of learners who were in their second and third year of English were analysed.

Three main facts became visible:

1. Learners preferred simpler structures to the model text, most of all in predicates, but also in noun phrases and prepositional phrases. They would use for example,
   - predicates without modals instead of predicates with modals;
   - noun phrases without possessive pronouns instead of with possessive pronouns;
   - direct speech instead of reported speech.
   Learners also preferred the present to the past tense.
2. Learners preferred semantically simpler words than the model text. They would for example, exchange
   - be + complement for a verb lexeme;
   - not + adjective for an (opposite) adjective lexeme;
   - lexemes with general meaning for lexemes with specific meaning.
3. Learners tended to cut the cohesive model text into slices of independent miniature texts without sentence connectors. An exception to this was simply the insertion of *and*, which appeared more frequently than in the model text itself. (Examples are given in the Appendix.)

All three strategies can be seen as heading in the same direction. They produce a text which consists of a series of bare, unmodified assertions. Or, to put it negatively, they produce a text without modal and otherwise modifying elements and without explicit links between sentences (apart from *and*).

Keeping in mind the limitations of the data, we can hypothesise that learners had a sort of semantic nucleus in their performance, consisting of, for example, the simple verb phrase as a predicate in the present tense, which they fell back on in their own utterances. This nucleus could be enriched by more complex structures like the past tense and modals. Thus, *present, past, modals + present/past* obviously mark a sequence of learning from the easy to the more difficult which the learners run through in the opposite direction when they find that some communicative task is too demanding for them.

Other syntactic nuclei are *article + noun* which can be enriched by demonstrative and possessive pronouns and additionally by adjectives. Prepositional phrases together with the enveloping sentence are obviously felt to be more complex than two independent sentences, because they are re-worded in this way. Semantically, we can hypothesise that the unit of performance for verbs is, of course, the lexeme, but that the analytic paraphrase *be + adjective* is just as frequent and thus as fundamental as the simple verb lexeme and is indeed in many cases even preferred. In sentence structure, embeddings come after paratactic independent sentences.

This project is, of course, only of limited validity. It should be duplicated in order to gain generalisability and it will have to be extended to many kinds of texts if eventually a sequence of learning within the verb and the noun phrase is to be established. Criteria other than syntactic and semantic complexity will have to be observed, like contrastiveness. In the case described it was observed that the choice of lexemes, for example, was additionally guided by contrastive influences, but it did not become clear which was stronger, contrastive influence or the quest for simplicity. In syntactic structures no contrastive deviations were found.

Project 2 (Hüllen, 1982)

A stretch of classroom discourse was analysed with reference to impromptu elements used in it by teachers and by learners (Enkvist, 1982). Such elements are marked by spontaneity enacted in real time. It may, therefore, be doubtful whether they occur at all in classroom discourse, whose outstanding feature is formalisation and predetermined pattern.

In its most typical form, discourse in a foreign language class consists of an elicitation uttered by the teacher and a response uttered by a pupil which is followed by another evaluative utterance by the teacher (Lörscher, 1983). As a rule, learners in a class know the kind of response they are expected to give (though, of course, they sometimes do not know the response itself). Teachers elicit their learners' responses normally in a fairly calculated and text dependent way. So there seems to be nothing impromptu here. But the follow-up utterances, which express the teacher's evaluation of the learner's performance, are different. They consist of words like *yes, right, no, okay, wrong, well, ah, mhm* and/or non-verbal signs like shaking or nodding one's head, smiling, brow-beating etc. In one stretch of 150 acts there occurred 43 such evaluatives, sometimes chained together (*yes, right, okay*).

The follow-ups as the concluding third part of teacher–learner exchanges are very impromptu and they are also heavily dominated by the source language, which in this case was German. *Yes/ja, right/richtig, wrong/falsch, no/nein, perhaps/vielleicht* occur particularly often with *yes* holding the absolute record. This interference from German also accounts for the total absence of expressions like *fine, I see, well-done, good girl*, or others. Sometimes even teachers who usually make a point of conducting the entire conversation in English will fall back on German interjections like *ja, ach, aha*. Needless to say, the accompanying non-verbal signs are all German.

As the sequence *elicitation/response/evaluative* is the normal exchange unit in classroom discourse, its last member, the evaluative, gains particular importance. It is the sub-unit of discourse which leads to the next exchange unit. It is the point in classroom discourse where a step forward is made and which, therefore, calls for the special attention of teacher and learner alike. There is often a glide between this follow-up and the next elicitation which may be realised as a planning pause (empty or filled), and contains more false starts, repetitions and interjections than is usual. Most frequent is again *yes*. (Examples are given in the Appendix.)

Follow-up utterances together with these glides serve at least four functions:

1. They are planning spans for the teacher, who must think of what to do next.
2. They are lubricants in the discourse, avoiding embarrassing gaps of silence.
3. They give reinforcing or correcting information to the learner.
4. They manipulate the learner's attention.

The frequency and obvious functional load of such elements in the language of teachers has its obvious counterpart in the conspicuous absence of them in the language of learners. Though there are occasional hesitation phenomena and false starts, they occur much less frequently. The problem is how to account for this state of affairs.

Impromptu elements obviously signal planning phases which precede the realisation of speech. In these sub-units the teacher is busy reinforcing the learner and planning the next exchange at the same time; therefore, this is the moment when his or her linguistic ego is really at work, so much so that it does not control itself but utters uncontrolled and structurally loose pieces of language. This also explains why the source language intrudes more than it usually does at such moments. The stress of the planning task accounts for the fact that the speaker is dominated by utterances which he or she knows from his or her mother tongue.

The absence of such impromptu elements in the language of learners signals that they do not go through real planning phases at all, but that the elicitation of the teacher triggers a performative act by going back to some performance product stored in the mind. What learners produce in such moments is not creatively planned speech but remembered or coded speech.

These observations can lead to at least two quite important consequences:

1. If the creative planning of one's own speech is supposed to be an important act in language learning, because it obviously is an important act in the performance of native speakers, the learners should have a chance of going through it. Making it too easy for learners may be keeping them from an important exercise (Hüllen, 1983).
2. Mother tongue interference is not so much due to the similarities of the systems, but depends on the strain of the moment, on the mental 'depth' in which the speech act is created by the speaker. Absence of such interference, therefore, can indeed mean that somebody is able to plan his or her utterances in the foreign language — that his or her competence indeed equals that of a native speaker. It can, however, also mean that a speaker does not plan his or her utterances at all but just verbalises premeditated texts.

Project 3 (Hüllen & Loŕscher, 1979; Lörscher, 1983)

The description of classroom discourse allows us to identify certain types of acts and to find out which quantitative share each of them occupies in the whole discourse. Such acts are for example,

– *phatic* with various functions like planning phases or back-channel comments;

- *topic* referring to the subject/topic under discussion;
- *linguistic* referring to the language itself, that is, its meaning or its formal and pragmatic correctness;
- *organising* with the functions of opening and closing discourse and of allocating turns;
- *correcting* (with obvious functions);
- *commenting* which often overlaps with correcting acts;
- *evaluating* with the four functions mentioned above;
- *repeating* which seems to be particularly classroom specific;
- *aside* with no relation to the classroom discourse.

The distribution of such acts in classroom discourse is of course very uneven. To begin with, 75% of all utterances come from the teacher; only the remaining 25% from the learners. Learners utter very few phatic and linguistic acts — these are almost entirely the teacher's — and no organising acts at all. Topical acts comprise the bulk of what the learners say. According to this way of grouping, the learners' speech in the classroom is uniform when compared to the teacher's speech, but also when compared to everyday discourse. Furthermore, teachers instigate initiative and elicitative acts as well as commenting and evaluative ones, that is follow-ups, whereas learners are limited to responsive and reactive acts.

Such findings should, of course, not be used for criticising teachers and their role in class. They should be taken as an insight into the diversity of speech acts in communication for which learners must be prepared. With the exception perhaps of repeating acts, all the others also occur in everyday dialogue and must be mastered eventually by our learners, although in different wording and rhetorical patterns, since partners in communication do not confront each other in teacher and learner roles. From this quantifying analysis, the alienating character of classroom discourse can indeed be made clear; something which must somehow be overcome by teaching methodology.

The three projects described enter the wide area of investigations into classroom discourse at quite different points. The first is devoted to learning sequences for syntactic and semantic rules, the second to teacher speech planning under the special aspect of contrastiveness, the third to the rhetorical distribution of speech acts between teacher and learners. All three projects are of a preliminary character and beg for much more intensive research.

There are of course other topics to be observed, for example, communication strategies in a foreign language, for which no pilot study could be given (Faerch & Kasper, 1983). All these investigations treat the learning process essentially as a process of communication. Learning is indeed communicating under special circumstances and with special aims. The outward appearance of communication, however, is discourse.

Appendix

Project 1

1.   begin to laugh → laugh
      could not believe → did not believe
2.1   he came → he was at
      the bed measured → the bed was . . . long
2.2   mad → not quite right
      straight → not crooked
2.3   ask → say
      crash → fly against
      walked → went
3.   S (when he was listening to some music) → He heard music + S

Project 2

T: Your homework for today was to find out all the idioms or expressions that have to do with sport and find an equivalent in plain English. Can we go through this now. (5 sec)
      Yes, Angela
L: I think the first idiom from sport is 'sitting in the same boat' — and in modern English I would say, eh, 'we are all in the same situation.'
T: Right.
      We are all in the same situation.
      Good.
T: Does anybody remember the title of the story?
      Bert.
L: Herbert, the human radio.
T: Yes, okay.
      Now, who was Herbert?
      Do you remember anything about him?
      Yes, please Guido.
L: Herbert was a boy . . .
T: mhm
L: in England . . .
T: mhm

L: and he have, have a good mother.
T: Stop, stop, there was a mistake.
L: has a good mother.
T: Aha, will you please repeat the sentence.
L: He has a good mother.
T: Aha, but you said, he was in England. So you must use the past tense in the second part of your sentence as well.
L: He was a good boy and . . .
T: Let's see if we can remember the things that Mary put on the sand castles to make them look nice.
        What were they? The things she put on the sand castles . . .
        Yes, Judy.
L: It was a mushle.
T: What? Is that right?
        Eh, Steven.
L: shell.
T: A shell, that's the English word, isn't it?
        Shell, that's right.
        Okay.
        I said the *things* she put so . . .
        [NV$_{nomination}$]
L: shells.
T: They were shells.
        Okay.
        The right sentence, listen.
        The things Mary put on her sand castles were shells.
        The things Mary put on her sand castles were shells.
        Everyone.

Project 3

	Teacher	%	Learner	%
phatic	55	8.97	3	1.97
topic	7	1.14	5	3.29
linguistic	119	19.41	70	46.05
aside	12	1.96	9	5.92
organising	195	31.81	28	18.42
correcting	6	0.98	27	17.76
commenting	47	7.67	19	12.50
evaluative	80	13.05	0	0
repeating	58	9.46	19	12.50

References

DECHERT, H.W. & RAUPACH, M. (eds), 1980, *Towards a Crosslinguistic Assessment of Speech Production*. Frankfurt: Lang.

EDMONDSON, W. & HOUSE, J., 1981, *Let's Talk and Talk About It*. München: Urban & Schwarzenberg.

ENKVIST, N.E. (ed), 1982, *Impromptu Speech: A Symposium*. Åbo: Åbo Akademi.

FAERCH, C. & KASPER, G., 1983, *Strategies in Interlanguage Communication*. London: Longman.

FELIX, S.W., 1982, *Psycholinguistische Aspekte des Zweitsprachenerwerbs*. Tübingen: Narr.

HÜLLEN, W., 1976, Fremdsprachendidaktik und linguistische Pragmatik. *Die Neueren Sprachen 75*, 217–229.

— 1982, Observations related to impromptu elements in classroom discourse and to the function of such elements for foreign language teaching and learning. In N. E. ENKVIST (ed), *Impromptu Speech: A Symposium*. Åbo: Åbo Akademi, 207–219.

— 1983, On some didactic consequences from insights into the mechanism of language acquisition and language learning. In S.W. FELIX & H. WODE (eds), *Language Development at the Crossroads*. Tübingen: Narr, 145–150.

— 1984, Streitbare Anmerkungen zu S.W. Felix 'Psycholinguistische Aspekte des Zweitsprachenerwerbs'. *Studium Linguistik 15*, 102–109.

HÜLLEN, W. & JUNG, L., 1979, *Sprachstruktur und Spracherwerb*. Düsseldorf: Bagel und Franke.

HÜLLEN, W. & LÖRSCHER, W., 1979, Lehrbuch, Lerner und Unterrichtsdiskurs. *Unterrichtswissenschaft 4*, 313–326.

KASPER, G., 1981, *Pragmatische Aspekte in der Interimsprache*. Tübingen: Narr.

KLEIN, W., 1984, *Zweitsprachenerwerb. Eine Einführung*. Königstein/Ts.: Athenäum.

LÖRSCHER, W., 1983, *Linguistische Beschreibung und Analyse von Fremdsprachenunterricht als Diskurs*. Tübingen: Narr.

NICHOLAS, H. & MEISEL, J., 1983, Second language acquisition: The state of the art. In S.W. FELIX & H. WODE (eds), *Language Development at the Crossroads*. Tübingen: Narr.

SINCLAIR, J.McH. & COULTHARD, M., 1975, *Towards an Analysis of Discourse: The English Used by Teachers and Pupils*. London: Oxford University Press.

STUBBS, M., 1976, *Language, Schools and Classrooms*. London: Methuen.

WODE, H., 1981, *Learning a Second Language: Vol. 1. An Integrated View of Language Acquisition*. Tübingen: Narr.

8 The Linguistics of Enunciative Operations and Second Language Learning

DANIELLE BAILLY

Introduction

It is our basic assumption that the theory of enunciative operations (TEO), developed by Antoine Culioli, represents a powerful model for the structuring of L2 input and the presentation of metalinguistic explanations in L1 about L2 to students in tutored second language acquisition. The precise framework within which we have worked is the teaching of English as a foreign language to French 11-year-old learners.[1] The efficiency of theoretical linguistics in this context appears to be threefold:

1. It seems to provide coherent criteria for the selection and delimitation of samples which are considered to be fundamental and thus suitable for teaching material. If L1 and L2 may be assumed as two specific modes or sets of traces which human subjects use to express generalisable language operations, linguistics may provide the theoretical framework to describe source and target languages, as being identical in depth and different on the surface. We expect this procedure of the selection of linguistic essentials common to both to be an encouraging way for the modelling of a system of representations that actually maps subjects' real speaking activities.
2. Linguistics enables the didactician to transpose his or her theoretical knowledge into ready-for-use pedagogical material without disregarding the specific linguistic status of such a transposition. Whereas, for instance, natural communication is constrained by genuine spatio-temporal, modal, referential/textual phenomena, that is to say, a real here-and-now discourse anchoring for a given set of communication partners, or a retraceable narrative status for a

given text, L2 comprehension/production in the classroom is different from this, remains communicatively non-functional and simulative. This biases any communication in the classroom, and verbal interaction in particular, and entails particular modal shifts and determinative blurrings. It is the task of the linguist to analyse them.

3. Finally, linguistics helps the didactician to take into account two kinds of complementary requirements of the material as well as of the strategies: first, the classical L1–L2 interference, as for instance, in the case of the aspectual system for a Frenchman learning English as a foreign language and second, the developmental and conceptual difficulties inherent in the apprehension of certain linguistic notions, as in the case of terms like *comparison, generic, hypothesis*, and so forth.

Since the raising of learners' consciousness of linguistic functioning is assumed to facilitate their L2-acquisition — together with intensive practice, of course — it is the applied linguist's task to materialise alternative choices in concrete experiments. Let us concentrate on two pedagogical devices which are typical for our approach:

(a) concerning the arrangement and presentation of teaching material: a well structured *grammatical progression*, and

(b) concerning the sequences of teaching: a *conceptualisation phase*, conceived of as a strategic element in the teaching process.

Grammatical progression links each unique micro-system in the sequence of the total course (for instance, the tenses, the determiners, and so on) to the other micro-systems both in a communicatively plausible and linguistically coherent way. The conceptualisation phase covers a very short period of time, in fact about twenty minutes a week in a total of four hours' teaching. It includes individual and collective reflection on the L2 in the L1. This phase we believe to be original in our concept. It differs from the traditional grammar lesson as well as from the communicative approach, currently practised in language teaching. It aims at making learners aware of language operations such as location, determination, quantification. The metalinguistic explanations given to them focus on the cognitive and cultural symbolisation through language(s). Learners are thus led not only to follow the organisation of L2 norms as such and as distinctive from their L1, but also to express their own interlanguage activities. They test their individual hypotheses on L2 functioning; they evaluate the degree of accuracy of their own and others' productions. Such metalinguistic reasoning depends on an effort of justification and a search for structural as well as communicative coherence criteria.

As for the teacher, this approach requires the use of a suitable metalanguage; he or she will classify and label text units and text arrangements and specify them in relation to the classes of extralinguistic situations they correspond with. It is the learner's task then to internalise such concepts as time–tense relationship modality, voice, determination, deixis and anaphory as linked to topological abstract locations elaborated from a given discourse origin. Thus the learner is trained not only to identify and combine elements of surface L2 semiosis, but to recognise the invisible language invariants that lie behind them. In course of time he or she must increasingly become aware of such speaker–addressee types of relationships and be able to define such thought experiences behind the experimental speech situations. And behind the lexical diversity he or she is likely to be confronted with, a single meaning value in a given context and environment will be evident, even if the marker(s) used are potentially polysemic. Technically, the metalinguistic devices applied in the classroom include denominations, manipulations, comparisons, representations, simulations involving L2. As such, these devices are classical, but their content is made as rigorous, linguistically speaking, as possible. Such a conception of linguistics prevents us from separating syntax and semantics, formal grammar or rules and the pragmatic communicative function they have. In proceeding toward near native L2 competence, learners are meant to 'decentre'[2] themselves in a gradually increasing metalinguistic awareness, without ever being able to be experts in linguistics. The teacher, as far as his or her part is concerned, should strive to be a fully competent linguist, if not an inventor.

For the second language acquisition (SLA) researcher it is extremely valuable to become aware of metalinguistic and epilinguistic data,[3] especially elicited during the maieutic dialogue which we call conceptualisation phase. They provide deep insight into the classificatory and argumentative activities of second language learners and contribute tremendously to a better understanding of the salient or vulnerable aspects of second language acquisition. Such a kind of research is necessarily multidisciplinary and complex. Various methodologies must indeed combine in such implicated experiments, the object under study itself being heterogeneous and variable. Therefore, we as SLA researchers must borrow our tools not only from theoretical linguistics but also from psycholinguistics, psychology, sociolinguistics, institutional analysis,[4] the educational sciences, and so on. In language pedagogy we may even have to create more than we can borrow.

We shall now examine more closely the linguistics of enunciative operations.[5]

The theory of enunciative operations (TEO) is both a formal theory and a descriptive theory of the singularity of speech of the human subject as a variable speaker. *Formal* stands for a metalinguistic system of representation according to which numerous sets of variable occurrences of texts may be analysed, in order to extract a few hypothesised abstract invariants from them. Conversely, it serves to predict and account for surface forms and values above these deep invariants. Different levels of units and relations are thus hypothetically revealed and reconstructed.

At the most fundamental level of general language activity, the linguist finds a set of primitive notions. They convey semantic and logical value; they are ordered in presyntactic relations according to referential properties such as degree of animacy, intentionality, agentiveness, modes of unfolding of events, kinds of intrinsic determination and relatedness, and so on. On this basis, predicative relations, linked to syntactic structures are produced/ recognised by speaking subjects and reconstructed by the linguist. These relations are dependent on the rules which specify a given language, including the morpho-syntactic and lexical compatibility requirements. The linguist lastly distinguishes the enunciative relations which account for the speaker's own location and viewpoint on reality: his or her personal and interpersonal judgements and adjustments, and so forth.

This method of linguistic theorising may be illustrated by the following notation

$$<\text{arb}> \in \underline{\ } \mathscr{S}\text{it}(\mathscr{S}/S, \beta/T)$$

It means that, for a given speaker

1. who is characterised by his or her *enunciative coordinates* (which are expressed with the rounded letters)
   (a) $\mathscr{S}$it. symbolising his or her enunciative situation,
   (b) $\mathscr{S}$ symbolising one or more actants (speaker(s)/hearer(s)) in the discourse, and
   (c) β: symbolising an enunciative space/time anchoring for the utterance;
2. there is an utterance, symbolised by the complete *formula*, which is the trace of *location* operations, performed by a *location operator* $\in$, and the location of a *predicative content* $<\text{arb}>$, whereby a stands for the primitive *source elements*, b for the *target elements*, and r for the *relator*. This predicative location is modalised and thematised enunciatively by the speaker's relating of his or her enunciative coordinates to
   (a) what he or she perceives as the *theme S* of the utterance and

(b) that which contributes to its *location T*.

That is to say, the overall textual content organises the elements <arb>, S, and T, starting from and according to the original anchorage imposed by the *extra-linguistic* elements $\mathscr{S}$, β, $\mathscr{S}$it, and $\in$. If, for instance, a speaker identifies a predicative content with his or her own situation so that the time of speaking coincides with the present time and deictic reference in the utterance, then the present progressive will express the speaker's proximity to the message content:

(1) *Look! John is eating an apple [now].*

This proximity appears in the co-reference with the addressee '*Look!*', as well. In this example $V + $ *-ing* in the present tense conveys a β/T relationship of the type: T identical with β, or T $\in {}_i\beta$, or: same value for message as speaker's situation is identical or associated with predication <arb>. In this same example the relationship $\mathscr{S}$/S is of the kind *different from*, as 'John' refers to a third person, who is talked about, and the speaker being the first person talking to an addressee, the second person (S $\notin \mathscr{S}$).

Let us now take an example of a different type:

(2) *Men are mortal.*

In this generic utterance no apparent or specified speaker takes charge of the content; the epsilon location is of the absence of relation type between speaker and predicative reference $<$ *for men, to be mortal* $>$. In turn, both $\mathscr{S}$/S and β/T relationships are of the same impersonal and general type, the speaker deliberately choosing to appear uninvolved.

The communicative aspect of the theory, however formal it may be, can be seen from this simplified example. It does indeed give a precise description of the variable language activity of human beings (and not an idealisation of an abstract speaker/hearer). It rather attempts to specify the unique conditions of production/comprehension for each analysed utterance. This implies the consideration of its space/time and notional discourse universe, be it pragmatically real or fictitious. This may concern simple deixis, the inclusion of extralinguistic ostensive or orientational foundations of speech, or more complex constructions which disclose the speaker's paraphrastic modulations on a given matrix, depending on their enunciative viewpoint.

We may, for example, compare the following two sentences:

(3) (a) *A thief stole three paintings from the museum.*
     (b) *Three paintings were stolen from a museum (by a thief).*

From a semantic perspective these two sentences are equivalent. From an enunciative perspective they are not. Normally one would rather be inclined to choose the second version in order to focus on the object (*Three paintings* . . .).

The theory must account for rhetorical, stylistic, or argumentative variation, not only syntactically through active versus passive constructions, but also by establishing a link between some speaker perspective and some equivalent linguistic device. In the preceding example (3) (b) communicative emphasis and symbolic focus thus converge toward an inanimate goal (*the paintings*), which becomes the surface grammatical subject. Morpho-syntactic choices between two structures, the second, a passive structure, being derived from the first one, an active structure, are symbolic for subjective, or for socially coded, speaking perspectives.[6]

The same kind of symbolic perspective may be seen on a radically different semiosis, in the core of the TEO treatment of a semantic item such as the lexeme *by*, for instance. In this case we are dealing with one marker only, but a highly polysemic one. The question is what kind of relationship may connect the various shades of its meaning, how native speakers produce and perceive them in their speech community, and how they are individually capable of differentiating and interpreting each particular meaning value, however specific and singular it may be in light of the context in which it occurs. *By*, for instance, as we know, can convey many different meanings, such as *agent, means*, or *manner*. It may also mean *during* (*He travelled by night*.) or *for* or *with* (*It's all right by him*.). All these different shades of meaning may be derived from one elementary component whose significance is disclosed in sentences such as

(4)   (a) *The house was located down by the riverside.*

in which the phrase '*down by the riverside*' means *next to* (equivalent to the German *bei*). This formal and semantic nuclear unit basically means *near, adjacent to, accompanying the neighbouring element with a dominated status related to that element.* Etymology will confirm this interpretation. From this primitive accompaniment-operation we may, for instance, derive an agent-complement-value, for in the agent-action-goal relation in a passive sentence with the concluding formula *by x*, the agent complement is *together with* the affected goal and dominated by it, as for example in

(4)   (b) *The house was decorated by the children.*

Actually, we thus find a comparable kind of location operation in 4 (a) as well as in 4 (b), although the meaningful construct in 4 (b) where it is symbolically metaphorised from 4 (a) is more elaborated. In both cases non-salient elements

$$(4) \quad (a) \; . \; . \; . \; the \; riverside.$$

and

$$(4) \quad (b) \; . \; . \; . \; the \; children.$$

are referred to other cognitively more salient elements

$$(4) \quad (a) \; The \; house \; was \; located$$

and

$$(4) \quad (b) \; The \; house \; was \; decorated \; . \; . \; .$$

Similarly, the sentence

$$(5) \quad It \; is \; all \; right \; by \; him$$

expresses topological approximation with the derived meaning effect of relatedness or concernment. '*Him*' acts both as a border and as a located or comparative element. '*It is all right*' acts as a locator or referential point since it is the element that is stated and qualified.

A psycholinguistic corroboration of the locator/located element or dominant/dominated dissymmetry in the accompaniment operation may be, for instance, found in the phrases

$$(6) \quad (a) \; a \; door \; \textbf{with} \; a \; lock$$

or

$$(b) \quad an \; apartment \; \textbf{with} \; a \; kitchen$$

as contrasted with

$$* \; a \; lock \; with \; a \; door$$

or

$$* \; a \; kitchen \; with \; an \; apartment.$$

What is enunciative in these examples is not a speaker's choice between two formal, structural arrangements to which he or she attributes symbolic value, but a speaker's symbolic activity with the help of a formal sign, namely the markers *by* or *with*, which correspond to an accompaniment operation and produce metaphorically a series of context-sensitive meanings.

Syntactic and morpho-semantic modulations represent an intermediate kind of procedure. Let us, for instance, consider the two following sentences:

(7) (a) *I've been writing (and writing) all morning.*
(b) *I've written a lot of letters this morning.*

The tense in both sentences is the same (present perfect), but 7 (a) is continuous and 7 (b) is not (which is, by the way, rather difficult for a French learner of English). The only other differences are: in 7 (a), absence of an object, emphasis on the process, the use of a temporal quantifier expressed through a 'scanning' operation: *all*; in 7 (b) presence of a quantified object, the establishment of deictic and punctual temporal reference: *this*. In a way, the speaker has had an enunciative choice between two ways of referring to the same 'objective' temporal reality; however, the emphasis on a very long process in 7 (a) or the 'final assessment' of a situation in 7 (b) is different. The speaker's perspective can be analysed through a topological approach of aspect: in 7 (a) the 'open' continuous aspect $V + ing$ accounts for the speaker's modal implication toward the event related, still in existence at the time of speaking; in 7 (b), the 'closed' non-continuous aspect signals the speaker's mutative-resultative rupture between past and present. But in both cases, the speaker has used the formal category of aspect (continuity or rupture), together with a morpho-syntactic device (a tense), evaluative semantemes (*all, a lot of*), and intonation patterns to construct symbolically his or her feelings. However diverse the constructions may be, the theory models abstract distances, or changes, or deformations, and specifies them in relationship with a starting point: the speaker's enunciative coordinates, or, more broadly, a human being's locative evaluation (quantification/qualification determinative criteria) of the elements of the world he or she chooses to refer to.

This type of psychogenetic interpretation of linguistic markers may be relevant for the study of child speech development. If one considers language traces as compounds of fundamental values, it is enlightening to know, for instance, that an eight-year-old child was found to invent the deconstructed and logically simpler phrase: *juste que (just that)* to express *sauf (except)* which he was not able to master yet (cf. Franckel, 1984, personal communication).

In this same line of thought, pragmatics can be treated as a symbolical network of constructed meanings, a hyper-syntax, so to speak. Indeed, relationships between human beings can be formalised and assumed to correspond to a set of language rules. For instance, the psychological and social extralinguistic dominance relationships between people can be linguistically expressed through the modality system (deontic/request, desiderative/will, and so on). Not only speaking situations, but parts of human interaction and of the status of the objects of the world can find their semiotic, transferred echo within language.

In conclusion of this very superficial survey of TEO, considered as both a formal *and* communicative theory, two aspects which are generally antithetic, let us then outline one of its main epistemological characteristics. Although conceived as a multilevel set of heterogeneous operations, partly semantic, morpho- and phono-syntactic, but also cognitive, semiotic, socio-cultural, and so on, this theory hypothesises operations as linked to each other through an endogenous complexification. This reveals a post-Piagetian *constructivist* psycholinguistic approach to linguistic causality: that is, a precise cognitive conception of symbolic activity displayed through language. From deep preconstructs to first occurrences of notional domains and more elaborated constructions in surface structures, a sort of history of utterances can then be traced back by the linguist, which is composed of a continuous series of articulated determinative and locative acts. This whole process from emergence to realisation thus appears to be logically unified, the theory itself being a highly metalinguistic reflection of speakers' language production as a sophisticated but natural behaviour.[7] Wht we have been looking for and believe to have found in the theory of enunciative operations is not only a powerful explanation of the reality of language and of interlanguage phenomena, but also a theoretical approach that is compatible with what is known of learners' way of reasoning and problem-solving strategies in general.

Experiment [8]

Methodology

We have observed some of the linguistic and cognitive strategies employed by French learners acquiring English, within the theoretical framework of TEO. The didactic setting was an English class of twelve and thirteen year old children in a Parisian suburb. It was observed and tape-recorded for an entire year. The classroom teacher had been trained in TEO and knew how to adapt it to the pedagogical situation. As stated above, the teaching material included grammatical progression and conceptualisation phases. The recordings provided data which we analysed from different points of view.

Description of data

The tape recordings provided data that were classified according to different kinds of epilinguistic (spontaneous, intuitional, and semi-conscious) and metalinguistic (conscious, formally verbalised, and controlled) processes related to L2 learning activity. Particularly investigated were the interactions between metalinguistic input from the teacher and the learners' treatment of such input. Teacher input and learner output were classified under three specific labels: *objects, categories*, and *notions*. We also classified the processes which were responsible for these data as either cognitive or semiotic. The former concerned various mental activities from *effectuation* (realisation) and *representation* to other activities initiating systems of *classification* and *argumentation*. The latter involved *verbal, semiverbal*, and *nonverbal* processes.

What we called *objects* were the L2 elements provided by the teacher as well as the learners' interlanguage. By exposing the learners to L2 sequences, the teacher aims at leaving their semispontaneous organising capacity free to interpret such material: that is, he or she attempts to enable them to identify units and combine them in structures, and recognise their stability in spite of their diverse lexical and situational 'clothing'. The learners' interlanguage constitutes a somewhat indirect trace of their gradual discovery.

What we called *categories* was linked to sets of explanatory concepts about the functioning of L2 which are basic to the teacher's and learners' formulations. These concepts were discussed in L1. Whatever the semiotic medium may be, definitional or metaphorical words, comments, paraphrases, figures, diagrams, the analytical material presented to the learners helps them to internalise the linguistic status (the function and referential value) of a given L2 surface unit or textual arrangement. This refers to the field of validity of morpho-syntactic rules (paradigmatic and syntagmatic classes and relations) as well as lexical compatibility with such rules. But it also refers to the communicational and discursive motivation for each grammatical transformation. Essentially it involves predicative relations. It may either imply working on traditional parts of speech or on linguistic paradigms proper (flexions, cases, prepositional phrases, syntagmatic contrasts, etc.).

To give an example: when explaining the categorical phenomenon of aspect, the teacher makes the learner aware of the different ways a speaker may perceive and/or express the process or state of an event as it takes place (beginning, duration, end, repetition, punctual occurrence, and so on), in relation to the different markers, sometimes morpho-syntactic, sometimes lexical, sometimes both at the same time.

What we called *notions* also concerned metalinguistic explanatory material. This material deals with the general referential operations a speaker constructs to apprehend reality: it may be as diverse as proper semantic concepts, or enunciative characteristics, or even textual organisation in relation to the extralinguistic data which it maps — for instance, concepts of obligation, of certainty, or number, or degree of specification, or temporal relation, or anaphora, and so on. In all these cases it is the teacher's aim to enable the learners to become conscious of these notions and verbalise them clearly. Such analytical tools as the elements of enunciative coordinates (speaker, utterance, deixis, factual or counter-factual judgement or projection, occurrence(s), location, etc.) must, one way or another, be mastered. The pedagogical work on these notions implies more argumentative than classificatory procedures: it involves more hypothetico-deductive and inductive reasoning than mere mechanical listing.

The internalisation of the three kinds of phenomena — objects, categories, notions — implies cognitive activities related to effectuation and representation. Effectuation, as for example the production of L2, comprises role-playing, reading, writing, problem-solving, and sequence manipulations and mobilises sensory-motor, graphic, gestual, imaginative acts of all kinds. Representation, like naming, autonomously manipulating language, symbolising phenomena, and so on, mobilises more abstract behaviour both of differentiation and generalisation. Cognitively these activities concern reasoning processes, and semiotically they concern the concrete coding used to convey such mental contents.

Results

Our results seem to indicate that tutored learning of L2 depends on two apparently contradictory but possibly equally powerful determining factors: on the one hand, it appears that tutoring strategies inspired by TEO linguistics decisively and positively influence the way learners acquire a second language. In other words, a metalinguistic approach of second language teaching, which explicitly deals with generalisable language operations and with the interlanguage as related to them appears to influence the substance of interlanguage activity itself: rhythm of evolution, permanence, and degree of mastery of L2 acquisition. On the other hand, at the same time general cognitive, and even linguistic, mechanisms do interfere with this influence.

As far as cognitive mechanisms are concerned, our study, like many others, confirms the permanent influence of such phenomena as simplification, regularisation, and analogy. They persistently prevail over the teacher's methodological endeavours whether it is plain drills or scientific explanation. The teacher has to resign him or herself to learners' irrational associations, erroneous hypotheses, segmenting mistakes, polyvalent interpretations, avoidance strategies, and the like.

As to linguistic mechanisms, what our investigation specifically emphasises is the difficulty encountered by second language learners in acquiring the value of L2 markers that refer to indetermination. There are particular learning obstacles inherent to everything that implies a *conceptual distance* or estrangement from the learner/speaker, either in reference or in enunciative location and evaluation: anything that is perceived as distal, multiple, uncountable, iterative, interrogative, indifferent, negative will tend to be uninteresting and matterless. In short, whatever conveys a notion of vagueness, whatever is opposite to 'what is close, what is good, what is me' (cf. Tanz, 1980) in linguistic terms or as we might say: whatever implies a blurring in the distinctness of topological borders, either in the apprehension of occurrences linked to notional domains, or in the enunciative location activities, inhibits learning. Such difficulties are strongly linked to problems of communicative, that is affective, attitudinal, or even socio-cultural motivation. When, for instance, role-playing in L2 simulations are practised in the classroom, the observer frequently realises how learners can lose motivation when such activities are situated outside real space and real time. Motivation and learning efficiency grow, inversely, whenever deictically proximal/ostensive, concrete, speaker-associated L2 contents are involved. Even when the class deals with fictional material (sketches, cartoons, narrations), one notices the strong impact on the acquisition of easily evocative themes. These observations corroborate with the principle of cognitive psychology, that the 'figurative underlies the operative'.

The selection of linguistic features that correspond to such motivation, namely L2 items illustrating the 'here and now' aspects with regard to agentivity, place, experience, personal identification and so on is essential for the teaching of L2, at least in the beginning stages of learning.

Lastly, our study tends to demonstrate that, on a very general and systemic level of analysis, a four-pole interactive network relates the *auto-* and *hetero-references* of both teacher and learners, in the organisation and regulation of second language acquisition. These four spheres enclose the pedagogic actants in specific interpretative micro-universes which are far from always coinciding. There remain differences in metalanguage, in sensitivity to problems, in relevant saliences, in background. On their articulation, though, depends the success or failure of learning.

This does not render the theoretical question of the relative amount of invariance and variation in learning, which is crucial in SLA research, more predictable in respect to a given input and to given data processing causalities and determinisms. The analysis is complicated by the fact that the systemic network, which governs each type of actor intervention, seems to produce each time a unique combination of interpretable language events in the classroom. And yet, it would be essential for SLA research to provide the answers to such questions, if it is to contribute significantly to the improvement of learning. 'Everything-works-as-if' and 'black-box' models are not satisfactory in this respect.

Samples from data[9]

Learner motivation due to explicit grammatical conceptualisation has been one of the topics of particular interest in our study. Out of the 50 classroom episodes selected for analysis in our study ten, almost all of them have in one way or another shown learners' enthusiasm and active effort to understand and apply their acquired knowledge. This motivation became apparent in many ways, such as positive answers to observer's questions, exuberant joy in the classroom, remarks to the effect that time was passing very quickly, in one word: pleasure. The learners' reactions were unanimous. Whenever we observed such classes, we were struck by the students' affective as well as intellectual involvement. This was confirmed in the observations of other researchers between 1969 and 1985.

The subjective reasons for such success are easy to find: throughout the process of making the learner aware of linguistic phenomena, the teacher appeals to his or her personal language experience in L1 and makes use of this in L2. For instance, when a teacher asks an adolescent learner such questions as: 'What does certainty mean to you? How do you analyse its components — source, circumstances, object, and so on?', or when he or she asks an 11-year-old learner what the difference is between the determiners in: 'Bring *a* chair!' and 'Hold *the* chair!', the teacher gives every possible clue to help the learner to master the non-arbitrariness of each specific marker in the linguistic micro-system. This is no longer formal grammar, but living psycholinguistics in action. It only remains to be verbalised, in the learners' own words first, and then in a more standardised form. Rules are only one way, among many, to formulate major language functions. This way children feel free to pool their individual ideas on the notions and marker values under study, express them intuitively first, and then metalinguistically.

Extract 1

Topic: Tense/aspect location — the preterite.
Subjects: 11-year-olds, first year of English as a foreign language.

The point summed up by the teacher is the double aspectual value[10] of the preterite, either referring to *once* or to *several times* for the same *-ed* marker.

She writes the following two sentences on the blackboard:

'*Last night*, I watched television.'
'*Last summer*, I watched television *every night*.'

Then she asks what difference the learners can perceive:

Learner 1:   'Both are ended.'
Learner 2:   'Both say what happened, but not how long it went on for.'
Learner 3:   'In one, it happened once; in the other, it happened several times and long ago.'
Teacher: 'How am I going to represent the second case?'
Learner 3:   (comes to the blackboard and draws):

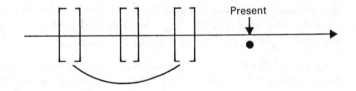

He says: 'I need three.'

The teacher writes on the blackboard:

(a) 'I'*m* watch*ing* T.V.'
(b) 'I *watch* T.V. every night.'
(c) '*Yesterday*, I watch*ed* T.V.'
(d) '*Last summer*, I watch*ed* T.V. *every night*.'

She asks: 'What do you notice?'
L1:   'There's *watch* everywhere.'
L2:   'Something's changing.'
L3:   '(b) is past and future as well.'
L4:   '(c) is past.'
Teacher: 'Once or several times?'
L5:   'Several.' (The others yell indignantly at the mistake.)
Teacher: 'Is there a difference between (c) and (d)?'

L1: 'In the past, it's always the same, but in the present it isn't.'
L3: 'Oh yeah, it's funny!'
Teacher: 'What's most certain?' (silence)
           'What's least certain?'
L2: 'Preterite.'
Teacher: 'Most certain?'
L4: 'Real present.'
Teacher: 'Why?'
L5: 'It's happening just now.'
Teacher: 'And why is preterite less certain?'
L1: 'Because you can't see again.'
L3: 'The only thing you can do is remember.'

Extract 2

Topic: Modals — change of tense.

    She writes the following two sentences on the blackboard:

    'Jane is a baby now, she *can't* walk.'
    'But in 1990, she'*ll be able to*.'

Teacher: 'Have we seen something like that already?'
L1: 'Yes, with *must*.'
L2: 'Yes, with *must*, too, you got to put another stuff.'
Teacher: 'And in the preterite?'
L3: 'Also.'
Teacher: 'Why did we have to change the auxiliary, when we changed tenses?'
L4: 'In the future, you're not sure it's gonna happen, so you got to say it!'
Teacher: 'And in the past?'
L5: 'Well, this time you're sure.'
L1: 'Oh really? You had to do something, but nobody's sure you did it!'
L2: 'Yes, *I* was sure; but maybe *you* didn't know!'
L5: 'Anyway, in the past, it's always flabby.'
L4: 'Yes, mentally, intellectually (!!!)'
Teacher: 'So, here, with *can*? What happens?'
L3: 'Well, you do the same, but not with the same stuff; or if you don't want to do nothing, you just do nothing.'

Extract 3

    Topic: Noun determiners.

Teacher: '*Some* chocolate, what kind of quantity is it?'
L1: 'You don't know.'
Teacher: 'Suppose I want to be more precise: What would I have to say?'
L2: 'Two cups.'
L3: 'Or: You just keep an eye on it!'
Teacher: 'Why do I have to use a measure or weight unit if I want to be more precise? Would it be the same with a word like *orange*?'
L4: 'What about *milk* or *sugar*?'
L5: 'Well you know, in England they've got powdered sugar, so you got no problem! But we have lumps, one, two, three.'
Teacher: 'Let's come back to chocolate: Can you say *one chocolate*?'
L3: 'Well, I'm in a pub, I don't ask for chocolate, I say: Give me white wine!'
L2: 'Chocolate, you got bars or little squares'.
Teacher: 'Tell me the difference between: "give me *some* chocolate powder" and: "give me *some* apples".'
L1: 'Well, you got the plural.'
L2: 'Same thing, but you could count the apples, even if you don't want to: the chocolate powder, even if you wanted to, you couldn't.'

These three episodes illustrate why TEO is specifically suited to elicit learners' cognitive activity. TEO aims at making language operations as apparent as possible, so that teachers may explain and learners may understand them, even in a very simplified and approximate way. Since this understanding has been found to facilitate L2 acquisition, all conditions are met to have learners' cognitive activity surface, and therefore make it accessible to SLA research.

These examples demonstrate that learners may be brought to discriminate between the formal values in lexical or morpho-syntactic items.

Extract 1

In Extract 1, the *-ed* verb ending must be understood as potentially bivalent, that is, punctual or iterative. Lexical phrases like *last night, every night, last summer* are to be understood, respectively, as punctual or iterative/durative. Besides, the person and tense marking depends on the modal force the speaker grants to the process of reference, according to his or her involvement in the evoked time–tense relationship. In other words, the semantic and grammatical context-sensitiveness must be analysed. Every bit of formal information must be given a status, a denomination, a valid application, and so on.

Extract 2

In Extract 2, every surface marker change must be understood to correspond with referential value change; here, it does not only mean a change of time/tense location, but an insight into the speakers' perspective on events when they change modals: the discussion about degrees of certainty shows the relative enunciative freedom of choice left open to the speakers. This freedom delights learners.

Extract 3

Extract 3 reveals that the reference cuts, according to languages, is an object of wonder for children. A cultural difference such as the shape of sugar in France and in England, for instance, entails a linguistic change of noun determiners according to the noun classification (uncountable or countable) characteristic for each language.

These examples may not be earth-shaking in terms of linguistic science, but in the classroom dynamic, they will arouse the children's lively interest and concern for language analysis. Such a positive attitude towards analytic reasoning will have the effect that they both assimilate what they learn more quickly, and remember it better.

Discussion

Confirmation of hypotheses

There is no doubt that appealing to the intelligibility of thought experiences contributes to making the learner understand that languages are paraphrases of one another in respect of language invariants. He or she therefore shifts more easily from one to the other. The autonomy learners acquire helps them control their pre- and post-error correcting systems, and to evolve more rapidly from one stage of interlanguage to the next one; they realise that they are progressing, and feel that their efforts have been rewarded. This does not mean, though, that this approach, in the end, will necessarily be more powerful than natural second language acquisition.[11]

Principles for further research

The first stage of our experiment (1969–1984) has led us to define a more controlled array of research questions. It is necessary to raise, test, and validate clearer preliminary hypotheses which are likely to constitute the outline of a SLA model. First, it seems to us necessary to 'learn the lesson' from the previous *Charlirelle* teaching experiment and draw the psycholinguistic conclusions for a future design. From this point of view, the observation of a didactic setting within the school system appears not to be the best. There are indeed too many diverse variables that bias the causes and effects the researcher is looking for in the data. These variables are socio-institutional, pragmatic, and affective. This means that no stable results can be predicted. We are all familiar with the vulnerable and dominated status of a learner and the pressures he or she is submitted to: artificial communication (in emergency), evaluation bias (marking and selection), sometimes fear and inhibition. All these phenomena interfere with a purely cognitive analysis. These factors may be, if not eliminated, at least diminished, in a different kind of didactic setting: a tutorial one, for instance. A more supple organisation might allow the researcher to examine the acquisition of single linguistic concepts. This leads us to protocol-research.[12] Such a type of research implies the construction, application, and evaluation of new teaching material under controlled conditions.

The subjects will be a small group of French adults, complete beginners of E.F.L. Adults, indeed, are supposed to have a full mastery of formal cognitive operations.[13] Learners, teacher/observer,[14] pragmatic parameters of the didactic situation (space, time, objects, simulated actions and L2 production and so on) will be specified and correlated in every possible way. Each change in the situation will itself be given a status, as well as the linguistic effect observed in the verbal and non-verbal data. For a better metalinguistic analysis of the whole corpus the learners' conflicts of choices, strategies, hypotheses, and problem-solving procedures, must be traced back. The learners must be made capable of identifying the salient clues of the situational dynamic, so that they may regulate their behaviour accordingly. They must be conscious of their activities. They must work out their own representations. They must anticipate and generalise their strategies.

The teacher must anticipate what part of the linguistic system needs to be explained. Rule-coordination must be insured, in relation with the gradual adding of new complexities. Learners' errors, what they feel to be allowed or forbidden or what they are unsure of, will be observed. Criteria for 'incorrectness' will be specified. Different types of learners, the *explainers* and the *producers*, will be sorted out. Methodological (probabilistic and not linear) precautions have to be followed in data-processing.[15]

The linguistic hypotheses we shall test will be roughly the following:

Hypothesis 1: there are language invariants, partly linked to language acquisition invariants through topological deformability laws; unstable systems are therefore related to stable ones through modulation, depending on the situational and contextual constraints of the learning situation.

Hypothesis 2: the complementary components of language acquisition invariants are related to general cognitive acquisition invariants. Even intensive metalinguistic training cannot influence them.

Hypothesis 3: in spite of this, the development of metalinguistic awareness channels interlanguage in predictable stages and provides 'short-cuts' for acquisition.

Hypothesis 4: the didactic situation biases the laws of linguistic determination in a specific way.

Hypothesis 5: consequently, interlanguage topological constructions display corresponding shifts in speech locations ('anchorings' and saliences), compared to natural communication.

Hypothesis 6: verbal and non-verbal observables are the traces of all these operations, but are not in a bi-univocal relationship with them.

The study will be longitudinal, either concerning the subjects' personal evolution or the input–output collective dynamic.

Conclusion

TEO appears to us as a promising theory both for language didactics and for psycholinguistic SLA research. Few studies have as yet been conducted in this field, but we think, if they are done systematically, they are likely to offer a better understanding of invariance/variation interaction, not only in language learning, but in discursive activity in general.[16]

Notes to Chapter 8

1. Work done by the Charlirelle research group, an acronym for Department of Research in Language Learning, Institut Charles V, Université Paris VII.
2. We use this word in a Piagetian sense: acquire a larger and more abstractive capacity to relativise speech phenomena by moving away from one's own 'here and now' situation.

3. 'Epilinguistic' refers to the subconscious, natural reflection a speaker may apply to language (from A. Culioli).
4. That is, interpreting classroom activity according to the behaviour and role which each social agent — teacher, learners — assumes in the school setting.
5. As mentioned before, the theory of enunciative operations was developed by Antoine Culioli.
6. It sounds indeed more natural if one says *John eats an apple*, than **an apple eats John*, but a fantastic style might of course inverse these properties: language, as we know, is spontaneously speaker-associated and symbolical. From such criteria, a surface sentence like *that car sells well* might seem contradictory: unintentional reference for *car* as transitively incompatible with intentional verb *to sell*, and with absence of object. But the anomaly is only apparent, since the unspecified agent indirectly appears through the obligatory modifier (*well*), and since the determined status of *car* (cf., *that*) enables it to be thematised. The <arb> structure is deeply instantiated, though not in a S V O surface way: *Somebody sells that car well*.
7. If we had to compare Culioli's model with, for instance, Halliday's, perhaps we could very briefly say that the differences are important, although some resemblances do appear: Culioli is not a structuralist, whereas Halliday seems to have remained one, his formalisation aims being compatible with logic and psychology, whereas Halliday appears to be more of a speech acts pragmatician. Lastly, Culioli shows a dialectic preoccupation with accounting for the dynamics of language elaboration, whereas Halliday rather seems to be inclined to give a systemic, methodologically stratified, description of language products and features. In a word, perhaps: taxonomic interpretation (Halliday) versus calculative model (Culioli).
8. Compare also 'Behind the Words,' Equipe *Charlirelle* (1975 & 1976).
9. Compare also *Eléments de Didactique des Langues*, Bailly (1984).
10. This is an example for a topic that was chosen at this early stage of teaching.
11. In this respect, we agree with Krashen's distinction between *acquisition* and *learning*, but we do not think they should be separated (not even methodologically), as they are highly interactive mental operations. The formal *monitor*, if psycholinguistically conceived, must follow the schemes of natural mental operations, while developing awareness and control, without changing their nature.
    The monitor will then permit the comparison of L2 with L1 and with interlanguage, as being, all three of them and each one in its own way, submitted to the organisation of language invariants. Rule-obedience therefore rather comes to equate the learner's metalinguistic assent with the coherence and necessity of such rules, and his or her consequent application of them in L2 production.
12. This methodological approach has been applied in a later phase of the project.
13. In the Piagetian sense of the word.
14. A linguist who was trained in cognitive science as well.
15. According to models developed in Artificial Intelligence and Cognitive Science.
16. I wish to express my sincere thanks to Mrs Margaret Bordez and Mrs Wendy Halff for reading over my English and suggesting improvements in style.

Bibliography

BAILLY, D., 1984, *Eléments de Didactique des Langues*. Paris: Les Langues Modernes.

BERTHOUD, A.C., 1982, *Activité Métalinguistique et Acquisition d'une Langue Seconde*. Bern: Peter Lang.

BESSE, H. & PORQUIER, R., 1984, *Grammaires et Didactique des Langues*. Paris: Crédif - Hatier.

BOUSCAREN, J., BYRAMJEE, B., CHUQUET, J., COTTIER, E., DEMAIZIÈRE, F., FILHOL-DUCHET, B., HERLIN, O. & MAYER, A., 1984 & 1985, *Cahiers de Grammaire Anglaise*. Paris: Ophrys.

EQUIPE CHARLIRELLE, 1975 & 1976, *Behind the Words*, 6e & 5e (Méthode d'enseignement de l'anglais), OCDL - Hatier distribué par M.D.I., Parc des Arpents, B.P. 69 - 78630 Orgeval Cedex.

CAIN, A., 1980, *Théorie Linguistique et Apprentissage de l'Anglais*. Unpublished doctoral dissertation, Université Paris VII, Paris.

CULIOLI, A., 1965–1984, Articles, cours, séminaires, disponibles au Département de Recherches Linguistiques, (D.R.L.) Université Paris VII, Paris.

CULIOLI, A. & DESCLES, J.P., 1982, *Système de Représentations Linguistiques et Métalinguistiques*. Paris: Laboratoire de Linguistique Formelle.

FRANCKEL, J.J. & FISHER, S. (eds), 1983, *Linguistique, Énonciation, Aspect et Détermination*. Paris: Editions de l'Ecole des Hautes Etudes en Sciences Sociales.

GAUTHIER, A., 1982, *Opérations Énonciatives et Apprentissage d'une Langue Étrangère en Milieu Scolaire*. 75013 Paris: Les Langues Modernes.

GROUSSIER, M.L. & CHANTEFORT, P., 1976, *Grammaire Anglaise et Thèmes Construits*. Paris: Hachette.

GUILLEMIN, J., 1982, *La Traduction, Syntaxe Comparée du Français et de l'Anglais*. Paris: Ophrys.

TANZ, C., 1980, *Studies in the Acquisition of Deictic Terms*. Cambridge, MA: Harvard University Press.

TRÉVISE, A., 1980, *Eléments d'Analyse de l'Activité Langagière des Étudiants Francophones Apprenant l'Anglais en Milieu Institutionnel*. Unpublished doctoral dissertation, Université Paris VII, Paris.

Part 3
Reference in Second Language Acquisition

9 The Development of Means for Temporality in the Unguided Acquisition of L2: Cross-Linguistic Perspectives

COLETTE NOYAU

Introduction

This article deals with the acquisition of temporality in French by adult Spanish-speaking immigrants. The European research project on Second Language Acquisition by Adult Immigrants organised by the European Science Foundation (E.S.F., Strasbourg, France) and coordinated by the Max-Planck-Institute for Psycholinguistics (Nijmegen, The Netherlands) bears on the acquisition of five target languages (TL) by speakers of six source languages (SL). The longitudinal study of the development of L2 over the first three years of stay in the host country is based on monthly recordings with each informant, with the same data collection procedures and agenda for all SL–TL pairs (see Perdue, 1982). After completion of the data collection phase, the cross-linguistic analyses are under way, following the preliminary analyses of data from one SL–TL pair which have been conducted during data collection.

The main approach in the analysis is a conceptual one (see Stutterheim & Klein, 1986, henceforth S&K). The question is: how does an adult acquiring a second language through his or her communicative needs in a TL environment construct the means for referring to a given conceptual domain in L2 — in our case, temporality — adjust them to his or her concrete needs for communicating, and progressively expand them towards the TL?

The overall organisation of research allows us to look for recurrent developmental steps among informants across SLs and TLs. It is thus hoped to come to a clearer picture of the general structure of second language acquisition (developmental sequences and dynamics of acquisition), as well as of some of the factors at play (cognitive factors, propensity factors linked to learners' needs, attitudes and motivations, exposure to TL).

The present article deals mainly with the development of temporality in French by three Latin-American refugees — among the Spanish-speaking informants of the Paris team within the European project.[1] The results obtained for the language pair Spanish SL/French TL will then be confronted with results from similar studies for other language pairs, in order to check the impact of the proximity of languages (and the representation of this proximity by the learners) on the acquisition process.

Methodological issues

The *knowledge* of L2 by a learner is not directly observable, but has to be accessed through the *uses* of L2, that is mainly through the *discursive activity* of the learner in given communicative situations. In addition to the learner's production, complementary data may be found in punctual clues from his or her comprehension activity (where it fails: when misunderstanding or incomprehension arise, cf. Trévise & Hérédia, 1984), and from his or her spontaneous metalinguistic activity (hesitations, reformulations, metalinguistic verbalisations, cf. Noyau, 1984, also Giacobbe & Cammarota, 1986).

The individual L2 system of a learner at a given moment, or 'learner language', is *unstable* by definition, given the tensions that push it to evolve towards the TL (the linguistic environment, the needs to communicate, and the propensity to learn: see Perdue, 1982). The learner language is also *permeable* to the linguistic varieties it comes in contact with (see the discussion of this feature of learner languages by Frauenfelder, Noyau, Perdue, & Porquier, 1980, which we refer to for this whole theoretical framework), but it has *systematicity*, and can therefore be described linguistically.

For studying the acquisition process of a second language, we have to proceed at different levels:

1. Describe individual systems (learner languages), which are to be considered as unknown languages of which the learner is the unique

    speaker, at different moments of the acquisition.
2. Reconstruct the psycholinguistic processes underlying the observable outcome of the linguistic activity.
3. Seek explanations of the processes under study.

To do so, the linguist has to part from his or her global understanding of the discursive productions of the learner. This enables him or her to reconstruct the meaning of these productions, an activity which is distinguished from the understanding of the learner's discourse in a situation by the native hearer. For the linguist, from the global interpretation of the productions in their situational context, the task is to look for regular relations between linguistic markers and semantic values — which need not be parallel to those encoded by either the SL or the TL (Trévise & Porquier, 1986, address this issue on examples of L2 analysis from different linguistic domains).

This leads to the search for an analysis framework which would not be linked to one particular language, thus imposing the filter of a given set of categories on the data. A conceptual approach of L2 acquisition provides such a framework.

The first step consists of a language-independent analysis of the conceptual domain, which gives a representation of the conceptual categories that may be encoded by a speaker in language. The second step is to look at the way in which a given language — a learner language, his or her SL, the TL — encodes some of these conceptual categories, and at the devices used for it.

One may hypothesise that the path of development in L2 is partly dependent on the conceptual knowledge which the adult speaker already has. As a consequence, explanations of the linguistic acquisition will be related in some way to the conceptual level.

A message intention has to be represented in terms of a language-independent conceptualisation (Pottier, 1974). As regards temporality, the studies available by logicians/linguistics since Reichenbach bring to the fore the main components of this conceptual area which are likely to be encoded linguistically by speakers in their language in one way or another:

1. External temporal features of the events. The location of events on a time axis, which we can refer to with the label temporal location: this location is achieved in relation with a zero point (an origo) on the axis, which can be given in different ways:
    = the location is achieved by an oriented temporal scale

given in the culture of a group, like a calendar (*calendaric temporal location*);

= the location is established in relation to the moment of speech, which determines a before and an after in the flow of time, and gives the frame to the (linguistic) *deictic temporal location*;

= the location is achieved in relation to another event or process which is already located in time: in this case, we can speak about *temporal relation*.

In all cases, the relations imply conceptual categories like order and inclusion (hence the notions of *after, before, simultaneous,* [totally or partially] *included in*, for example).

2. Internal temporal properties of events, which may be either objective properties (durative / punctual / iterative . . . events, cf. Aktionsart at the linguistic level) or from the point of view of the observer (events seen as completed or not / ongoing / habitual, etc., cf. aspect in some languages).

Although the natural logic of human beings may not be using all the (combinations of) categories of formal logic, every linguistic utterance of a speaker implies some of the above mentioned temporal dimensions and has to locate an event in time in relation to some reference point or to other events, or to specify some of their temporal characteristics. We may assume that every language is able to encode all possible temporal notions, be it obligatorily or optionally, giving them a more or less 'central' place, directly or indirectly, and at a low or high cost. This may imply in principle all the structural levels of the language.

At the early stages of acquisition of an L2, a learner still lacks the mastery of the obligatory markers of the TL (for example, morphological markers appear rather late in L2 acquisition). He or she will then leave many more aspects to implicit or indirect marking than is the case in the TL or than he or she does in his or her SL. Hence the crucial importance of looking at the discursive activity of the learner in concrete communicative tasks, in which the role of the context and of the situation are clear.

Data base

As for temporality, it is important to distinguish between particular tasks in the data base. For example, a film retelling task requires the expression of sequences of events with temporal relations between them. But no event need be situated in relation to the speech time and the recount of the events may be situated in a fictitious past space as well as in a fictitious present (atemporal) space. Other tasks used in the European Project, like route directions or stage instructions, may be located in a future space, or treated as pure injunctives by the speaker. But we get the richest picture of temporality in free conversation, where the informant may relate things which happened to him or her recently or at a more remote time, may talk about intentions and projects in the future, or about present situations. And in conversation the personal narratives are the most temporally structured discursive samples. Therefore personal narratives constitute the main data base for our analysis of temporality.

For the present study, data from the first 18 months of individual monthly recordings with three of the longitudinal informants of the Latin American group acquiring French were analysed:

AL, Colombian male informant, first recording after eleven months in France;

BE, Chilean female informant, first recording after four months in France;

GR, Chilean female informant, first recording after three months in France.

For each one, the earliest sample of narrative from after one year of acquisition approximately (henceforth T1) is contrasted with a second narrative from about one year later (T2). However, the inventories of linguistic devices available to an informant at a given time bear on the whole individual recording which the narrative is extracted from (60 to 90 min.).[2]

Linguistic means for referring to time in French L2 and their development

Temporality in discourse

Narratives are highly structured discursive objects. Many studies on narrativity have described the different components of this discourse genre (see Labov, 1972; Kintsch & van Dijk, 1975; Adam, 1978; among others). As regards the temporal dimension in narratives, the *orientation* establishes the reference to persons, places, time location, circumstances. The *development* brings sequences of events which may be organised into sub-sequences or *episodes*. Those events which constitute the *plot*, or story-line, are linked in different ways to secondary information (the *background*). Finally, we may find an evaluation, which often closes the narrative as such.

An interesting and very frequent sub-case is the 'dialogue narrative', in which the sequence of reported events is a sequence of speech acts. This is not a peculiarity of L1 or L2 learners' discourse, as is shown for example by the studies of Tannen (1983, forthcoming) on 'constructed dialogue' in conversational and literary narrative.

The sequences of narrated events need not be structured in a linear way. A given event may be sub-divided into sub-events later on in discourse, or a series of smaller scale events may be clustered into one. These are decisions of the speaker, who may choose to *segment* or to *condense* in various degrees the contents he or she refers to (see Bowerman, 1984, for this phenomenon in children's narratives).

An adult L2 learner masters these skills in the SL, and need not acquire them anymore. He or she also knows how to rely on knowledge he or she supposes to share with the hearer, for leaving part of the information to convey to indirect or even implicit mention.

Informant BE was recorded from four months after her arrival, at a time when she knew virtually no French. Her early narrative passages are mere question–answer sequences in which all the temporal information is given in the interviewer's turns. The first narrative as such, which she takes the initiative of, is found after 13 months of stay, and contains still many SL sequences, non-verbal predicates, and prosodic structuring of discourse.

BE + 13 Narrative 1 : Danger of drowning (1st version)[3]

1. eh [ʒe] hm + quand eh petit +
   'hm I hm + when hm little'
2. la mer comme ↑ ça (geste de peur) +
   'the sea like that' (gesture of fright)
3. mais moi la ↑ mer +
   'but me the sea'
4. mais *cómo se llama* les [ßaɣ–a] *cómo se* [di] + +
   [me] (geste)
   'but how do you call the (waves) how do you say + +
   me (gesture)'
      <ah t'entraînait? ... la mer t'emportait?>
      'oh was dragging you ... the sea was carrying you
      away?'

oui oui
'yes yes'
　　<et alors?>
　　'and then?'
5. *y* moi *me afirmé de un* pied *de un* ↑ garçon ...
　　'and I I cling to a foot of a boy'
6. *y él* ↑ [sorti se] ...
　　'and he get out ( )'
7. et ↑ maman + '[a parti] tout ↑ suite!'
　　'and mum + go right away'
　　(6–7 = he took me out and mum (said): 'we must leave
　　right away')
　　　　<oh la la la la + tu as eu peur hein>
　　　　'oh + you were scared, weren't you?'
　　↑ oui!
　　'yes'
8. maman [ne pa de] la mer ↑ ↑ jamais jamais ↑ ↑ eh
　　'mum not of the sea never never hm'
9. '[sorti(r)] ↑ ↑ tout suite ici ↑ ↑ ' ...
　　'get out right away here'
　　(8–9 = mum said 'I (don't want/don't go to) the beach
　　never never,
　　get out of here immediately)
　　　　<et tout le monde a vu?>
　　　　'and everybody saw?'
　　si
　　'yes'
10. et moi à côté [ʒue] (x) la ↑ rue
　　'and me beside play ( ) the street'
11. *y* après comme ↑ ça
　　'and after like that (gesture of fright)'
　　(10–11 = and then I played in the next street and I was
　　scared)

Although the linguistic means proper are very scarce, we already find differentiated discourse functions which build a full narrative: background information, explicitly connected events, sequences of reported speech, and a closing (resultative situation). But the informant relies heavily on the cooperation of the TL speaker. Fourteen months later she tells another TL interviewer the same story:

BE + 27 Narrative 2 : Danger of drowning (2nd version)

    ... [paske ʒe] peur à la mer
    '... because I'm scared at the sea'
    <ah bon + pourquoi?>
    'is it? why so?'

1. ouais [paske + kwand ʒo ete] petit
   'yeah because when I was a child'
2. [ʒe] un accident dans la mer ↑ hmm
   'I have an accident in the sea'
3. ouais [paske se] très fort la mer *en* au Chili
   'yeah because it's very strong the sea in Chile'
4. *y yo* [ʒe] peur
   'and me I'm scared'
5. [paske] la mer [me a me a tumb]/
   'because the sea has fall- me'
   el comment [se apel] la / * no sé cómo* [s apel el] /
   'the how is called the I don't know how it is called'
   cuando [ko'mensa] à [sortir]
   'when it starts coming out' (= the waves!)
6. *y* [me a tumbe]
   'and it has fall- me'
7. *y* après [ʒe swe] dans la mer
   'and afterwards I am in the sea'
8. *y por* ça [ke ʒe] peur à la mer
   'and for it that I'm scared at the sea'
9. et [solamã] à côté
   'and only aside'

The learner has practically no more verbless utterances, and uses more diversified connectors, including connectors like '*por* ça que' and [paske] (= because) for relating an event to a previous one with an additional causal link.

Informant GR produced only very short narrative sequences in the first six months of recordings, like the following:

GR+6 1st narrative sample

1. *yo* [arriße] à -- à C -- [ke] un foyer de *tránsito* ---
   'I arrive(d) in C which is a transitory refugee camp'
2. et ah eh ah [reste] *como se dice* [du] *mes* en C
   'and remain(ed) how do you say two months in C'

3. *y de ahi* [sorti] à F
'and from there go to F' (another refugee camp)

The first long narrative is introduced through her initiative, as an illustration to a general question of the interviewer about racial discrimination:

GR+16 Narrative on racialism

1. <et tu penses que les Français ont la même attitude pour les Chiliens et pour les Africains par exemple?>
'and you think that French people have the same attitude towards Chilean and African people for example?'
non
'no'
non? tu as remarqué des differences?
'no? did you notice any differences?'
oui ––– [paske]
'yes because'
un fois [ʒe regard / ʒe ale] *por* [tʃerʃe le vestimān]
'once I look/ I go for getting the clothes'
por mes enfants et *por* moi
'for my children and for me'
2. et[se] un/un madame [ke di]
'and there-is a lady who say'
3. "vous [reste] ici vous vous [pase] madame"-
'you stay here you come here Mrs'
4. *y* [ʒe/ʒe arriße] eh à dix heures
'and I arrive at 10'
5a. et le monsieur [se]/- comment [se]? [no se pa] comment [se di]
'and the man it-is/how is it? I don't know how to say'
5b. [se le primjer] personne [ke se- ave] un rendez-vous-pour lui (...)
'it-is the first person wh- there-is an appointment for him'
6. [il (= elle) di]
'he (= she) say'
7. non—vous [reste] ici
'no—you stay here'
8. et [se] la/la dame [ke ke pase]
'and it-is the lady wh- come'

'and you were the lady?'
9. "oui" – *yo* [di]
'yes – I say'
10. "non [se] Monsieur"-
'no-it-is this man'
11. "non" [me di]
'no say to me'
12. "[el reste] ici"
'he stay here'
<et le monsieur c' était qui?>
'and who was the man?'
13. [se] un noir [se] un Africain
'it-is a black it-is an African'
⟨et tu penses que c'était à cause de ça?⟩
'and you think that it was because of that?'
14. oui [paske se/se vjolent] la/la dame avec le monsieur
'yes because it-is violent the lady with the man'
15. et [ʒe pens ke se por/por le] couleur
'and I think that it-is because of the colour'
<tu penses oui?>
'do you think so?'
16. oui et [ʒe le di]
'yes and I say to her'
17. 'non [ʒe ne aʃete] pas de [vestimãn] merci'
'no I don't buy (= take) clothes thank you'
18. et [ʒe parti] à ma maison très *furioso* (laughs)
'and I go home very angry'

			-15-		-13-		
background	1	5	14				
reported speech			3	7–8	10	12	17
plot							
backmove	4						
chronological			2	6	9	11	16	18

The temporal sequence[4] is straightforward, with the exception of 4, which goes back to a time *before* the starting point of her story. She lacks the right linguistic devices for it, expresses her feeling uncomfortable, and finally finds a solution with a numeral. She still lacks direct devices for 'moving back' in time.

Let us see another example the very simple although lively narrative of GR at T2, made of a linear sequence of five narrative propositions, closed by an evaluation (10: oh la la!).

GR+27 Narrative 2

1. *y por* [paje] le métro le ticket de métro [je ne paje] pas [paske]\
   'and for paying in the metro the metro ticket I don't pay because'
       <tu passes en dessous>
       'you go through under the ...'
2. oui ... l'autre jour .. un inspecteur [me di]
   'yes the other day an inspector tell me'
3. 'votre ticket'
   'your ticket'
4. 'ah' [le di]
   'ah say to him'
5. "*no* [ʒe ne a] pas de argent
   'no I have no money'
6. "[ʒe swi] en [ʃoma]" (= chômage)
   'I am unemployed'
7. [ʒe le mostre] ma carte de [ʃoma]
   'I show him my unemployment card'
8. "ah" [me di]
   'ah tell me'
9. "ça [fe] rien"
   'no problem'
10. "oh là là" (laughs)

```
background      =1=                    10
reported speech »3   =5-6=        9
plot             2     4    7    8
          - - - - - - - - - - - - - - - - -+ - -→
```

Let's look now at AL's first narrative sample (his first recording, AL + 11), where he tells how he went to register at the unemployment office:

AL + 11 Narrative 1: Registering for unemployment[5]

'you did not speak French but yet you registered for
unemployment?'
oui [je meskri] *al* chômage
'yes I register for unemployment'
<alors comment ça s'est passé?>
'so what happened?'

1. eh + *un* ami de mon frè(re) + [me di ke]
   'hm + a friend of my brother + tell me that'
2. *el* [parla]
   'he speak'
3. *el* ami *el* [↑ parla] français +
   '*the* friend *he* [speak] French'
4. *y él* [me di ke]
   'and he tell me that'
5. *para* inscription [ilja] *el* chômage +
   'for register there be the unemployment'
6. et [a] un monsieur
   'and (be, have, to) a man'
7. [ke parla] espagnol italien français beaucoup de langues
   'who speak Spanish Italian French many languages'
8. *y él* [me di ke]
   'and he tell me that'
9. pas *problema* ../
   'no problem'
10. *y yo* [swi ale] avec lui
    'and I go with him'
11. *y* 'si [sere] possible
    'and if be possible'
12. [ke je meskri]'
    'that I register'
13. [paske] *el señor* B +
    'because mister B'
14. *él* [s apel] B + *él* [me]/
    'he be called B + he me'
15. [je parle] avec lui
    'I speak with him'
16. [lesplike] *el problema* de moi *y* de ma *familia* ...
    'explain to him the problem of me and of my family'
17. *y él me* / *él* [ekri le formular] *y todo*
    'and he me / he write the form and everything'
18. y* pas *problema* +
    'and no problem'

19. après eh + [ʒe] un rendez-vous ˚con una˚ mademoiselle
    ↑
    'after hm + I (have) an appointment with a miss'
20. ˚y yo˚ [ne puße parle] bien +
    'and I can not speak well'
21. [paske le di ke]
    'because tell (him, her) that'
22. [je ne parla] français
    'I not speak French'
23. ˚y˚ après elle [parle ke]
    'and after she speak that'
24. [je n se pa krir] ...
    'I can not write'
25. ˚yo˚ [solaman/ dʒaprendi solaman] ˚decir˚ eh [dir]
    'I only / I learn only say hm say'
26. '[je ne parlœ] pas français [je ne parlœ] pas français'
    'I not speak French I not speak French'
27. ˚y entonces y + y [le komprende]
    'and then and + and understand (him, her, it)'


```
summary          0
background           -3-      -6-7-          -14-
reported speech -2-    -5-     -9-          »11-12 -26-  -22-     -24-
plot :
backmove               13-15-16                  25    21
chronological   1     4     8    10 × 17 18        19    20    23    27
– – – – – – – – – – – – – – – – – – – – – – – – – – – – – – – +
```

O = A + B + C
Episode A = 1(2–3)–› 4(5)
Episode B = –6–7–, –13–14–: 15–› 16–› 8(9)–› 10–› (»11–12)–› 17–›18
Episode C = 25(26)–› 19–› 21(22)–› 20–› 23(24)–›27

AL is a faster learner. From the figure above[4] it appears that after 11 months of stay he is able to produce a very complex narrative: it is introduced by a summary, the temporally ordered events of the story line are linked to background information and grouped into three episodes, and the chronological order is interrupted by backmoves. All this is achieved with restricted linguistic means (see section 'Lexico-syntactic means for temporality' below) without consistent morphological variation on the verb, and with only a few connectors and lexical expressions.

At T2 (22 months of stay), the linguistic repertoire of AL has not changed drastically (apart from an obvious increase in lexicon). The complexity of the narrative capacity still finds its limits where morphological distinctions would be needed for time location, as in the following misunderstanding on time:

> <et tu retourneras à la préfecture pour le
> logement?>
> 'and will you go back to the préfecture for the
> lodging?'

1. oui [ʒo / japre + jale] autre fois
   'yes I (after) I go other time'
2. [paske] toujours [ija] logement + aussi de la mairie
   'because always there be lodging + also from the
   townhall'
   > <hm + tu y es allé ou tu iras?>
   > 'hm + have you been or will you go there?'
3. non + [jo ire] /
   'no + I go /'
4. non [ʒe] déjà [ʒo ale] là-bas/ oui? +
   'no + I already I go there yes?'
5. après [ʒo ale] autre fois (laughs) + [ʒo ire] autre fois
   'after I go other time + I go other time
   > <hm + donc tu ne l'AS pas fait? ou tu l'as fait?>
   > 'hm + so you haven't done it? or have you done it?'
6. non + déjà [ʒœ la fe] oui? +
   'no + already I do it yes?'
7. APRES [ʒœ la fere] autre fois + oui?
   'after I do it other time yes?'
8. chaque [vente] jours chaque mois [ʒo ale paske ...]
   'every twenty days every month I go because ...'
9. [paske il fo] toujours ↑ non? +
   'because one must always no?'
10. [paske] la personne [k il vwa] ...
    'because the person wh he or she see'
11. [il va krwaje]
    'he will believe'
12. [ke ... dʒe] besoin de l'appartament' non?
    'that I need the flat no?'

(10–12 = because if the person sees me he or she will be convinced that I need the flat)

The TL interlocutor is puzzled by the contradiction — in terms of the TL — between markers which point to the past: [ale], *autre fois*, and her question about future perspectives. In terms of AL's interlanguage, [ale] still does not bear temporal information, 'autre fois' is an SL derived adverbial for repetition (cf. Span. *otra vez* = another time). For solving the problem he tries out with a marked form for expressing future: [ire] (cf. Span. *iré* = I will go), [fere]. The final solution, which breaks the misunderstanding, is the use of quantitative information (see line 8).[5]

For comparing the learners' L2 knowledge between speakers or at a year's distance (T1 – T2), the degree of complexity of produced narratives does not appear to be a reliable index of development in itself, it depends also very much on the intrinsic complexity of the events to refer to, on the discursive style of the individual speakers, and on the opportunities of a given conversation for eliciting narratives. But all these stories remind us that an adult learner puts to use a fully developed speaker competence in L2 acquisition.

For establishing the comparisons, we have to relate the structure of the narratives obtained with the linguistic means, lexico-syntactic as well as morphological, available to the learner at the same acquisition phase.

Lexico-syntactic means for temporality

In this section we give a short account of the lexico-syntactic means (adverbials and adverbial clauses) for expressing time location and relations and their evolution between T1 and T2 for all three informants (for detailed analyses see Noyau, 1986; see also on GR, Trévise, 1984; and on BE, Vasseur, 1985).

The slowest informant, BE, relied a long time on the cooperation of the native, which she knew how to elicit (see the two narrative samples above!), and on SL or SL-derived expressions. This is the reason why we find a few instances of temporal clauses with *cuando* / [kwan(d)] / *quand* much before she would be able to use verbal clauses consistently. After 13 months of stay, she had still only a few calendaric expressions without Prep or with SL *en*, which we may assign a punctual (location by distance from a reference point) or a durative value according to shared knowledge or plausibility, a marker of consecution: *après*, and no proper deictic expression (for *now*, *yesterday*, etc.). After 27 months of stay, she had acquired deictic expressions like [mannō] (= now), *aujourd'hui* (= today), and used a diversified inventory of calendaric expressions: predominantly NPs, and PrepPs with *après, jusqu'à* (= after, until), as well as formulas like [(s)a fe], [ilja] (= — ago). She showed a clear generalisation of deictic expressions to anaphoric values: *ce soir* (→ in the evening), *maintenant* (→ then), and had acquired no proper anaphoric expression.

As for GR, at T1 she used deictic adverbials like [ajerswa] (= yesterday evening), various lexical expressions with durative, punctual or iterative values, and had already frequent temporal subordinations with *quand*. After 25 months in France, she had diversified her inventory of lexical expressions, allowing more quantitative precision for distance and frequence.

For AL, we could not observe the initial steps, as after 11 months he had already reached a state of development which was broadly comparable to BE's or GR's state at T2. The development in the second year of stay brought more diversified lexical expressions, but above all their syntactic complexification:

la dernière fois [ke jo vjen] ici
(= last time I come here)
vous [vene el kel] jour que je le [marke] un rendez-vous
(= you come back that day wh- I write down an appointment for you)

For all of them, we notice the late appearance (if at all) of anaphorics, and the tendency to resort to some connectors which are recognised and memorised due to their close resemblance to SL (Preps as well as subordinators), from early stages on.

Morphological means for temporality

For BE, the first stage shows few verbal lexemes at all, or she resorted to SL verbs. Then, at T1 of this study, she acquired verbs as mere lexical units with a unique form. At T2, the verbs tend to appear under more than one form (short form: V- Ø / long form: V-e/i for the regular verbs), but without any temporal distribution. Towards the end of the data collection period (29 months of stay), she would use some preverbal morphs, precursors of Aux ([a] V, [e] V, [swi] V), in non-actual contexts (completed events and also for prospective events), but with a tendency to overgeneralise them to actual events also. She had not yet reached a developmental state in which morphology can support tense.

GR's morphological development follows similar lines, with the variation V-Ø / V-[e] showing overgeneralisation of the last form to non-past events in subordinate clauses whereas the first one is not found any longer for past events at T2.

AL's first steps in discovering verbal morphology could not be observed, but although his lexicon contained an important number of verbal lexemes from T1 on, these appeared often in a unique form, or showed overgeneralisation of V-[e] until late. After 44 months of stay (end of the study), some preverbal morphs were used and V-Ø / V-[e/ i] or Aux+V were contrasted in temporally contrasted contexts (actual / completed) for a limited number of verbs. Tense distinctions were just about to settle.

Evolutionary trends

The main evolutionary trends for Spanish-speaking learners of French, on the basis of these case studies and of observations from other informants, are the following (for more details see Noyau, 1986). As regards indirect means:

— heavy reliance on pragmatic inferences based upon world knowledge or shared information, and on context, particularly on aspectual properties of the verbal lexemes or the reported situations, above all in the first stages;

— use of discursive configurations which support an implicit temporal structuring of events (like the 'natural order', the use of reported speech, and the frequent contrasts, which appear to be a favourite figure of the rhetorics of learner languages). This imposes quite a burden on the hearer for the reconstruction of the temporal information;

— specialisation for temporal indications of linguistic means from other areas, as spatial expressions, and causal connectors for moving back in time.

As for the linguistic means:

— initial reliance on lexical expressions (with idiosyncratic syntactic insertion: Prep Ø, then Preps influenced by SL use), which diversify both syntactically and in their precise semantic functions, mostly with a quantifier / numeral + a calendar unit;

— predominance of deictic expressions, which tend to be overgeneralised to anaphoric uses;

— progressive syntactic complexification of adverbials, and rather early temporal subordination;

— late appearance of verbal morphology, which diversifies and progressively finds a distribution which contradicts less often the TL, without being able to bear tense categories in a consistent way until the end of the longitudinal study (about four years of stay) (see Noyau, 1986).

Cross-linguistic perspectives on the acquisition of means for temporality in L2[6]

A central question in the development of temporality in L2 is the following: Why do some features appear before others in the learners' systems? Some potential explanatory factors come to mind:

(a) the conceptual structure as such;
(b) the discursive needs of the speaker;
(c) the SL ways of encoding the conceptual structure;
(d) the intrinsic relative difficulty of acquisition of the linguistic means in TL.

Cross-linguistic studies are a necessary step to a better understanding of the acquisition process, because they are likely to provide evidence of the relative weight of such factors in the construction of the learner language. In the results available so far from analyses of temporality in L2 learner varieties both within the E.S.F. project on second language acquisition by adult immigrants and on other data, some strong convergences appear, and some differences which can lead to preliminary hypotheses on the factors at play.

Among the convergent features are the following:

— early use of lexical devices for temporal location and relations;
— late acquisition of morphological categories, which develop on given favourable verbal lexemes first. (Conceptual factors such as the inherent semantic properties of the verbs are likely to be studied at a global cross-linguistic level while others like frequency of given forms in input, relative degree of morphological complexity, saliency, transparency, have to be envisaged across SLs for a given TL);
— initial reliance on the sequential ordering of events in discourse for temporal relation, and more generally on some discourse organisation principles;
— massive use of quoted speech, which permits to fall back to a (derived) deictic anchoring.

Differences across SL/TL pairs (as far as the current state of the studies allows to generalise) are the following:
— early / late appearance of PrepP and of subordination in the adverbial means;
— earlier / later morphological marking of tense;
— predominance or not of aspectual categories over temporal categories, which allows learner varieties to differentiate morphologically foreground and background events (for example for Punjabi learners opposed to Italian learners of English, cf. Bhardwaj, 1986a,b).

Many of the convergent features might be explained from a cognitive point of view in terms of the conceptual structure of temporality, or in terms of the discursive needs linked to this conceptual structure, more likely than in terms of linguistic universals. But some of the cross-linguistic differences may also be linked to the conceptual level, in terms of the more or less central place of a given category which is encoded in a TL in the linguistic systems of different SLs. Other differences may be explained in terms of the intrinsic relative degree of difficulty of acquisition of the linguistic devices across TLs (here, additional evidence might be drawn from parallel cross-linguistic differences in the acquisition of these languages as L1s).

Let us look at each of these potential factors more precisely.

The influence of the conceptual structure itself on the path of development

As the conceptual knowledge of the speakers serves as a framework in producing and understanding discourse, predictions like the following one can be formulated: The appearance of a given L2-form for production in the learner's language depends on 'the degree to which the given temporal category can be conveyed implicitly' (Stutterheim & Klein, 1986). Let us take some examples:

Example 1: For establishing a reference point in time, explicit means are generally required — this can only be left implicit when the temporal reference is already given by the interlocutor, in his or her question for example; hence the early use of adverbials and generally lexical means. This temporal information is usually given at the beginning of the sentence, resulting in a pattern:

temporal location – event.
quand petit – la mer comme ça (BE + 13)
en el mois de avril – me [apel] por téléphone (BE + 15)

Example 2:   For expressing the relative order of a sequence of events, if the events are expressed in an order which is parallel to the order in which they follow each other in time, no explicit means are required. But if for some reason, the order of mention differs from the order of succession in time, it has to be made explicit. This is done either by relocating the events in time, or by expressing the temporal relation — sometimes by both, in many discursive contrasts.

Example 3:   The speaker has to convey the difference of function between foreground events, which form the temporal story-line (each one functions as reference time for the following utterance), and background ones, which give a frame to the events of the story-line. If the verbs involved have some inherent temporal characteristics (e.g. punctual on the one hand, durative on the other hand), the relation between foreground and background is easy for the hearer to reconstruct, as a relation frame-embedded event.

Example: quand [ili abite] là-bas — mon garçon
(=when (we) live there my son
[ili kase] un bras
he break an arm)

But if both verbs are, say, punctual, an explicit marking of their relations is required, for example in the form of an aspectual marking of completion. It is in such cases that the first uses of *ge*-V are found in German. In French, we then find occurrences of semi-Aux like [fini] + V, [komens(e)] + V. The need for making clear this conceptual relation gives an account of the observed development of *aspectual distinctions* before purely temporal distinctions in learner systems of many language pairs (Houdaifa, 1983, Arabic/French; Schlyter, 1984, Swedish/French; Kumpf, 1984, Japanese/English; Andersen, 1984, English/Spanish; Stutterheim, 1984, Turkish/German).

The influence of the conceptual structure involved leads to similarities in the development of L2 across language pairs, which need not be tied to *linguistic* universals. We may also consider if the similarities in the earlier construction of aspectual categories with respect to temporal ones in children's acquisition of L1 may be linked to the conceptual structure — although as regards the acquisition of L1, the task of the child is both a conceptual as well as linguistic one, which leads us to be careful in inferring similar processes from L1/L2 acquisitional similarities.

The influence of the discursive needs

At any stage of acquisition, the learner has to cope with the task of reporting temporally complex clusters of events. He or she may refrain from doing so in some cases by topic avoidance or by simplification of the contents, feeling that his or her capacity in L2 won't do. He or she may rely on the help of the native and on the scaffolding offered by the interlocutor (see BE's narrative 1 above), which provides at the same time good input for the acquisition to continue. But in that case, the learner may choose implicitly to let the elements provided by the interlocutor form part of the jointly constructed discourse, like in BE's first and second cycles of data, or may take them over to his or her own production, repeating or adapting them in his or her own utterance, like BE starts doing in the third cycle of data (cf. Vasseur, 1985). He or she may finally take the risk of expressing the complex realities he or she has in mind with his or her limited linguistic means (like AL does right from the beginning of the data collection period, see his narrative 1 above).

At the initial acquisition stages, when the grammatical devices are still poor, the learner must rely heavily on the *lexicon*, for locating events in time, and on some unrisky *discourse organisation principles* for conveying the temporal relations, like the chronological order principle. This results in a very frequent three-part discursive structure which is found in data from all the existing studies on temporality in L2:

RT – E1, E2, E3, . . . En – Clsg
initial reference time – sequence of events – closing

The first element of the structure gives the reference time of the first event in the following sequence:

before
en keer, en gang, un fois (= once)
l'autre jour (= the other day)
en vecka sen (= one week later)
en Chili (= in Chile)
ich kleine kinder (= I small child)
[ʒe] quand petit (= I when young)
moi quand [ili vjen] ici (= I when he-come here)

The second part of this typical structure consists of a sequence of events, (E1 to En) either juxtaposed, or linked together by 'and', 'et', *y*, . . . or by 'after', 'und dann', '(en) dan', 'och sen', *y* après', ...

The reference time of the first event is usually given by the initial segment, but the temporal location of an Ei+1 is to reconstruct as consecutive to the location of Ei, when a marker of consecution is given, or as either simultaneous or consecutive in the case of mere juxtaposition or coordination.

The third element of the discursive structure may be

(a) a conclusive marker:
   et [se] fini
   et [se] tout
(b) an evaluation:
   y pas problème
   ah la la!
(c) a summary.

Obviously, all one wants to tell cannot fit in such a simple structure, and the speaker (or the hearer) faces the limitations of it when a comment, or backmove to an anterior period of time, comes up (see the understanding problem in AL's extract from a narrative on housing proceedings at T2).

Various studies have found a differential morphological treatment of foreground events in opposition to the rest of the text (Kumpf, 1984; Schlyter, 1984, for example), but with apparently opposite solutions. Kumpf's Japanese learner of English seems to use the base form for all foregound events, marking past (or more precisely completiveness) in the background only, whereas Schlyter's Swedish unguided learners of French seem to use Aux-V forms for punctual events which move the plot forward, for actions of human beings, and root V-forms for states and background actions linked by a causal subordinator. Here again, different idiosyncratic formal solutions point at a general process in the learners at a functional level.

The influence of the SL

The role of SL in the acquisition of L2 can be seen at two different levels at least. In the early stages of acquisition, SL provides the learner with an initial hypothesis set as for (a) which conceptual categories are central in the language, that is, are likely to be represented in grammar, and as for (b) which types of structural devices are likely to bear this conceptual information.

Obviously these initial hypotheses are modified soon as acquisition proceeds and they are confirmed, or replaced, or abandoned by the learner. In the E.S.F. project, the most 'exotic' SLs as regards temporal categories are Turkish and Punjabi.

For Turkish learners of German, previous cross-sectional studies (Aksu, Dittmar, Klein, & Stutterheim, 1982; Stutterheim, 1984) have shown that they tend to specialise lexical means for obligatory grammaticised conceptual categories of their SL, as the oppositions between

— witnessed past / non-witnessed past (marked by learners with 'vielleicht' (perhaps);
— near past / remote past, marked with 'vorher' / 'ganz vorher' respectively.

But this does not imply that 'additional' (from the viewpoint of TL) categories taken from an SL are likely to bias strongly the path of acquisition of L2. They only give a special value to given lexical units, which tend to appear overfrequently. 'Missing' grammaticised categories in the SL ought to have a deeper influence on the course of L2 acquisition.

Punjabi (see Simonot, 1983; Bhardwaj, 1983, 1986a,b) is a tense-free language. The verb forms categorise aspectual distinctions like completed / incompleted, ongoing, habitual or potential, and a relational category as 'completed before another event', but no deictic temporal category at all. Punjabi learners of English tend to construct L2 verbal systems in which the base form is opposed to the -ing form:

base form — completed processes + definite future
-ing form — ongoing or uncompleted processes + ordinary future
(For future, the opposition is a modal one.)

The location of events in time is left to lexical means and to discourse principles, in all the Punjabi data of English studied so far. The task of constructing deictic tense categories appears in fact to be very difficult for Punjabi learners, who in the light of their SL, have no reason to be sensitive to this aspect of the values of English verbal morphology. It will be crucial to look at further developmental stages from Punjabis, and to compare their development with the Italian learners of English, who have deictic tense categories in their SL, and seem to construct a basic tense opposition past / non-past (see Bhardwaj, 1986a,b).

Let us look at the linguistic side of the potential influence of SL on the acquisition of temporality in L2, that is, the types of structural devices for conveying the conceptual information that may be inferred from the SL.

Italian and Spanish-speaking learners tend to make early use of temporal PrepP and of temporal subordination:

wann. . ., wenn. . . in German L2
cuando, [kwan], quand. . . in French L2

whereas Turkish learners do not. Here is an example of a minimal narrative by a Turkish learner of German (Stutterheim, 1984):

mein mann unfall – krankenhaus zwei monat (my husband accident – hospital two months)

Compare this with the narrative of BE above, at a very undeveloped acquisitional stage.

For French L2, one might argue the proximity of languages and the formal similarity of certain Preps and conjunctions. For German L2, this argument does not apply. One hypothesis could be that Italian and Spanish-speaking learners have given expectations as regards the structural devices which are likely to bear the temporal information in the sentence, based on structural properties of their SL. Here again, Spanish-speaking learners of Swedish on the one hand, who seem to acquire early Preps and subordinators, and Arabic-speaking learners of French on the other hand, who do not, should provide additional evidence.

The relative intrinsic difficulty of acquisition of given linguistic means in the TLs

Let us look at the oral morphology of French verbs. The [-e] ending is likely to correspond to:

regular infinitive
regular past participle
imperfect (the 3rd ps sg + 3rd pl) for all verbs
present (2nd pl + politeness form) for almost all verbs

[e] as preverbal Aux may correspond to:

'avoir' 1st ps sg present
'être' 2nd and 3rd ps sg present

and for a learner with an SL phonology like Spanish, who does not distinguish between /œ/ and /e/, a quantity of preverbal morphemes:

pronouns: 'je' 1st sg subject,
the clitics 'me,' 'te,' 'le,' 'les' as object or dative

the reflexive 'se'
the negation 'ne'

may (or may not) be blended with Aux [e]. Generally speaking, the main possible markers for past are all but salient for the learners. Only a few markers are salient and unambiguous:

the Aux [a], [ave], [swi], [sō]
(for forming passé composé)
endings like [-ra], [-rō] (for future).

The whole verbal morphology of French can be said to be opaque to the learners. As a consequence learner productions, even if they do not raise understanding problems at the level of communication, are far from easy for the researcher to interpret.

Comparatively, in German morphology the regular markers for preterite [-te( )] and for past participle [ge-] as well as the Aux forms 'hab (e),' 'hat', 'bin,' 'sind,' . . . have a high saliency. This may help to understand why in the French data base, positive morphological markers for tense appear so late (see section 'Morphological Means for Temporality' above), whereas the Turkish and Italian learners of German construct an opposition base form / ge-form relatively soon (cf. Stutterheim, 1984 and Aksu, Dittmar, Klein & Stutterheim, 1982).

Concluding remarks

From the analysis of these first longitudinal samples of data from two years of early acquisition, it appears that the problem of the learner in acquiring devices for a conceptual domain like temporality is multiple.

He or she can rely on an important body of knowledge drawn from the experience of being an adult speaker of a fully developed language, and on all his or her capacity to grasp the world and infer broader principles from limited evidence. He or she may make the most out of a limited repertoire of linguistic means for communication, with his or her ability to combine linguistic and non-linguistic information for giving the interlocutor enough cues for reconstructing the message intention. These resources allow him or her to communicate while he or she is learning.

But meanwhile, he or she has to analyse and identify the peculiar sets of choices of the TL in structuring the perception of the world, and there his or her competence as a native speaker of another language helps and creates problems at the same time.

Beyond the construction of grammar by the learner, a concept-oriented approach in the study of second language acquisition will allow a better understanding at a deeper level, of how and why some categories tend to be constructed more or less easily in the interlanguage. A cross-linguistic approach in this perspective will give access to the influence on this process of the conceptual categories which are privileged in the SL or TL, and allow us to weigh the relative importance of the different levels of organisation of language in the acquisition process.

Notes to Chapter 9

1. The data which are used in this study have been collected and transcribed by all the members of the Paris team of the E.S.F. Project. Thanks to all of them also for the discussion of these analyses.

2. Informant's months of stay at

	T1	and	at T2
AL	11		22
BE	13		27
GR	16		24

When we refer to samples of data, the notation is the following: NN+18 = the initials of the informant's pseudonym + length of stay in months.
3. The transcription conventions are the following:

porque	SL segment
[paske]	segment in phonetic transcription
+,++,+++	short, medium, long pause
nnnn /	self-interruption
|	rising intonation
ΠnnnnΠ	sequence with a high tone of voice.

The numbers are used to identify the narrative segments. The formulas and diagrams with these Roman numbers represent the temporal organisation of the narratives.
4. The diagrams are meant to represent the relation between the narrative sample and (a) the chronology of events, along a time axis; (b) the discursive levels. A few additional symbols are;

--+-->	the time axis, with the utterance time as origo
-2-	durative situation
»5	prospective event

5. These two narratives, as well as GR's Narrative 2, have been analysed in some detail in Noyau, 1984, and in a more exhaustive way in Noyau, 1986. See also for GR, Trévise, 1984; for BE, Vasseur, 1985.
6. This section owes much to Stutterheim & Klein, 1986.

References

ADAM, J.-M., 1978, La cohésion des sequences de propositions dans la macrostructure narrative. *Langue Française 38*, 101–117.
AKSU, A., DITTMAR, N., KLEIN, W. & STUTTERHEIM, C. VON, 1982, *On the Acquisition of Temporality in German by Adult Migrant Workers.* Paper delivered at the Second European-North-American Workshop on Second Language Acquisition, Göhrde, F.R.G.
ANDERSEN, R., 1984, *The Development of Verbal Morphology in the Spanish of English Speakers.* Working paper, Workshop on Temporality, Max-Planck Institut für Psycholinguistik, Nijmegen.
BHARDWAJ, M., 1983, January, *Aspectual and Temporal Reference in the Punjabi Verb System and the Influence of this System on the Natural Acquisition of English as a Second Language.* Paper delivered at the SSRC Workshop, Southall.
— 1986a, *An Analysis of Temporality in Interlanguage Narratives.* ESF Project paper.
— 1986b, *Reference to Time by Two More Acquirers of English.* ESF Project paper.
BOWERMAN, M., 1984, *Event Segmentation.* + *Event Segmentation, Continued: More on Event Condensation.* Working papers, Workshop on Temporality, Max-Planck Institut für Psycholinguistik, Nijmegen.
FRAUENFELDER, U., NOYAU, C., PERDUE, C. & PORQUIER, R., 1980, Connaissance en langue étrangère. *Langages 57*, 43–60.
GIACOBBE, J. & CAMMAROTA, M.A., 1986, Learner's hypotheses for the acquisition of lexis. *Studies in Second Language Acquisition 8* (3), 327–342.
HOUDAÏFA, T., 1983, La référence personnelle et temporelle dans le récit d'un apprenant en milieu naturel. Acquisition du français par des travailleurs marocains. *Papiers de Travail 1*, 125–140.
KINTSCH, W. & VAN DIJK, T., 1975, Comment on se rappelle et résume des histoires. *Langages 40*, 98–116.
KUMPF, L., 1984, Temporal systems and universality in interlanguage: A case study. In F.R. ECKMAN, L.H. BELL & D. NELSON (eds), *Universals of Second Language Acquisition.* Rowley, MA: Newbury House, 132–143.
LABOV, W., 1972, *Language in the Inner City: Study in the Black English Vernacular.* Philadelphia: University of Pennsylvania Press.
NOYAU, C., 1984, The development of means for temporality in French by adult Spanish-speakers: linguistic devices and communicative capacities. In G. EXTRA & M. MITTNER (eds), *Studies in Second Language Acquisition by Adult Immigrants.* Tilburg Studies in Language and Literature 6. Tilburg, The Netherlands: Tilburg University, 113–137.
— 1986, *L'Acquisition du Français dans le Milieu Social par des Adultes Hispanophones: La Temporalité.* Unpublished doctoral dissertation, Sorbonne University, Paris.

PERDUE, C. (ed), 1982, *Second Language Acquisition by Adult Immigrants. A Field Manual.* Strasbourg: European Science Foundation.

POTTIER, B., 1974, *Linguistique Générale, Théorie et Description.* Paris: Klincksieck.

SCHLYTER, S., 1984, *L'Acquisition des Formes et des Fonctions Verbales Françaises par des Apprenants Suédois.* Paper delivered at the Ninth Congress of Scandinavian Romanists, Helsinki.

SIMONOT, M., 1983, January, *'Long Time Go': Narrative Techniques of a Second Language Speaker.* Paper delivered at the SSRC Workshop, Southall.

STUTTERHEIM, C. VON, 1984, *Der Ausdruck der Temporalität in der Zweitsprache: Eine Untersuchung zum Erwerb des Deutschen durch türkische Gastarbeiter.* Revised doctoral dissertation, Freie Universität Berlin. Berlin: Walter de Gruyter.

STUTTERHEIM, C. VON & KLEIN, W., 1986, A concept-oriented approach to second language studies. In C.W. PFAFF (ed.), *First and Second Language Acquisition Processes.* Rowley, MA: Newbury House.

TANNEN, D., 1983, 'I take out the rock — dok!': how Greek women tell about being molested (and create involvement). *Anthropological Linguistics 25* (3), 359–374.

— (forthcoming). Introducing constructed dialogue in Greek and American conversational and literary narrative. In F. COULMAS (ed.), *Reported Speech Across Languages.*

TRÉVISE, A., 1984, *Some Remarks on the Expression of Temporality in the Speech of a Spanish-speaking Adult Acquiring French in a Natural Setting.* Working paper, Workshop on Temporality, Max-Planck Institut für Psycholinguistik, Nijmegen.

TRÉVISE, A. & HÉRÉDIA, C. DE, 1984, Les malentendus: Effet de loupe sur certains phénomènes d'acquisition d'une langue étrangère. In C. NOYAU & R. PORQUIER (eds), *Communiquer dans la Langue de l'Autre.* Paris: Presses Universitaires de Vincennes.

TRÉVISE, A. & PORQUIER, R., 1986, Second language acquisition by adult immigrants: Exemplified methodology. *Studies in Second Language Acquisition 8* (3), 265–275.

VASSEUR, M.T., 1985, *BE: A Longitudinal Study of Temporality in a Spanish-speaking Learner's Personal Narratives.* ESF Project paper.

10 Reference and Discourse Structure in the Learning of French by Adult Moroccans

DANIEL VÉRONIQUE

Introduction

The aim of this paper[1] is to explore the relationship that exists between reference and discourse organisation in the early stages of the acquisition of a second language in a naturalistic setting by adult learners. If we hypothesise that in his or her first attempts at production in L2, the learner can only rely on the following resources:

(a) knowledge of language production activities and communicative interaction in L1;
(b) use of non-verbal signals (be they source culture specific or not);
(c) knowledge of some general principles for organising the information to deliver;
(d) lexical items in L2,

it follows that giving information about objects, their state and change of state, about degree of acquaintance with a person or object, and about the spatio-temporal correlates of actions and processes (i.e. the basics of productive activities) is one of the most influential factors in the shaping of utterances and discourse in L2.

In this paper, I would like to investigate the extent to which the acquisition and use of the L2 pronominal system and of referential expressions in the target language, of spatial and temporal marking are discourse dependent. It is my contention that the Bickertonian specific/non specific or state/non state dichotomies in language acquisition and language evolution do not apply to L2 learning. I shall support the view that in the data available at least, referential values for lexical items are contextually bound and are independent of the TL semantic and pragmatic values of the determiners that happen to occur in the learner system. I am aware that it can be retorted in answer to the criticism levelled at Bickerton's (1981) dichotomies that adults cannot be expected to activate their innate bioprogram in second language learning. This is no argument for me since I believe that we can satisfactorily explain language acquisition without recourse to such a construct.

I would thus like to assess how far discourse constraints such as those involved in the task of story-retelling affect the marking of referential activities. I further wish to evaluate the share of means other than those tied to reference, such as word order or connectors for example, to the structuring of discourse activities in a particular task.

The first section of this article 'Reference and Discourse Structure' develops the theoretical framework of the study and reviews some of the relevant literature on the acquisition of reference and discourse structure in French as a second language. In the second section, 'Acquisition of Reference in French by Adult Moroccans' I summarise previous work on the acquisition of reference by Moroccan adults including findings on Abdelmalek's interlanguage (IL), one informant for this study. In the third and fourth sections 'The Informant' and 'The Charlie Chaplin Experiment' I introduce the informant and the design of the experiment. The findings of the study are presented and discussed in the final sections 'Findings' and 'Discussion'.

Reference and discourse structure

Referential activity can be approached from two different perspectives: as a component of what Givón (1984) calls propositional semantics, that is, at the clause level or in relationship to cohesion (Halliday & Hasan, 1976) or discourse pragmatics (Givón, 1984). Obvious links exist between the functions of referential expressions within the proposition and its pragmatic roles in relation to the preceding and subsequent utterances. When mentioning these two levels of function, it should be borne in mind that reference is but one of the linguistic domains that help foster the discourse fabric. Predication is another one of these linguistic realms that contribute strongly to discourse organisation.

Halliday & Hasan (1976) very carefully distinguish between discourse structure and what they call cohesion. According to them, discourse structure refers to some type of structure larger than a sentence such as a paragraph for example, whereas cohesion is a semantic and pragmatic entity. I use the term discourse in a very broad sense to refer to the way in which sentences are bound and related together to form larger entities the prototype of which is the narrative (Labov, 1972). Discourse structure then is not a static device situated at a rank above the sentence, but a cover term to designate the set of means and the pragmatic effects they produce which enable the speaker and the hearer, each within his own perspective, to distinguish for instance between background and foreground information, or evaluation and summary within a narrative.

In this article, I have singled out referential activity as one of the major sets of means by which discourse comes into being. Doubtlessly, many other means contribute to discourse fabric. It is my contention that the origin of syntax must be sought in discourse. In that respect, I share Givón's view (1979) that the distinction between discourse structure and sentence structure is, in some sense, an arbitrary one. However, I must admit that linguistic research has very clearly demonstrated that constraints intervene at the clause level — such as, for instance, those that tie classes of NPs to given classes of verbs — which, although they might originate in discourse, do not affect the discourse level *per se*. On the other hand, the existence of specific patterns of discourse organisation which are not strictly dependent on the clause level, such as those analysed by Deulofeu (1980) for spoken vernacular French, can be demonstrated as well.

Reference and discourse structure in L2 acquisition

The theme–rheme distinction and its application to the analysis of data produced by learners in their first stages of L2 acquisition has been discussed recently in various articles by Dittmar (1984), Schumann (1983), and Trévise (1986). I have singled out for discussion the important cross-linguistic analysis by Klein & Perdue (1986) which deals partly with data from a French L2 learner. I shall also summarise en passant work done by Giacomi (1986) and Deulofeu (1986) on Moroccan Arabic learners of French.

Klein & Perdue (1986) attempt to understand how a learner who does not possess 'the normal syntactic devices' available to a native speaker, organises his or her utterances. They list a series of principles of linearisation of lexical items which could be applied by a learner lacking syntactic means either because of L1 influence, of the learner's metalinguistic awareness of L2, of his or her attempt to facilitate his or her interlocutor's understanding, or because the principle is deemed universal. One objection to this approach can be raised: what is hypothesised by the authors to be the special case of the L2 learner could be the case of the native speaker, as well. The native speaker can use an array of both syntactic and thematic means to organise his or her utterances without doing it by default, so to say.

Analyses of the 'Charlie Chaplin' retelling by Italians learning German and English, and by a Spanish speaker learning French reveal the following. In the case of Vito, the Italian learning German, the arrangement problems encountered in his IL are solved according to the following distinctions:

1. Presentationals have a final NP, others an initial NP.
2. When two NPs are present, the agent occupies first position.

Although other complicating factors do occasionally intervene, Vito's utterances seem to follow these constraints. They can also be found in Rudolfo's retelling. It seems, however, that he makes extensive use of an associative contextualisation. Besides, rules of reference do not operate in cases of subordination, and different intonation contours are used to mark introductions and conclusions to episodes.

Ramon's retelling, the only case of a learner of French as L2, is the most intricate one. The assessment of the main type of utterances used by Ramon discloses that in the sequences $\emptyset$ - V and *Nominative clitic - V*, $\emptyset$ and nominative clitic are complementarily distributed. This may be explained either as maintenance or change of function of the preceding referent. In the former case $\emptyset$ is used, except when the span of reference is above two utterances, and in the latter case clitics are used. Re-introduction of an entity is done through a lexical N.

According to Klein and Perdue (1986), the maintenance of reference by pronouns or $\emptyset$, or their re-introduction seem to be determined by episode boundaries which Ramon has devised for himself, independent of the material presented to him. This would explain the frequency of occurrence of N-V and N-clitic-V patterns.

The findings of Klein and Perdue concerning the use of NPs in relation to V forms confirm previous work by Givón. They are also quite in accordance with what was found in Abdelmalek's retellings, as we shall discuss later. They correspond with Trévise's (1986) findings on the use of [se] in Gloria's data, a Spanish learner of French.

In order to fully appreciate our findings in the Abdelmalek study, it is necessary to contrast it with previous work on the acquisition of utterance patterns by Moroccan Arabic speakers.

Deulofeu (1983) identifies three main topic/comment patterns in the first two encounters of Abderrahim, another Moroccan informant:

(a) without any 'constructional' element,
for example, *monsieur José monsieur Tayeb directeur*
(mister José mister Tayeb director)

(b) with an 'elementary' verb
for example, *la musique [se] bien*
(music it's good)

(c) with 'full' verbs
for example, *le facteur [zədone] enveloppe par*
le monsieur par la maison
(the postman [I give] envelope by
the man by the house)

Deulofeu argues that in all these cases the first term is a topic because:
(a) it is not compulsory;
(b) it is never indefinite;
(c) it could not be 'translated' by an agent or a subject in the target language (TL).

Deulofeu (1986) assumes that during L2 acquisition both grammatical and discursive structures are learned in parallel. He believes that although the syntactic organisation of IL does not differ much from that of the TL from a qualitative point of view, its interpretation by a TL speaker might prove to be difficult. Deulofeu shows that one Moroccan informant, Abdelmalek, is able to use all the discursive devices available to a native speaker to structure the information he wants to convey. Despite this 'knowledge', however, misunderstanding crops up in the learner's interaction with a TL investigator because of the manner in which he uses the discursive devices, a manner partially if not totally different from that of a TL speaker. It is the communicative styles which seem to differ.

Giacomi (1986) studies the structuring of utterances through the interplay of questions and answers in the first, fifth, and ninth encounters with Abdelmalek. He draws up a list of the lexical means used by the informant in his interaction with the investigator: repetition of a lexical item given by the investigator — one-word answers. He also mentions another device frequently used for the structuring of utterances by Abdelmalek: propositional accumulation. In his analysis of data comparable to Deulofeu (1986), Giacomi (1986) comes to slightly different conclusions. Although he agrees with Deulofeu that there is no great difference between a narrative told by a TL speaker and told by a learner, he draws attention to the specific use of *parce que*, *après*, and *y en a* by Abdelmalek. Those markers seem to be used either to introduce background (*y en a*) or foreground items (*parce que, après*). We will come back to this point later.

Finally, Houdaïfa (1986) in his analysis of data from the first cycle of investigation with Abderrahim gives some information on the way his utterances are structured. He notes that although the status of predicate can be assigned to a given lexical item in a given utterance, no satisfactory criteria are available to distinguish between nouns and verbs in Abderrahim's utterances. Houdaïfa stresses the frequency of zero anaphora in subject position in various discourse (such as mention of the topic in a previous clause) and syntactic contexts (with interrogatives or negation, for instance). He finally mentions the use of a word order pattern based on the thematic–rhematic dichotomy and the frequent use of thematic markers *c'est* and *il y a*. Houdaïfa argues that a parallel must be drawn between the development of pronominal reference and the growing syntactic structuring of the informant's utterances.

Acquisition of reference in French by adult Moroccans

The referential activities of Abdelmalek, one Moroccan informant, can best be studied if seen within the general framework of the acquisition of means to refer to people, space, and time as used by Moroccan adults. Such a study of the development of linguistic means to refer to self or others and to spatio-temporal correlates of events and processes across individual learners shows many commonalities.

Nominal reference

Coupier (1983) presents a study of the acquisition of pronominal reference. It is based on extracts from the first six encounters with Zahra, a female subject who, at the time the data collection started, had been in France for approximately one year. Coupier notes that the informant's utterances tend to be organised according to a theme–rheme division. She further notes that in Zahra's interlanguage morphology is of no help in deciding to which syntactic class a given lexical item belongs. She draws attention to the plurifunctionality of morpheme-like elements like [e] or [li] and their variants. Coupier's study is centred on such morpheme-like items immediately preceding the rheme-predicate in Zahra's utterances. During the three first encounters, self-reference is mainly expressed through the following:

$$\begin{bmatrix} \text{moi} \\ \begin{Bmatrix} \text{moi} \\ \varnothing \end{Bmatrix} \end{bmatrix} + \begin{bmatrix} \varnothing \\ [\text{le}] \\ [\text{i}] \end{bmatrix} + \text{Predicate}$$

Je or *moi je*, which are the usual TL forms in subject or thematic position, are used very infrequently in the examined data, but tend to become important by the end of the observation period. In contexts where TL would have *je* or *moi je*, Zahra frequently resorts to (moi) + $\begin{Bmatrix} [\text{āna}] \\ [\text{se}] \end{Bmatrix}$.

Exophoric reference is expressed mainly by $\begin{Bmatrix} \text{le} \\ \text{i} \end{Bmatrix}$.

Coupier's study of Zahra confirms a previous study by Véronique (1983) on pronominal reference in Abdelmalek's IL. It seems that during the first steps in L2, the main information as to whether reference is to self or not, lies in the use or non-use of *moi*, given that zero anaphora is a frequent feature, governed by thematic continuity (see also Houdaïfa, 1986; and Deulofeu, 1986). As soon as the distinction between full and clitic pronouns as well as a possible distinction between theme and grammatical subject seem to be mastered, pronominal reference in the IL tends to become similar to that of the TL.

Houdaïfa (1986) describes pronominal reference in Abderrahim's IL. For self-reference, *je* and *moi je* are used, but also *il* as is the case with Zahra. For reference to the addressee, *tu* is used as in the TL. To refer to some other person, *je* + predicate or *il* + predicate are used. Thus, the acquisition of pronominal reference by Abderrahim seems to proceed along similar lines as with Zahra and Abdelmalek. A clitic form from TL (either *je* [TL + speaker pronoun] or *il* [TL-speaker-addressee pronoun]) is appended to the predicate and this unanalysed (?) block is used as such. Specific reference to self or others is made through the use of full pronouns or through the context. It should be added that zero anaphora as well as presentative and existential reference are used when the topic is clearly in the foreground.

Véronique (1984) gives support to this trend by pulling together data from Zahra (see Coupier, 1983), Rquia (first three interviews), Abdelmalek (first eight interviews) and Abdessamad (first interview). It would even be possible to group informants on an acquisitional scale indicating whether:

(a) they add a morpheme-like unanalysed form to the predicate
— be it [li], [le], [i] or even [3ə] — or not;
(b) they refer to self preferentially by means of *(moi)* + *je* or through

$$
\text{a device like } \begin{bmatrix} \text{moi} \\ \begin{Bmatrix} \text{moi} \\ \emptyset \end{Bmatrix} \end{bmatrix} + \begin{bmatrix} \emptyset \\ [\text{je}] \\ [\text{li}] \end{bmatrix}
$$

(c) they use [jāna] / [ja] or [se] extensively to avoid reference to self through pronominal forms;

(d) reference to self or others is established mainly through the linguistic context rather than by explicit pronominal marking.

Véronique (1985a) analyses (see Table 1) the manner in which Abdelmalek and Abdessamad refer to persons and objects by looking at the types of NPs and pronoun-like forms they use during the first ten encounters of the data collection cycle. Concerning the acquisition and use of lexical referential expressions the main findings are:

1. In the first stages, the lexical items are acquired and used as such without any attention being paid to whether the item is preceded by a determiner or not, or to the semantic and pragmatic value of the given determiner.
2. Lexical NPs derive their referential value mainly through the linguistic context. This explains why zero determiners are employed in a manner similar to zero anaphora.
3. Half-way through the period of observation, Abdelmalek acquires the definite/indefinite distinction. He starts using referential expressions of the form indefinite determiner + Noun to introduce new referents and definite determiner + Noun to refer to known items. The definite/indefinite distinction has been mastered by Abdessamad already at the outset of the data collection cycle.
4. No demonstrative article is used by either informant during the phase of observation. This implies that sequences of definite determiner + Noun or even Ø + Noun must be endowed with specific deictic force in IL.

Spatial reference

Houdaïfa (1986) includes a study of the syntax and semantics of the verbs of movement, of direction, and of position in data from the first ten encounters with Abderrahim. The following verbs are analysed: *partir, arriver, sortir, venir, rester, aller, marcher*. Apart from a detailed specification of the syntactic distribution of each verb, Houdaïfa (1986) provides the following information about spatial reference in Abderrahim's IL:

(a) The main spatial prepositions used in conjunction with the

TABLE 1. *Pronominal reference (reference to self).*

	Zahra	Abdelmalek	Rquia	Abdessamad
Arrival in France	1981	09. 1981	1981	10. 1981
Period of data collection	6 monthly encounters between 18.11.82 and 23.07.83 (248 days)	7 monthly encounters between 13.11.82 and 25.06.83 (218 days)	4 monthly encounters between 18.11.82 and 05.03.83 (114 days)	Only the first encounter has been studied 20.11.82
Forms	formulaic use of je + [köprä] + [se] moi + Pred.* (moi) + {[le]/[i]} + Pred. (moi) + {[jăna]/[se]} Beginning with the third encounter (after 111 days) the TL-like form (moi) + je + Pred. can also be observed.	formulaic use of [ʒə ne pa]/[ʒə krwa] (moi) + Pred. (moi) + (li) + Pred. (moi) + {[jăna]/[se]} Beginning with the fourth encounter (after 109 days) the TL-like form (moi) + je + Pred. can also be observed.	moi + Pred. (moi) je + Pred. (Self-corrections of *moi + il + Pred.* into *moi + je + Pred.* can be observed.)	In a narrative where reference to self occurs 63 times, the following can be observed: moi + Pred. (2) moi + {il/[lij]} + Pred. (2) moi + [jăna] (2) moi + je + Pred. (41) je +Pred. (16).

*Predicate

movement verbs are *à, avec, par*, and *à côté*. It should be noted that most spatial expressions have the form V + prep. + N in Abderrahim's IL;

(b) *partir* is used by Abderrahim wherever *aller* would be used in TL;

(c) some spatial prepositions are overgeneralised during specific encounters, for instance, *par* in the first three interviews or *avec* in the fifth.

Véronique (1985b) describes the acquisition of the linguistic means of spatial reference by Abdelmalek and Abdessamad. This study is based on conversations and specific tasks recorded during the first cycle of data collection. Its main findings are:

1. Despite some marked differences in the construction of spatial expressions, Abdelmalek and Abdessamad share the same verbs of movement: *entrer, rentrer, partir, monter, aller, venir, descendre, sortir, marcher, tomber, passer, rester, tourner*. This list is different from the one given above for Abderrahim.

2. The two informants diverge in the manner they build their referential expressions. From the start, Abdessamad like Abderrahim uses V + *preposition* + N, the preposition being in most cases *à*, whereas Abdelmalek starts out with V + Ø + N to end up with V + *à* + N at the end of our observation period.

3. The spatial expressions mustered by the informants vary due to the pragmatic constraints imposed upon them by the elicitation situation. Thus, it was observed that only a subset of the verbs available to Abdelmalek and Abdessamad was used by them in the recorded conversations and narratives.

4. This task variation can be further explained by the type of schematisation (Talmy, 1983) the informant needs to express in various discourse contexts. In some of the data elicitation techniques, both interactants can see the referents and share the situation where various spatial expressions must be produced by the informant. In other cases, in a different setting, the informant must reconstruct a spatial domain known to both partners. In other cases still, the informant must describe movements and spatial settings to the investigator, of which the latter is unaware. That is the case when narratives involving spatial reference are produced by an informant.

Houdaïfa & Véronique (1984) extend the analysis of Véronique (1985b) to two other informants, Zahra and Abderrahim. Only the main results will be summarised here.

In the Ash-Tray Experiment data the following is observed (see Perdue, 1982) for the four informants:

1. The canonical form of referential expressions in that task is

$$\begin{Bmatrix} V \\ \emptyset \end{Bmatrix} + \text{Referent} + \left\{ \begin{Bmatrix} \text{prep.} \\ \emptyset \end{Bmatrix} + \text{Relatum} \atop \emptyset \right\}$$

where V is a causative movement verb like *poser* (*to place*); the referent is usually specified lexically except when it is replaced by zero anaphora because rules of topic continuity apply and the relatum is often specified by a deictic rather than by a noun.

2. There is an important variation across informants in the way referential expressions are built. Abdelmalek and Abdessamad have a more important lexis for V than Zahra or Abderrahim.

3. Items common to all informants include causative verbs [*uvrir*] and [*ferme*] and spatial prepositions *dans* and *pour*.

4. Two main spatial schematisations are expressed in this task: movement towards a goal and inclusion of one object in another. The latter is expressed mainly through the use of *dans* and not by means of a causative of movement such as *mettre*.

Data on route descriptions yield the following common characteristics:

(a) The order of description follows the spatio-temporal configuration to be described;

(b) the description is ordered as if the narrator proceeded mentally from one salient reference point to another;

(c) the mention of a given reference point in the spatial description allows for digressions and comments;

(d) movement from one reference point to another is expressed mainly through verbs.

Route descriptions in L1 and L2 have one feature in common: the informant seems to journey across a mental map as he or she talks about the route. Differences between the two sets of data derive from the fact that the informants have a larger stock of spatial expressions in L1 than L2. Besides the reference points mentioned in both narratives differ because of cultural background. Thus in L1, places known to North African migrant workers are mentioned, whereas in L2 French culture based reference points are chosen.

Houdaïfa & Véronique's (1984) study confirms one important feature noticed previously: the various types of spatial expressions produced in various settings differ not so much in the verbs as in the prepositions and adverbs used.

Temporal reference

Houdaïfa (1983a,b) deals with temporal reference in the data of two informants, Abdelmalek and Abdessamad. Despite the fact that a fair amount of verbal morphology is observed in IL data — *entrer* for instance is found under the following forms: [eantre], [ãtre], [syiãtre] — it does not seem to fulfil specific temporal or aspectual functions. However, Houdaïfa notes that in Abdelmalek's data at least, the distribution of verbal forms seems to be determined by the existence of various dimensions in Abdelmalek's narrative. The story line is marked by *a + V forms* whereas *V stems* and *V + e* forms are used in the background. In Abdessamad's data, local constraints govern the distribution of verbal forms. Thus, if two verbal forms occur in succession, the second verb has a *V + e* form. Morphology being rarely used in IL to express temporality, temporal reference is expressed through the following devices:

(a) strict observance of the chronological sequence of events to be recounted and of their spatial settings — hence, the importance of dates;
(b) use of connectors such as *alors, après* which allow a contrast between what happens before and after the reference point;
(c) use of 'situants' such as *hier* and *aujourd'hui* which mark the point of departure from the sequence of events;
(d) recourse to aspectual operators such as *parfois, jamais* and *chaque fois*.

Summary

Among the most striking features observed in the acquisition of reference by the Moroccan informants, the following should be stressed because of their relevance:

(a) the apparently non-functional use of the definite article in the construction of nominal expressions;
(b) the progressive cliticisation of the segment appended to the predicate;
(c) the acquisition of locative prepositions in a determined order: Ø > à > dans > pour;
(d) the apparently non-functional motivation of verbal morphology in IL.

Another important hint provided by the preliminary analyses is the close links that may exist between the use of new lexical items, the activity of referring to persons, objects or space and the structuring of utterances in terms of the theme–rheme dichotomy. In effect, such discourse constraints as topic continuity, referential continuity, or topic switch apply with reference to persons and space as well as with the structuring of utterances. It would seem that an implicational relationship holds between the mastery of the TL pronominal system, and more precisely of the clitic *versus* full pronoun dichotomy (where it exists), and the marking of obligatory subject.

The informant

Abdelmalek, the main informant for this study, is one of the four longitudinal informants we have worked with during the past three years in the European Science Foundation (ESF) research project on second language acquisition (Perdue, 1982). At the time data collection started, he was twenty and had been living in France illegally for approximately twelve months (he was granted amnesty in 1981). His first language is Moroccan Arabic and he knows some Spanish from living in Northern Morocco and from having spent some three years in Spain. Abdelmalek attended primary school in Morocco but dropped out after two years.

Since that time he did not receive any type of instruction except for a one hour language course he attended in France during his first year of stay or so. After his migration to France, Abdelmalek has worked as a fisherman on a boat owned by a boss of Italian origin, then as a clothes seller in a market whose current customers are speakers of Arabic. Abdelmalek proved very cooperative during the course of our field work and thought that participation in the study would help him improve his mastery of French. He is a very good storyteller as all the data collected from him has proved.

At the time when the first Charlie Chaplin Experiment was submitted to Abdelmalek, his IL had the following characteristics in the domain of reference to persons and objects:

(a) reliance on context for the referential values of lexical NPs;
(b) full pronouns filling the thematic slot while 'the would be' clitic paradigm seemed to be reduced at one stage to one item *li* alternating with Ø;
(c) rarity of prepositions, be it to mark semantic links between NPs or for any other purpose.

This study can be viewed as a further exploration of the properties of Abdelmalek's IL in the referential and discourse domains.

The Charlie Chaplin Experiment

In this task devised by the Heidelberg ESF team, extracts of 'Modern Times' have been organised in two episodes. The researcher and the informant watch episode one together, then the researcher leaves the room and the informant watches episode two by himself. The researcher returns and the informant must retell the end of the film. Here is a summary of the contents of the 'Modern Times' extracts used in this experiment. This resumé is borrowed from Klein & Perdue (1985):

Episode 1
Subtitle: America 1930 — poverty, hunger, unemployment

Charlie gets into a demonstration against unemployment, is taken for the leader and put into prison. At dinner one of his fellow-prisoners hides heroin in the salt-cellar, and Charlie helps himself by mistake. With the drug he gains a heroical force: he foils an attempt to escape and frees the director who, in gratitude, releases him with a letter of recommendation for a job. Charlie doesn't feel too enthusiastic about this because in prison he is better off, he feels, than at liberty. Parallel with this we see a second story: a young girl (whose father is a widower, unemployed and without the means to feed his three children) steals food for her family. Her father is shot in a demonstration, and the children have to go to an orphanage. The girl manages to escape at the last moment.

Episode 2
Subtitle: Determined to return to prison

Charlie finds work in a shipyard. Clumsily he causes the launching of a ship that was not finished. He is immediately fired and is all the more determined to go back to prison. The girl roams through the streets hungrily, and steals a loaf of bread. When she tries to escape she runs into Charlie and both fall to the ground. A woman, who watched the theft, calls the baker. The policeman comes to arrest the girl. Charlie tries to claim responsibility for the theft but it doesn't work. The girl is marched off to prison.

Charlie tries again to get to prison. He goes to a restaurant, eats as much as he can, calls a policeman from the street and tells him that he has no money to pay the bill. He is arrested.

In the police-car he again meets the girl who stole the bread. In an accident they are both thrown out. The girl suggests that he escape with her, and he does. In the garden of a middle-class house they rest for a while, and watch the couple who live there say a tender good-bye to each other in front of their house. Middle-class conjugal bliss. Charlie and the girl dream of an existence like that. A few days later the girl has a surprise for Charlie, having found such a house for both of them. Of course, it is a ruined cabin in a miserable condition, so that a series of hilarious accidents happen when they first come to see it. But they won't let this disturb their happiness. In the last picture we see them walking on a long road that disappears into the horizon.

This task is of special interest for the study of reference and discourse structure:

1. On one hand, both interactants, speaker and hearer, have a shared knowledge of *some* characters and *some* events in the film. This common knowledge facilitates the task of processing the narration.

2. On the other hand, the informant with his limited linguistic resources must introduce information in the case of some *other* characters and some *other* events in the film which are new to the hearer.

In this experiment, he must refer to at least ten different characters, four different objects and six different places. Some of these are known to speaker and hearer whereas others are unknown to the hearer. Among the known figures are Charlie Chaplin, a young girl, the director of the prison, and so forth. The baker and the woman witness to the theft, however, must be introduced by the speaker. Among the unknown objects, there are a loaf of bread, a wood block and furniture in the house. Whereas the shipyard and the prison have been seen by speaker and hearer, subsequent places such as the restaurant, the police-car, or the cabin must be added by the speaker.

In examining the three retellings of 'Modern Times' by Abdelmalek which have been collected at a nine months' interval,[2] I shall be addressing the following issue: what are the elements which structure Abdelmalek's narratives and what is the contribution of referential activities to this structuring of the narrative? To achieve this purpose, the analysis will bear on the following points:

(a) the forms used in the first and subsequent mention of the characters;
(b) the means used to avoid referring to persons or events;
(c) the signalling of subevents of the two main episodes and the use

of such markers as *jāna (there is)*, *voilà (there is/it is)* or *après (afterwards)*;

(d) word order in relation to specific verbs.

The findings will be compared to those of Giacomi (1986) and Giacomi & Vion (1986) bearing on the same informant and to those of Klein & Perdue (1985).

Findings[3]

'Modern Times' cycle 1

In this first retelling which is approximately 357 words long, Abdelmalek chose to start his recounting at the point where the investigator left the room. In the subsequent experiments, he retold the whole story from the very beginning.

Participation and state of affairs (first and subsequent mention)

Characters can be mentioned through one of these possibilities: use of proper nouns and use of lexical items. To these two classes pronouns in their deictic functions must be added as well as anaphora (including cataphora), be it through a pronoun or zero. Once a character has been established in the fore, it is necessary to maintain continuity of reference unless a switch of reference occurs. This should then in turn be signalled (see Lyons, 1977; Givón, 1983).

Use of NPs: It should first of all be mentioned that in terms of the morphology of NPs and pronouns for that matter, no distinction of gender is marked and the same holds true for number. In version 1 and 2[4] of this first retelling of 'Modern Times', the main female character is introduced as *le/la femme* which could be + Presupposed and ± Specific in Bickerton's terminology. Charlie Chaplin is introduced by proper name. The second female character is introduced in version 1 as

[li] femme [ke garde ilavole] un restaurant[5]
(the woman who witnessed he stole a loaf of bread)

and as

[li] femme [sa le garde ilavole]
(the woman that she witnessed he stole)

in version 2. In both cases the clause appended to the lexical item *femme* bestows a + Specific feature to the referential expression. Secondary characters such as the policeman or the baker are mentioned with lexical NPs of the form *le* + *N* which could have specific or generic meaning according to context. Other characters such as the foreman or the fellow prisoner are just not mentioned.

Subsequent mention of Charlie is either through the use of a proper name (20 tokens in all) or through the 'all purpose' pronoun *il/li*. The two female characters are subsequently referred to as *la femme*. Linguistic context and shared knowledge enable the hearer to understand who is being referred to. The policeman is designated by *la police* which is ambiguous in so far as this expression has generic (referring to the police force) as well as specific meaning (viz. a policeman). In one case a numeral is used

[jāna] un police
(there is one police(man))

and in another case an approximation of policeman [pulisi] is resorted to. An examination of the structure of the NPs reveals that le/li/la + N is overwhelmingly used. Of the 21 different lexical items occurring in the text, 19 combine with *le* . . . to yield 55 tokens of that structure (see Table 2). Of the two lexical items which do not combine with *le*, *jardin* has a particular status because it always seems to be preceded by *un* in the informant's retellings of 'Modern Times'. One case of clear alternation in the use of *un* and *le* with the same lexical item has been noticed: the first mention of the loaf of bread is *un restaurant* and in subsequent occurrences, the sequence is *le* + *N*. Thus it would seem that at this stage in his learning of French, Abdelmalek's French reflects two types of referential assumptions:

1. A subset of lexical items associates better with given determiners despite the linguistic context.
2. The distinction between *un* and *le* + N is useful if one wants to mark an item of information as new and then refer back to it as given.

TABLE 2. *Modern Times cycle 1: The nominal phrase.*

$\left\{\begin{matrix} le \\ li \\ la \end{matrix}\right\}$ + N	$\left\{\begin{matrix} \text{œ̃} \\ yn \end{matrix}\right\}$ + N	Ø + N	beaucoup de + N
Tokens : 55	3	2	1

It must however be mentioned that the overwhelming number of pseudodefinite NPs in this and the subsequent retellings of 'Modern Times' need not indicate a specific trait of Abdelmalek's IL: in standard French discourse or in spoken French, *definite article + N* is probably the most frequent form of NP (Deulofeu, personal communication). In effect, it would seem that the great number of le/li/la + N in the data obtained from Abdelmalek could be accounted for by one or several of these factors:

(a) a markedness factor, *le + N* being less marked than *un + N* or *ce + N*;

(b) a task dependent factor, that is, in narratives most entities are usually referred to by *le + N* segments, at least in spoken French (Deulofeu, personal communication);

(c) a syntactic factor, *un + N* is much less frequent in the preverbal slot than *le + N*; in effect all cases of *un + N* are postverbal (Deulofeu, personal communication);

(d) a lexical factor, objects that pertain to the personal sphere or refer to such properties as profession and so forth, tend to be associated in French with *le + N* (Deulofeu, Houdaïfa, personal communication).

One last word about referential NPs in retelling cycle 1: the reliance on semantic equivalence as defined by the linguistic context. Thus, in one case *patron* is used instead of *boulanger* and in another case, a specific term *restaurant* is used instead of the cover term *pain*.

Use of Pronouns: The 'all purpose' clitic *il/li* is used to supplement terms which can be inserted in the subject/topic slot. Thus the gender marking is neutralised and occasionally the number marking, too. However, as has been mentioned before, the main characters are referred to by means of lexical items or zero anaphora after first mention. Here is such an example:

il [eveni] la police Ø [letrape] la femme
(it came the police Ø it took hold of the woman)

For reference to persons or objects that could occupy object position, Abdelmalek uses a postposed pronoun whose form is different from *il/li*, for example, *[itrape] le* (it seized it).

Two remarkable features in Abdelmalek's use of pronouns for reference are (although their functional status differs):

(a) Topic switch without any corollary pronominal switch. The same *li/il* used for the young woman is applied to the elder one in the

following utterance without any particular indication that there has been a switch of reference;
(b) recourse to a discursive device based on the use of full pronouns and of identificational *se*.

Such topic switch without a corollary change in pronouns leads to opacity as in the following passage:

[ilaparti] la boulanger [ilavole] un restaurant
[ilavole] comme le femme [sale garde ilavole]
il [madi] le patron la femme [ilavole] le restaurant
(he went to the baker he stole a loaf of bread he stole as the woman that s/he was looking he stole s/he told me the boss the woman s/he has stolen the loaf of bread)

The contrasting device through which a positive value is attributed to the topic is represented by a full pronoun and a negative value: [*se*] + negative modality. This is an efficient procedure, used in the three retellings we have analysed. Here is one instance of this device:

[se] pas le femme il [madi] moi [levole] le restaurant
(it is not the woman he told me I he stole the restaurant)

The signalling of subevents.

The narrative progresses very clearly through the use of *après* (*afterwards*) which marks both thematic and temporal successivity. [*Se*] (*it is*) and [*jāna*] (*there is*) are used for comments and background information. Such a discourse organisation has also been described for the first narrative collected from Abdelmalek, some three months before the first 'Modern Times' experiment (Giacomi, 1986). Within the realm of background information, [*se*] and [*jāna*] play different roles (see Trévise, 1986). [*Se*] is used for identification and direct deictic functions (this is why it is used in the contrastive rhetorical device described above), whereas [*jāna*] marks the existence of the subsequent term, states that

TABLE 3. *Modern Times cycle 1: Discourse markers.*

	après	[jāna]	[se]	voilà	bon	alors
Tokens :	13	4	6	Ø	Ø	1

the speaker 'possesses' a given object, which is to the right of [jāna], and frames temporal information. It should be noted that [se] freely combines with the negation (out of six tokens five are combined with pas); this is less frequent with [jāna] (one case of combination with that marker out of five tokens).

Deulofeu (1986) has observed very convincingly that in this retelling and the subsequent one of cycle 2 après acts as an episode marker which constrains the marking of the theme: whenever in the new episode marked by après a new theme is introduced it must be explicitly indicated by the use of a lexical item. Otherwise, it is implied that the main character of the plot Charlie is referred to. In this case pronominal reference through il or zero anaphora suffice. It is also at these boundaries that breaches in the canonical VX word order for verbs of emergence can be observed.

It should be noted that whenever interaction is supposed to take place between two characters, reported speech is introduced by the marker [madi]; [ilmadi] and [madi/la femme] are the two main sequences that serve to introduce the words assigned to the characters of this silent movie.

Verbs and word order

In version 2 of the retelling, there are 74 utterances comprising V.[6] Only 13 instances of VX order have been counted. The verbs involved are [trape], [marʃe], [mōte], [tōbe], [parti], [veni], and [madi]. They are mainly verbs of movement and a verb of saying. The case of [veni] is quite striking; out of eight tokens six follow the VX pattern. Many factors explain this particular VX order while the general trend is to use canonical XV word order. For example, in the source language the dominant pattern is VX. For typological and diachronic reasons (see Givón, 1984), it seems that verbs of appearance, of emergence and of grasping tend to follow a VX pattern. This trend is also illustrated in the TL. At least those two factors seem to account for the word order VX.

'Modern Times' Cycle 2

This second retelling is 640 words long. This time Abdelmalek narrates the whole film shown to him.

Characters and state of affairs (first and subsequent mention)
Use of NPs:

TABLE 4. *Modern Times cycle 2: The nominal phrase.*

$\begin{Bmatrix} le \\ li \\ la \end{Bmatrix}$ + N	$\begin{Bmatrix} \tilde{œ} \\ yn \end{Bmatrix}$ + N	Ø + N	beaucoup de + N	[de] + N	numeral + N
74	9	9	4	6	1

As in the retelling of the preceding cycle, most NPs are preceded by *le/la/li*. This confirms a trend signalled in a previous study (Véronique, 1985a) and already observed in the 'Modern Times' data from the first cycle. However, many more lexical items occur with contrasting determiners than in the previous task. Besides *un bateau* ~ *le bateau*, we find such other contrasting pairs as *le drap* ~ *des draps, un tableau* ~ *Ø [piti] tableau* ~ *beaucoup des tableaux*. It is obvious that in these cases, at least, the distinction between the sequences of determiners + Nouns is functionally motivated. The lexeme *jardin*, however, still associates only with *un*. Thus, Abdelmalek's IL in the domain of the use of NPs illustrates two diverging tendencies:

(a) generalisation of the plurifunctional marker *le/la/li* in this particular linguistic task. Other data confirm this tendency (Karmiloff-Smith, 1979);

(b) expression of referential values through the choice of the relevant determiners instead of pure dependence on the context.

Despite this development in the linguistic means for expressing referential values, the rules governing topic continuity still apply to the data analysed. Thus, in the following utterance, once reference to Charlie is established he is not mentioned for a while:

Charlie Chaplin [eveni] Ø [uvre] la porte
avec un tableau [imõt] Ø [tõbe] avec la tête
voilà il [prepar] les [mãʒe] + après Ø [uvr]
la porte et / et Ø [plõʒe] avec
(Charlie Chaplin came Ø opens the door with a board he climbs Ø falls with the head O.K. he prepares the food then Ø opens the door and land Ø plunge with)

Once there is a switch of reference as in the following example, then the relevant topic is mentioned:

avec le Charlie Chapline (Topic 1) [imarʃ] seul [imarʃ] avec la rue seul [jāna] des camions euh [jāna] des drapeaux pour [li] voiture voilà Ø [letrape] +++ [se] pas vrai ça comme le drap (Topic 2) [letōbe] le Chaplin (Topic 1) [iprā] le + [fo] le camion (Topic 3) voilà Ø
(with the Charlie Chaplin [Topic 1] he walks by himself he walks with the street alone there are lorries there are flags for the car O.K. Ø he takes +++ that's not true like the flag [Topic 2] it/he falls the Chaplin [Topic 1] he takes it + must the lorry [Topic 3] O.K. it falls)
(Reference through *voilà* and full NPs for each topic switch.)

Use of Pronouns: In retelling cycle 2, the most striking development occurs not in the sphere of personal pronouns, although he uses *tu* (*you*) which reminds one of *li*, for example, *voilà [eparti] avec petite fille déjà tu [vole]* (*so gone with small girl already you steal*), meaning *she steals*. Real progress is found in the realm of what French grammars usually call indefinite pronouns. *[Swila]* (*this one*), a deictic pronoun known to Abdelmalek quite early during the first cycle of data collection (Abdelmalek used *ça*, a 'would be' demonstrative pronoun in the first encounters), is used three times in contrast to *l'autre (the other one)* (8 tokens) and *quelqu'un (someone)* (2 tokens). Thus, besides the personal pronoun paradigm completed by a full use of *moi-je* which has been acquired during the first cycle of data collection (Véronique, 1983), Abdelmalek henceforth has recourse to a distal deictic pronoun *l'autre* and a proximal pronoun *[swila]*.

Although cases of zero anaphora can still be observed, it must be noticed that most cases of topic maintenance or topic switch are clearly marked at least by a clitic.

The contrastive discursive device *[se] pas X; moi X (it is not X; me X)* is again used in retelling cycle 2.

Avoidance of reference

In retelling cycle 1, *ilmadi/iladi* (*he told me/he told*) was used in two instances for introducing quoted speech. The same can be observed in retelling cycle 2. Through the use of this formulaic expression Abdelmalek is able to avert reference to such secondary characters as *the foreman* or *the director of the prison* by quoting speech attributed to them without explicitly naming them.

The signalling of episodes

As in retelling cycle 1, episodes seem to be mainly signalled through the use of *après* (*afterwards*). But this is also one of the functions of the polyfunctional *voilà* (*so, thus*). Besides, verbs of emergence do help to indicate change of episode. The rules which govern topic switch and topic maintenance in the vicinity of *après* (see Deulofeu, 1986) observed in retelling cycle 1 also hold for this narrative.

TABLE 5. *Modern Times cycle 2: Discourse markers.*

après	[jāna]	[se]	voilà	bon	alors
15	21	25	44	1	2

Discourse markers

The major change in narrative style is the massive use of *voilà*. Whereas in retelling cycle 1, there was a very clear-cut distinction between foreground and background markers, *voilà* is used on both dimensions. In the foreground, it is used in contrast with *après* (*afterwards*) for close-ups as it were, for example,

après [ireste] le prison [parte] il [mã3] avec: le / ↑ cuisine voilà [imã3e]

(then he stayed in prison went he eats with the kitchen here he ate)

In the background, it is mainly used in introducing quoted speech in conjunction with *[ilmadi]*. Besides, *voilà* has a phatic enunciative function in reported speech. The episode marking and the phatic functions of *voilà* are illustrated in the following example:

voilà [i/trap] la clé [uvr] la ↑ porte + +
voilà [vjē] la police voilà toi bien gentil
(so he snatches the key opens the door + + here comes the police so you are very nice)

Verbs and word order

Out of approximately 132 tokens of verbs, 121 are in an XV frame — however, some verbs have zero anaphora — and 11 in a VX frame. *Venir* (*to come*) accounts for seven cases, but not all tokens of *venir* are VX.

There are at least three cases of *venir* which are clearly XV. This change in word order seems to be linked to episode boundary.

'Modern Times' Cycle 3

The third retelling is approximately 780 words. As in retelling cycle 2, the informant chose to recount the excerpts he had watched *in toto*.

First and subsequent mention of characters

Use of NPs: NP structure is more complex in this retelling; in at least two cases this can be traced back to L1 influence, for example, *ton père de elle* (*your father of she*, meaning *her father*). *Le + N* is, however, predominantly used. *Un + N* is always used to refer to objects, never to refer to persons. This is constant throughout the three retellings. Still, the use of *un + N* for unknown items and of *le + N* to refer to them once they have been mentioned continues.

TABLE 6. *Modern Times cycle 3: The nominal phrase.*

$\left\{\begin{matrix}\text{le}\\ \text{li}\\ \text{la}\end{matrix}\right\}$ + N	$\left\{\begin{matrix}\text{œ}\\ \text{yn}\end{matrix}\right\}$ + N	Ø + N	beaucoup de + N	[de] + N	numeral + N	l'autre + N	poss. + N
75	6	3	Ø	6	2	1	1

One case of regression in the lexicon can be observed. In the first narrative, the two female characters are referred to as *le femme* and *le femme + 'wh'-phrase*. In retelling cycle 2, they are lexically contrasted as *la femme* and *la dame*. In narrative 3, Abdelmalek refers to *le elle* as the main female character and *l'autre* as the second one.

By the same token, it should be noted that Charlie Chaplin, the main character's proper name, is mentioned only nine times whereas in the preceding retellings, it totalled twenty tokens. This drastic reduction is tied to greater syntactisation.

Use of Pronouns: No case of zero anaphora is observed. This implies that the informant masters the TL's clitic system. If in the case of topic continuity there is a clitic trace in VP, the morphology of V proper is deviant. In retelling cycle 3, practically all tokens of V are preceded by an overgeneralised element *m* which probably comes from TL *me* (*me, myself*) in reflexive verbs.

In this retelling, *l'autre* and *quelqu'un* are used as in narrative 2. Here is one case of contrast marked by pronominal switch *quelqu'un* ~ *lui*:

il [maparti] la prison + + [jāna] quelqu'un
il [mafe] des drogues par exemple . . . il [mareste] [mōnʒi] + lui il
[pās] de sel . . .
(he goes myself the prison + + there is someone he has taken myself drugs for example . . . he stays myself eat him he thinks of salt)

It should be noted that even in the third cycle cases of avoidance of pronominal reference through the use of [se] can be observed, for example:

[ilmadi] voilà bon [se] gentil
(he told me so well it is nice)

Avoidance of reference

Cases of non-mention of secondary figures through the use of formulaic expressions [*ilmadi*] can be observed as in the previous narrative.

Discourse markers

As the informant masters more of the TL, the organisation of his narratives tends to become more intricate with the use of plurifunctional items such as *voilà* or, in this version, *bon*. This new essentially phatic element takes over some of the functions of *voilà*, that is, it serves to mark episode boundaries, it appears in collocation with [*madi*] and has a conclusive value. However, *bon* is never used to introduce a character as was the case with *voilà*. At times, both markers co-occur.

TABLE 7. *Modern Times cycle 3: Discourse markers.*

après	[jāna]	[se]	voilà	bon	alors
6	4	19	13	28	Ø

Verbs and word order

As in the two previous retellings, the dominant word order is XV. Approximately 139 tokens have been counted; 13 tokens of VX provided mainly by verbs of motion such as *venir* (*to come*) (four cases out of six), *arriver* (*to arrive*), *sortir* (*to depart etc.*) and so forth, verbs of grasp such as [*trape*] (*to seize, to grasp*) and of saying such as [*mɑdi*], have been counted.

Summary

The following features of reference and of discourse organisation have remained constant across the three retellings despite the time factor and the structural reorganisation of Abdelmalek's IL:

(a) the overwhelming predominance of *le* + *N* for referential lexical expressions when referring to persons, whether already mentioned or not;
(b) the use of [*se*] to identify characters and the [*se*] *pas moi . . .* discursive device ([*se*] bearing more frequently a negative modality);
(c) the use of [*jāna*] to express possession and existence, and to introduce spatial and temporal reference;
(d) the non-signalling of given episodes or given characters through the use of quoted speech and of [*iladi/ilmadi*];
(e) the use of *après* as episode boundary marker.

The three most remarkable changes across the three versions of 'Modern Times' are:

(a) a gradual disappearance of zero anaphora as pronominal marking on VP becomes more constant;
(b) an extension of the non-personal pronominal paradigm with the use of proximal [*swila*], distal *l'autre*, and definite *quelqu'un*;
(c) a change in the organisation of the narrative from monofunctional markers such as [*jāna*] and *après* to more plurifunctional items such as *voilà* and *bon*.

Discussion

I would finally like to

(a) discuss the possible influence of L1 by taking a quick glance at the L1 'Modern Times' version;[7]
(b) compare the findings of this article with other findings about Abdelmalek's IL;

(c) comment upon similarities with the findings of Klein & Perdue (1985);

(d) speculate about possible explanations for the modifications in discourse structure that have been observed especially *vis-à-vis* referential activity.

L1 influence: If I apply the same grid of analysis to the Arabic data obtained from Abdelmalek, the following features can be observed:

1. For the main characters, Charlie Chaplin is always referred to as *he*, whereas a lexical opposition *lbent* (*the girl*) ~ *lamra* (*the woman*) makes it possible to distinguish characters.
2. Among secondary characters, the father is mentioned through lexical item, whereas the director of the prison is not and the foreman is designated by *laxor* (*the other one*).
3. Obviously, the full system of L1 determiners is used to mark given and new items, the use of *demonstrative article + N* must particularly be stressed.
4. Objects that are always indefinite in the IL version are definite in the Arabic version if needs be; this is the case of the borrowed item [*eʒʒardē*] (*the garden*).
5. Avoidance of naming in the case of the prison director is especially practised through *gālu* (he said).
6. The main discourse markers used are *ʔu* (*and*) and *maelli* (*when*).
7. Obviously, all the verbs occurring in the Arabic version of 'Modern Times' are VX, except for two unclear cases.

From this quick glance through the L1 data it is quite clear, however, that the influence of L1 in the shaping of the retelling cannot really be evoked. The only possible influence could be the use of formulaic [*ilmadi*] which plays the same role as *gālu*.

Abdelmalek's IL: When the findings of this study are compared to other studies on Abdelmalek's IL (see Giacomi, 1986; Giacomi & Vion, 1986) a remarkable measure of convergence can be observed. In the first retelling of 'Modern Times', Abdelmalek uses [*jāna*], *se* and *après* in exactly the same way as in the early narratives of the first cycle of data collection (for instance narrative 1.1 in the Giacomi corpus). The overwhelming use of *voilà* in the second retelling of 'Modern Times' is precisely comparable to what Giacomi and Vion observe in narrative 2.1.

Comparison with Klein & Perdue (1985): Many of the findings of that paper apply to the data from Abdelmalek. Thus, the rules for

TABLE 8. *Discourse markers in other linguistic tasks (from Giacomi & Vion, 1986).*

interview	11	21	17	14
linguistic task	narrative	narrative	role play	conversation
'voilà'	0	158	7	2
'il [madi]'	0	69	4	14
'moi je [di]'	0	33	0	1

maintenance and shift of reference described by these authors are on a par with what was found in Abdelmalek's retellings. The difference in coping with the agent/topic slot and with the object slot was also observed. The use of [se] for identificational purpose was also noted in Abdelmalek's data.

One major point of difference lies in the sensitivity of episode boundaries in Abdelmalek's data as compared to the rules applying to data from Ramòn. The marking of episodes by Abdelmalek results from various factors including the use of *après*, *bon* or *voilà*, and word order. However, no other constraints seem to apply besides the rule that at an episode boundary the unmarked case is reference to the main character, Charlie, and that in other cases lexical specification is expected. Subordination, for instance, does not seem to exert any particular influence on maintenance or switch of reference.

Causal factors: L1 influence cannot by itself explain the structuring of the three narratives analysed. Still it could, however, explain the extensive use of [*ilmadi*]. Besides task dependent factors such as acquaintance with the investigator and mainly the requirements imposed on the informant's discourse, two other factors can be thought of. Certain features of Abdelmalek's IL could be explained by typological trends. Such seems to be the case of the VX order with elementary verbs ([*jāna/ se*]), verbs of motion, of emergence and of grasp. However, in this particular case L1 verbs of this category follow the same pattern.

Besides typology, another major factor is the dynamics of language acquisition itself. It seems quite clear that a full-fledged pronominal system affects reference maintenance and reference shift by preventing ambiguity. It is also clear that the acquisition of a marker that takes over part of the functions fulfilled by another form, affects the whole fabric of discourse.

Conclusion

I started off with the aim of testing how far the acquisition of reference to person, but also to time and space, was discourse dependent, and conversely how far referential activities contributed to the shaping of discourse. It seems to me that the relationship between discourse structure and the mention of characters and objects has been established. However, it has also been established that other means such as the use of specific discourse markers or of word order contribute to the marking of discourse. One striking feature on that count is the evolution from the use of rather monofunctional markers such as *après* to more polyfunctional items such as *bon* and *voilà*. It is as if mastery of TL morphology led to greater freedom in the choice of words which relate events and actions.

Notes to Chapter 10

1. I wish to thank Abdelmalek for his cooperation and Diego Ruiz for his help at various stages of this article. The data have been collected by Et-Tayeb Houdaïfa and Daniel Véronique, transcribed by Tayeb Houdaïfa and checked by Daniel Véronique. I extend my thanks to Houdaïfa. All errors are, of course, of my responsibility.
2. The cycle 1 experiment took place on 02.04.83, the cycle 2 experiment was on 29.02.84 and the last experiment was performed on 20.04.85.
3. I would like to thank José Deulofeu and Tayeb Houdaïfa for the stimulating discussion of the retellings of Abdelmalek. Some of their ideas are represented in this section.
4. For technical reasons, the informant had to be interrupted in his retelling (version 1). When the interview resumed, the informant spontaneously started anew from the beginning of his retelling (version 2). Counts have been made only on version 2 but data from both texts are used for linguistic analysis.
5. For the sake of simplicity, the data has been transcribed with minimal phonetic sophistication.
6. A word of caution is in order here. Obviously, it is not clear in Abdelmalek's IL whether all predicates are verbs, whether he uses a real pronominal system, and whether the NPs he uses have the same form as those found in TL (let alone the same range of referential values). All those labels are used here for the sake of convenience.
7. Transcribed and glossed by Et-Tayeb Houdaïfa.

References

BICKERTON, D., 1981, *Roots of Language*. Ann Arbor, MI: Karoma Press.

COUPIER, C., 1983, *Acquisition de la Référence Personnelle en Français par une*

Jeune Femme Marocaine. DEA thesis, Aix-en-Provence: Université de Provence.

DEULOFEU, J., 1980, Organisation discursive et constructions grammaticales dans les énoncés de français parlé en relation avec le problème de la variation en syntaxe. Communication au 15ème Congrès International de Philologie et de Linguistique Romanes, Palma de Majorque.

—— 1983, Premières remarques sur la constitution de la grammaire dans l'interlangue d'un informateur. *Acquisition du Français par des Travailleurs Marocains. Papiers de Travail 1,* 64–79.

—— 1986, Sur quelques procédés de hierarchisation de l'information dans les récits d'apprenants marocains en milieu naturel: Pour une conception souple des rapports entre phénomènes de micro- et de macro-thématisation. In A. Giacomi, & D. Véronique (eds), *Acquisition d'une Langue Étrangère: Perspectives et Recherches.* Aix-en-Provence: Publications Université de Provence, 263–284.

DITTMAR, N., 1984, Semantic features of pidginized learner varieties of German. In R. W. ANDERSEN (ed.), *Second Languages: A Cross-linguistic Perspective.* Rowley, MA: Newbury House, 243–270.

GIACOMI, A., 1986, Processus de structuration de l'énoncé en acquisition et interactions. In A. GIACOMI & D. VÉRONIQUE (eds), *Acquisition d'une Langue Étrangère: Perspectives et Recherches.* Aix-en-Provence: Publications de l'Université de Provence, 287–303.

GIACOMI, A. & VION, R., 1986, Metadiscursive processes in the acquisition of a second language. *Studies in Second Language Acquisition 8,* 355–368.

GIVÒN, T., 1979, *On Understanding Grammar.* New York, NY: Academic Press.

—— 1983, Topic continuity in discourse: The functional domain of switch reference. In J. HAIMAN & P. MUNRO (eds), *Switch Reference: Typological Studies in Language.* Amsterdam: John Benjamins.

—— 1984, *Syntax: A Functional-typological Introduction.* Amsterdam: John Benjamins.

HALLIDAY, M.A.K. & HASAN, R., 1976, *Cohesion in English.* London: Longman.

HOUDAÏFA, T., 1983a, L'organisation de la référence temporelle dans une interlangue. *Acquisition du Français par des Travailleurs Marocains. Papiers de Travail 1,* 95–114.

—— 1983b, La référence temporelle et personnelle dans le récit d'un apprenant en milieu naturel. *Acquisition du Français par des Travailleurs Marocains. Papiers de Travail 1,* 141–154.

—— 1986, Quelques aspects de la grammaire des verbes et, en particulier, des verbes de mouvement dans l'interlangue d'un migrant. In A. GIACOMI & D. VÉRONIQUE (eds), *Acquisition d'une Langue Étrangère: Perspectives et Recherches.* Aix-en-Provence: Publications de l'Université de Provence, 447–473.

HOUDAÏFA, T. & VÉRONIQUE, D., 1984, La référence spatiale dans le français parlé par des marocains à Marseille. In G. EXTRA & M. MITTNER (eds), *Studies in Second Language Acquisition by Adult Immigrants.* Tilburg: Tilburg University, 211–261.

KARMILOFF-SMITH, A., 1979, *A Functional Approach to Child Language. A Study of Determiners and Reference.* Cambridge: Cambridge University Press.

KLEIN, W. & PERDUE, C., 1985, The learner's problem of arranging words. Nijmegen: ESF Working Paper.

—— 1986, Comment résoudre une tâche verbale complexe avec peu de moyens linguistiques? In A. GIACOMI & D. VÉRONIQUE (eds), *Acquisitions d'une Langue Étrangère: Perspectives et Recherches*. Aix-en-Provence: Publications de l'Université de Provence, 305–330.

LABOV, W., 1972, *Language in the Inner City: Study in Black English Vernacular*. Philadelphia: University of Pennsylvania Press.

LYONS, J., 1977, *Semantics* (Vols. 1–2). Cambridge: Cambridge University Press.

PERDUE, C. (ed.), 1982, *Second Language Acquisition by Adult Immigrants: A Field Manual*. Strasbourg: European Science Foundation.

SCHUMANN, J. H., 1983, Utterance structure in Basilang speech. In G. G. GILBERT (ed.), *Pidgin and Creole languages: Essays in Memory of John E. Reinecke*. Ann Arbor, MI: Karoma.

TALMY, L., 1983, How language structures space. In H. PICK & L. ACREDOLO (eds), *Spatial Orientation: Theory, Research and Application*. New York: Plenum Press, 225–282.

TRÉVISE, A., 1986, Topicalisation, is it transferable? In E. KELLERMAN & M. SHARWOOD SMITH (eds), *Crosslinguistic Influence in Second Language Acquisition*. London: Pergamon Press, 186–206.

VÉRONIQUE, D., 1983, Observations préliminaires sur *li* dans l'interlangue d'Abdelmalek. *Acquisition du Français par des Travailleurs Marocains. Papiers de Travail 1*, 155–180.

—— 1984, Apprentissage naturel et apprentissage guidé. *Le Français dans le Monde 185*, 45–52.

—— 1985a, De quelques aspects de l'apprentissage de la référence nominale en français. *Acquisition du Français par des Travailleurs Marocains. Papiers de Travail 2*, 97–133.

—— 1985b, Acquisition de la référence spatiale en français par des adultes marocains: observations à partir d'une enquête longitudinale. *Acquisition du Français par des Travailleurs Marocains. Papiers de Travail, 2*, 135–167.

Part 4
Cross-linguistic Interaction in Second Language Acquisition

11 Effects of Transfer in Foreign Language Learning

HÅKAN RINGBOM

Today it is generally acknowledged that language transfer is an important subject of study which plays a subtle and pervasive part in L2-learning. Transfer can, rather generally, be described as the ways in which knowledge of the mother tongue (and other languages) influences the learning of another language. It presupposes some cross-linguistic similarity that the L2-learner has perceived. When the L2-learner tries to facilitate his learning task by making use of whatever prior knowledge he or she has, he or she will also rely on the knowledge that originates in his or her L1, provided that he or she can perceive this L1-knowledge of some other language as a workable reference frame.

If we, then, accept that transfer exists, we have to investigate *how* and *when* and *why* learners transfer *what*, and *how much*. We should also remember that hypotheses about the L2 can be formed not only on the basis of L1-knowledge or L2-knowledge separately, but also as a result of *interaction* between L1- and L2-knowledge.

A distinction often made, particularly in transfer studies some 10 to 15 years ago, was that between positive and negative transfer. Positive transfer means that the L1 has a facilitating effect on language learning whereas negative transfer, or interference, causes the learner to make errors. In recent years, however, many scholars (e.g. Gass & Selinker, 1983; Faerch & Kasper, in press; Sajavaara & Lehtonen, 1988) have disapproved of this distinction. They do so primarily because the two distinct types of transfer apply only at the product level, whereas the distinction is not seen as relevant to what these scholars are primarily concerned with in their research, that is, the underlying processes in the learner.

However, it does not seem to be necessary to do away with the distinction altogether, as long as we can make it quite clear that we are here indeed discussing on another plane, the product level, not the process level. For practical *and* theoretical purposes, the question whether and to what extent the mother tongue has a facilitating or an inhibiting effect on L2-learning is by no means a trivial one. So far, the discussion of transfer has been much coloured by the fact that it has almost without exception occurred in the context of error analysis and what can be seen as tangible evidence of transfer has almost invariably been negative transfer. It is a relatively straightforward task to compare differences of the learner's end product, his interlanguage, with the L2-norm and on the basis of these differences conclude that transfer is very nearly synonymous with negative transfer. It is much more complicated to specify where or how the learner's L1 has facilitated his L2-comprehension or -production. There are very few investigations analysing how the learner can profitably make use of his automatised L1-knowledge by extending it, and perhaps modifying it in the process, to L2-learning (see, however, Faerch, Haastrup, & Phillipson, 1984).

Only in vocabulary learning has the facilitating effect of cognates been studied in any detail (cf. e.g. Hammer, 1978), but we still lack comparative studies which would also consider other linguistic areas than lexis, with the aim of placing cognates in a more general perspective of language transfer. To study transfer we should, with Ard and Homburg in the recent comprehensive anthology by Gass and Selinker on Language Transfer (1983), emphasise the importance of comparing data from speakers of different language groups. Ard and Homburg compare Spanish-speaking and Arabic-speaking subjects who took the Michigan Test of English Language Proficiency. The problem with studying such different immigrant groups in order to learn something about transfer is, however, that it is impossible to say to what extent the differences between the Spanish and the Arabic speakers might be due to inevitable cultural and educational differences of a general nature rather than to the linguistic differences between the groups.

One country where the situation is uniquely favourable for investigation of transfer is Finland. Finland is a bilingual country with two official languages, Finnish and Swedish. Finnish is spoken by 93% of the population, whereas Swedish is spoken by a little over 6%. The Swedish-speaking population is concentrated to the coastal areas in the south and west of the country. The great majority of the Swedish-speaking Finns regard themselves not as Swedes living in Finland, but primarily as Finns, merely with a mother tongue different from that of the majority of the population. For more than

40 years there has been no language conflict between these groups, which do not differ much from each other as far as culture and education are concerned. Thus, although there are great differences between the Finnish and the Swedish languages, it is possible to regard Finland as a bilingual, but almost unicultural country, or at least as unicultural as it is possible to find anywhere in the bilingual countries in the world.

If we start to study how these two language groups learn a third language, English, we can expect to find some interesting differences which can be referred back to the totally different mother tongues of the two groups, whereas the cultural and educational differences are negligible. Since Swedish is closely related to English, but Finnish is totally unrelated to the Germanic languages, these differences can be seen as typifying the differences between learning an L2 related to L1 and an L2 unrelated to the mother tongue.

To a non-Scandinavian audience, however, it needs to be especially emphasised that the context of learning English in Finland is very much that of a foreign language learning situation, where the teacher and the classroom are very important, whereas there is little chance for the students to practise their English by talking to native English speakers. Most American studies, on the other hand, deal with immigrants or students learning English in a natural setting where they are surrounded by the target language. The role of transfer is hardly the same in these two learning situations. Though not much is known with certainty about the different extent of L1-influence on these two different situations, it is nevertheless most plausible that there is more transfer in classroom learning situations than in the situations of unguided second language acquisition (cf. Meisel, 1983; Tarone, 1979).

Since Swedish and English are closely related, a large number of Swedish words are similar, near-identical or even identical to English words in form, and with meanings that are often close to English words, though by no means always identical. Finnish, on the other hand, belongs not to the Indo-European but to the Finno-Ugrian family of languages. It is an agglutinative language, which makes especially great use of endings to indicate linguistic functions. Some linguistic categories which are basic to the Germanic languages, above all articles and prepositions, are not found in Finnish.

The word stress in Finnish is always on the first syllable, without exception. In lexis, too, resemblances to the Germanic languages are extremely few and insignificant, since Finnish has traditionally taken a very restrictive attitude to loanwords.

A research project has been going on for some years at the Department of English at the Swedish university of Åbo Akademi in Finland. In general terms, its starting hypothesis is that Swedish-speaking Finns, or Swedes, as I shall call them in the following, would do better in any test of English than an equivalent group of Finns. It can be expected that the advantage of the Swedes who learn a related language, compared with the Finns who learn an unrelated language, will appear at all levels and stages of learning. With one minor exception, that of English spelling, this hypothesis has also been borne out in all experiments.

Analysis of the results, however, shows that the differences between Finns and Swedes make themselves felt differently in different types of tests. In this article I can deal with only some of these analyses, and for more detailed studies I refer to the papers on the project listed in a separate bibliography (cf. pp. 218), and, especially, to my book on the role of the L1 in foreign language learning (Ringbom, 1987).

Table 1 shows the mean figures for the listening and reading comprehension tests of a multiple choice type in the National Matriculation Examination, where English is a compulsory subject.

Table 1 reveals that the candidates from the Swedish schools in Finland attain consistently higher marks than the candidates from the Finnish schools,

TABLE 1. *Results in the National Matriculation Examination in English in Finland (mean scores of candidates)*

	Listening Comprehension (max. 30 p.)		Reading Comprehension (max. 30 p.)	
Year	Finnish school	Swedish school	Finnish school	Swedish school
1974	19.7	22.4	24.1	25.7
1975	21.6	24.8	22.8	24.7
1976	18.5	22.4	18.6	22.0
1977	18.5	23.2	23.4	25.3
1978	22.1	25.2	22.9	25.2
1979	23.3	26.4	19.4	21.6
1980	20.9	25.0	18.4	19.9
1981	22.5	25.4	22.1	25.0
1982	21.2	24.6	23.6	26.4
1983	22.8	26.1	23.3	25.4
1984	25.6	28.3	22.3	24.4
1985	19.6	23.0	20.5	23.4

Number of candidates:
Approximately 12 × 25,000 Fi. = 300,000
12 × 1,500 Sw. = 18,000

and further shows that each year the difference is greater for the listening comprehension exam (except for 1981, when the difference is the same for both listening comprehension and reading comprehension).

Tests of partial dictation given to Finnish and Swedish groups of learners show the same trend. Listening comprehension appears to be a skill where Finns, compared with Swedes, have especially great problems, even though some tests of vocabulary knowledge, grammar or translation given to the same populations have revealed relatively insignificant differences.

A test given to the applicants for university entrance showed that there was practically no difference between the Finns and the Swedes in an English sound recognition test, whereas a partial dictation test, where the candidates had to provide a coherent version of a text, gave significantly better results for the Swedes. The time pressure present in any situation involving comprehension of a coherent text was obviously relevant, and a detailed analysis of the individual words in the dictation showed that the greatest differences between the Finns and the Swedes in error frequency occurred not in low-frequency words, but in words like *to, in, had, of, the,* and *him* occurring in contexts next to 'difficult' words or phrases that posed problems to both groups. To give an example, in the given context 'it would be made up to him in other ways' 88.5% of the Swedes but only 35% of the Finns included the preposition *to* in their renderings.

The only aspect of the English language where Finns regularly do at least as well as, and usually better than Swedes, is spelling. Finnish learners of English make relatively few spelling errors, if we here exclude their marked problems of distinguishing between voiced and unvoiced stops which, in fact, is an indication of perception difficulties, not of spelling difficulties. The Finns' good spelling ability may also be thought to indicate the other side of the coin, as it were, of their problems in coping with the time pressure of a listening situation. As foreign language learners in a Finnish context they normally meet with written forms of English words more often than the spoken forms, and even at a fairly advanced stage of learning, some learners may have stored the words in their graphemic, not phonological form. Thus some Finnish learners may store the word /p ə :s/ in the form /p ʊ rse/, since that is how an equivalent Finnish word would have been stored if it existed. At the earliest stages of a foreign language learning situation this is not an unnatural thing to do, but Finns may well go on with this way of storing words longer than the Swedes do, partly because of the close relation between spelling and pronunciation that exists in the Finnish language.

If such a method of storing gives Finnish learners a good ability to spell words, it is a highly uneconomical process in a listening situation. The Finnish learner is then landed with the extra task of drawing an equivalence between the actual heard form and the written form stored in the mind. Under the time pressure of a listening situation it will often take too long to activate the word, and this frequently results in faulty comprehension or staccato speech with awkward pauses.

As far as production of lexical terms is concerned, cross-linguistic similarity without identity may, of course, often lead to errors, but as far as comprehension is concerned, it does not normally take very long to acquire a vague or partial understanding of simple texts written in a language closely related to one's L1. An important characteristic of receptive skills is, in fact, that the communication aspects are in focus: the listener/reader normally concentrates on understanding the message without paying much attention to its structural details. Syntax is less important for comprehension than production (cf. Ulijn & Kempen, 1976: 495) and acceptability and grammaticality are concepts of much less importance to the listening/reading process than to speaking or writing. Thus, a vague knowledge of L2-lexis, which is primarily the result of inferencing on the basis of a related L1 (cf. Haastrup, 1984), may take the Swedish learner of English quite far. After having mastered a rudimentary knowledge of English grammar, he can combine this knowledge with relevant L1-knowledge to get a workable basis for figuring out the approximate general meaning of an English text. For production, this works to a much more limited extent: the learner will here need a much more extensive and a much more accurate skill in order to produce a language creatively. But even for productive skills, the fact that the learner of a related L2 has been able to attain a receptive knowledge in quite a short time puts him in an advantageous position, compared with the learner of an unrelated language. This is because we can assume that there is considerable interaction between receptive and productive skills in the learning process, and if the learner can anchor his learning in some kind of previous L2-knowledge, rather than having to start from scratch, his learning, especially of lexis, will be much facilitated.

However, even to attain an elementary receptive skill, the learner must have an idea of how the basic linguistic categories in the target language function. This is not necessarily the result of L2-teaching, or even of conscious L2-learning; in the learning of a closely related L2, the learner's L1 has already provided him with a considerable part of this essential knowledge automatised in his mind. If we compare Finnish learners of English with Swedish learners, the categories of articles and prepositions are of special interest, since Swedish basically uses the same system with these word classes as English, whereas these grammatical categories do not exist in Finnish. In Finnish, case-endings and, for articles, word order may express the functions expressed by articles and prepositions in Germanic languages, but simple one-to-one equivalences are here much harder to establish between Finnish and English than between Swedish and English.

Although the English articles and prepositions cause difficulties to all learners of English, as far as the productive skills go, the Finnish beginning learner faces especially great problems even for comprehension, since he cannot directly relate prepositions and articles to the linguistic reality he is familiar with. He has to learn the very principles of how these categories function, something the Swedish learner had automatised before he even started to learn English.

Earlier work on error analysis has, as expected, revealed that the use of articles is an especially problematic area for both Finns and other groups of learners whose L1 does not have the article system (Duškova, 1969, for Czech learners; Oller & Redding, 1971; and for Finnish learners, Herranen, 1978; Sajavaara, 1981, 1983; Granfors & Palmberg, 1976; Ringbom, 1978a; cf. also Kellerman, 1984). The research on Finnish learners shows that most of their errors, especially at early and intermediate stages of learning, consist of omitting the articles, above all the definite article, where they should have been included. At early stages of learning, and even after that, a Finnish learner may unconsciously perceive articles and prepositions as redundant (cf. George, 1972), in the same way as a native American or Swede starting to learn Finnish often perceives most of the fifteen Finnish case endings of the noun as redundant and frequently omits them.

If omission of these categories of high-frequency words are especially characteristic of Finnish learners of English, a frequency count may also be expected to reveal this. We can also expect clear differences between advanced and less advanced Finnish learners and between native and non-native speakers. The results of such a count of high-frequency words in learner language is reported in Ringbom (1985c). The corpus analysed consisted of 300 English essays written in the National Matriculation Examination. One hundred and fifty of these were from Finnish-language schools and 150 from Swedish-language schools. On the basis of their marks awarded by the examiners, these essays were divided into three categories: good, intermediate, and poor. The frequencies of these six groups of non-native essays were compared with three groups of native speakers. The first was the Brown Corpus, Section A, Press Reportage, as reported in Zettersten's word-frequency list (1978). The second group which from a maturational point of view is most comparable to the learners in Finland consisted of 50 American first-year undergraduates at Purdue University, Indiana, and the third of 50 essays written by 15-year-old pupils at Hookergate Comprehensive School in Rowlands Gill, Northern England.

The main hypothesis to be tested was that compared with the other groups the poor Finnish essays and to some extent also the intermediate Finnish essays would show lower frequencies of English articles and of those prepositions for which simple one-to-one correspondences to Finnish are particularly difficult to establish, especially *of*, *on*, and *by*. The frequencies of such common English prepositions where one-to-one correspondences can be found to work in the great majority of cases, that is *in* and *with*, were expected to show very little variation in all nine groups. The good Swedish essays were, on the other hand, expected to show all-round frequencies very similar to those of the American students.

It will not be possible for me to comment on the details of this frequency count, but its main points have been brought into the staple diagram (Figure 1). This staple diagram shows that the hypotheses have been verified. The figure showing the frequencies of the poor Finns is considerably different from the other figures, whereas the figure for the good Finns resembles that of both the good Swedes and the American students quite closely. The diagram also reveals some other interesting points. Thus, for instance, the low frequencies of *of* and *by* in the poor Finns, the poor Swedes and the English school-children no doubt indicate a very infrequent use of passives and the *of*-genitive. But the main result of this word frequency study supplements earlier error analyses in that it shows that less advanced learners tend to avoid using such linguistic features as are absent in the L1, and therefore easily perceived as redundant or perhaps merely 'difficult'.

It is obvious that the L1 of the learners is a most important variable accounting for the difference between high-frequency words in the less advanced learners. It is also obvious that this variable interacts with other variables, for instance with what might be called linguistic sophistication, since there are also considerable frequency variations between the three native-speaker groups.

Can the low frequency of articles and prepositions in the less advanced Finnish learners then be taken as an example of transfer? As I see it, the answer must be *no* here, since nothing has been directly transferred from the L1 and according to my definition transfer is based on perceived similarity. It is rather the result of *lack of transfer*, or perhaps preferably covert cross-linguistic influence, because what lies behind the Finnish avoidance of articles and prepositions is, in fact, the absence of a reference frame in the L1. At early stages of learning, in particular, transfer occurs

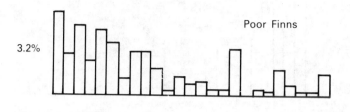

Poor Finns

3.2%

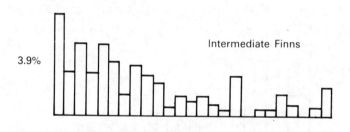

Intermediate Finns

3.9%

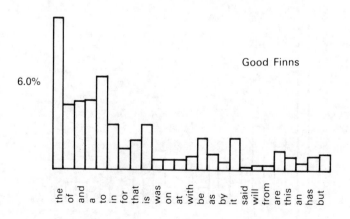

Good Finns

6.0%

the of and a to in for that is was on at with be as by it said will from are this an has but

FIGURE 1 *Word frequency study*

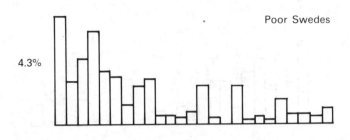

Poor Swedes

4.3%

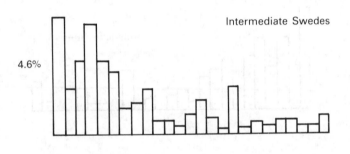

Intermediate Swedes

4.6%

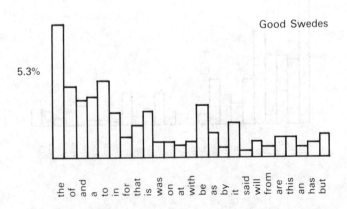

Good Swedes

5.3%

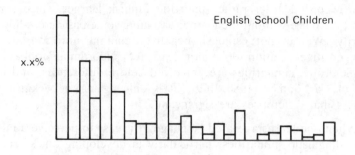

English School Children

x.x%

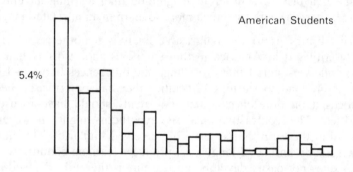

American Students

5.4%

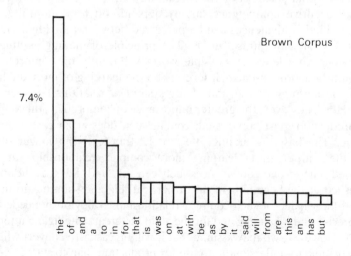

Brown Corpus

7.4%

the of and a to in for that is was on at with be as by it said will from are this an has but

☐ = 1.0%

in the Swedish learner rather than the Finnish learner, since transfer cannot take place without the learner assuming some basic cross-linguistic similarity. We do not establish negative relations until we are sure that a positive relation does not exist (cf. Noordman-Vonk, 1979). Psychologically, similarities are perceived before differences, and in the words of Carl James (1980: 169), 'it is only against a background of sameness that differences are significant'.

When one learns a related language, it is easy to perceive a number of cross-linguistic similarities, particularly in developing one's receptive knowledge. In all learning, the learner tries to simplify his task by making as much use of previous knowledge as possible, and a related L1 is here of primary importance. As Corder (1979) puts it, to learn a related language is a task of a different magnitude than learning an unrelated language: there is simply so much more to learn in an unrelated language.

This brings us to the contrastive analysis hypothesis, which was severely criticised in America in the late 1960s and 1970s. When Lado and his followers stated that cross-linguistic differences between L1 and L2 inevitably lead to learning difficulties they can be criticised because they focused on differences when they really should have focused on similarities. The contrastive analysis hypothesis might, however, be reinstated in the form that absence of perceived similarities, for instance between totally unrelated languages, produces learning conditions where transfer does not easily develop and learning is therefore delayed at the important initial stages. For the beginning learner the ease of achieving a basic receptive competence largely depends on how naturally rough and simplified equivalences can be perceived between individual morphological, lexical, and phrasal items. The principle of making as much use of previous knowledge as possible works differently on comprehension than on production and also differently on the learning of individual items versus the learning of the underlying system of relations between these items. Here, however, the greater importance of comprehension compared with production must be stressed, coming as it does at an earlier stage of learning. The basic facilitating effect of L1-transfer is no longer obvious when the learner starts learning more complex relationships than the simplified one-to-one-equivalences between L1 and L2 that he or she established at the beginning of his or her learning and soon has to modify. A good knowledge of such complex relationships is obviously needed both for a precise understanding and for the ability to create intelligible utterances oneself. However, we may assume that it will be easier to convert what one is already able to understand into use for production than to start to acquire the rules of production from scratch.

References

ARD, J. & HOMBURG, T., 1983, Verification of language transfer. In S. GASS & L. SELINKER (eds), *Language Transfer in Language Learning*. Rowley, MA: Newbury House, 157–176.

CORDER, S. P., 1979, Language distance and the magnitude of the language learning task. *Studies in Second Language Acquisition 2* (1), 27–36.

DUŠKOVA, L., 1969, On sources of errors in foreign language learning. *IRAL 7* (1), 11–36.

FAERCH, C., HAASTRUP, K. & PHILLIPSON, R., 1984, *Learner Language and Language Learning*. Clevedon: Multilingual Matters.

FAERCH, C. & KASPER, G. (in press). Perspectives on language transfer. *Applied Linguistics*.

GASS, S. & SELINKER, L. (eds), 1983, *Introduction to Language Transfer in Language Learning*. Rowley, MA: Newbury House.

GEORGE, H.V., 1972, *Common Errors in Language Learning: Insights from English*. Rowley, MA: Newbury House.

GRANFORS, T. & PALMBERG, R., 1976, Errors made by Finns and Swedish-speaking Finns learning English at a commercial college level. In H. RINGBOM & R. PALMBERG (eds), *Errors Made by Finns and Swedish-speaking Finns in the Learning of English*. AFTIL 5. Åbo: Åbo Akademi.

HAASTRUP, K., 1984, *Lexical Inferencing*. Paper read at the Seventh AILA Congress, Brussels.

HAMMER, P., 1978, *The Utility of Cognates in Second Language Acquisition*. Paper read at the Fifth AILA Congress, Montreal.

HERRANEN, T., 1978, Errors made by Finnish university students in the use of the English article system. In K. SAJAVAARA, J. LEHTONEN & R. MARKKANEN (eds), *Jyväskylä Contrastive Studies 6. Further Contrastive Papers*. Jyväskylä: University of Jyväskylä, 74–95.

JAMES, C., 1980, *Contrastive Analysis*. London: Longman.

KELLERMAN, E., 1984, The empirical evidence for the influence of the L1 in interlanguage. In A. DAVIES, C. CRIPER & A.P.R. HOWATT (eds), *Interlanguage*. Edinburgh: Edinburgh University Press, 98–122.

MEISEL, J.M., 1983, Transfer as a second-language strategy. *Language and Communication 3*(1), 11–46.

NOORDMAN-VONK, W., 1979, *Retrieval from Semantic Memory*. Berlin: Springer.

OLLER, J.W. JR. & REDDING, E., 1971, Article usage and other language skills. *Language Learning 21* (1), 85–95.

RINGBOM, H., 1978a, What differences are there between Finns and Swedish-speaking Finns learning English? *Papers and Studies in Contrastive Linguistics 7*, 133–145.

—— 1985a, Transfer in relation to some other variables in L2-learning. In H. RINGBOM (ed.), *Foreign Language Learning and Bilingualism. Publications of the Research Institute of the Åbo Akademi Foundation, 105*, 9–21. Åbo: Åbo Akademi.

—— 1987, *The Role of the First Language in Foreign Language Learning*. Clevedon: Multilingual Matters.

SAJAVAARA, K., 1981, *The Nature of First Language Transfer: English as L2 in a Foreign Language Setting*. Paper presented at the First European–North American Workshop on Cross-Linguistic Second Language Acquisition Research, Lake Arrowhead, CA.

—— 1983, The article errors of Finnish learners of English. In C.C. ELERT &

A. Seppänen (eds), *Finnish–English Language Contact: Papers from a Workshop. Umeå Papers in English 4.* Umeå: University of Umeå, 72–87.

Sajavaara, K. & Lehtonen, J., 1988, Aspects of transfer in foreign language learners' reaction to acceptability. In H.W. Dechert & M. Raupach (eds), *Transfer in Language Production.* Norwood, NJ: Ablex.

Tarone, E., 1979, Interlanguage as chameleon. *Language Learning 29*, 181–191.

Ulijn, J.M. & Kempen, G.A.M., 1976, The role of the first language in second language reading comprehension: some experimental evidence. In G. Nickel (ed.), *Proceedings of the Fourth International Congress of Applied Linguistics: Vol. 1.* Stuttgart: Hochschulverlag, 495–507.

Zettersten, A., 1978, *A Word-frequency List based on American English Press Reportage.* Copenhagen: Akademisk Förlag.

The Åbo Akademi Project: Separate Bibliography

Ringbom, H., 1978b, The influence of the mother tongue on the translation of lexical items. *Interlanguage Studies Bulletin – Utrecht 3* (1), 80–101.

—— 1982, The influence of other languages on the vocabulary of foreign language learners. In G. Nickel & D. Mehls (eds), *Error Analysis, Contrastive Linguistics and Second Language Learning. Papers from the Sixth Congress of Applied Linguistics, Lund 1981* [Special Issue]. *Iral 85–96.*

—— 1983a, Borrowing and lexical transfer. *Applied Linguistics 4* (3), 207–212.

—— 1983b, On the distinctions of item learning versus system learning and receptive competence versus productive competence in relation to the role of L1 in foreign language learning. In H. Ringbom (ed.), *Psycholinguistics and Foreign Language Learning. Papers from a Conference held in Stockholm and Åbo, October 25–26, 1982. Publications of the Research Institute of the Åbo Akademi Foundation 86,* 163–173. Åbo: Åbo Akademi.

—— 1985b, The influence of the Swedish on the English of Finnish learners. *Foreign Language Learning and Bilingualism. Publications of the Research Institute of the Åbo Akademi Foundation 105,* 39–71. Åbo: Åbo Akademi.

—— 1985c, Word frequencies in Finnish and Finland–Swedish learner language. *Foreign Language Learning and Bilingualism. Publications of the Research Institute of the Åbo Akademi Foundation 105,* 23–37. Åbo: Åbo Akademi.

—— 1986, Crosslinguistic influence and the foreign language learning process. In E. Kellerman & M. Sharwood Smith (eds), *Crosslinguistic Influence in Second Language Acquisition.* Oxford: Pergamon Press, 150–162.

12 Input from Within: Utrecht Research into Cross-linguistic Influence in Formal Language Learning Environments

MICHAEL SHARWOOD SMITH

Introduction

This paper will discuss various aspects of research into the acquisition of English as a foreign language which has been carried out at the University of Utrecht where the underlying aim has been, in equal measure the gathering of data from learners at Dutch schools and universities and the development of a richer theoretical framework for further investigation.

Over the last ten years, the department of English has been developing a programme of training and research into second language acquisition specially adapted to meet the needs of faculty and students. Part of this has involved the creation of a corpus, or rather corpora, for more or less descriptive purposes, and part of it has been the exploration of links between second language acquisition and other theoretical disciplines in order to improve the theoretical underpinnings. The aim of this paper, then, is to give some idea of the work that has been done so far. In view of space limitations, there will be two areas of focus, namely syntax and what we call *cross-linguistic influence*. This means, for example, that work on lexical and phonological aspects will be ignored and likewise the studies on attitudes and motivation will not be touched on: cross-linguistic influence (CLI) confines the discussion to how language systems interact within the learner.

First, a brief mention will be made of the way research is carried out at the department of English at Utrecht. Then the theoretical work will be discussed and this will be followed by illustration from projects carried out within the last few years.

The Utrecht programme

The English Department is responsible for training some five hundred students at one time in English language and literature: English is the medium of instruction. The language side covers theoretical linguistics, second language acquisition studies and instruction in English. Second language acquisition is now an official line of study as distinct from linguistics and practical language training. It also means that, although students may do their final thesis (after four years) on an 'applied topic', that is, one having to do with the pedagogical side of second language research, the obligatory programme in second language acquisition is 'non-applied', that is to say, it focuses on the theoretical aspects alone and the links with other theoretical disciplines. A typical student graduating in second language acquisition will do obligatory courses in linguistics and second language acquisition and a set of optional applied and non-applied courses involving term papers some of which may be published in working paper form. He or she will then graduate by writing a master's thesis (*doktoraalscriptie*). Some theses may be linked with a faculty research programme: this is encouraged but not required of students.

One of the ways students may do research is by investigating the development of fellow students in lower years: in this way data are collected which are of use as experimental and theoretical training but which may also serve the applied purposes of the language instruction programme. The other side of the coin is the way in which the language instruction programme is organised to facilitate second language research. For example, students are required to do a certain limited number of tests carried out for research purposes as part of their normal language training. Also, the three-year writing programme is structured in such a way that a student undergoing instruction actually collects data for the research programme. As far as the student is concerned, these data are not collected primarily for research purposes but first and foremost as a means of promoting instructional feedback. What students actually do is extract errors plus surrounding explanatory context from their written compositions and enter these onto specially designed sheets. In this way, during the course they each effectively create an individualised corpus of their own errors. This corpus is then used for the purpose of improving their English and takes the place of generalised commentaries about the errors that that student's particular group has made on a given written assignment. When that particular course is completed the corpus is absorbed into the larger corpus of written English much of which has been computerised. This larger corpus is then used by staff and students doing research into second language acquisition. Oral data are also collected from the various interview and role play tests that students have to undergo and these are also used for research purposes. However, it should be said that, despite the availability of such corpus material, a reasonable number of students prefer to do their work outside the Department and over a hundred Dutch secondary schools have been visited by students for the purposes of investigation into various aspects of the acquisition of English in formal contexts.

In addition to the locally constructed corpora and the easy access to Dutch secondary schools, there are other advantages enjoyed by the Department including close links with other departments in the Netherlands (in particular in Nijmegen) and abroad, for example in Poland, Finland, and the Federal Republic of Germany. This allows for a certain measure of cooperation whereby, for instance, elicitation tests constructed in one place may be carried out in another. Also, the *Interlanguage Studies Bulletin* has been edited here from its inception as is its successor, *Second Language Research*. Furthermore, Utrecht is the venue for the LARS[1] series of symposia, which brings staff and students into direct contact with active researchers from abroad and this has all contributed to the development of a favourable environment for research.

The theoretical framework

Over the last three or four years, a general framework has been developed whereby links between second language research and theoretical linguistics have been exploited. A key aspect of this is the clear distinction made between acquisition in the sense of *development of knowledge over time* and those processes which have to do with the accessing and integration of knowledge during performance at a given moment in time. One important stimulus for this explicit distinction has been the general dissatisfaction with the notion of acquisition as used by researchers such as Krashen (see Dulay, Burt, & Krashen, 1982) where the distinction is not paid much more than lip service. Consideration of the work in theoretical linguistics following Chomsky, where competence is distinct from performance mechanisms, as well as consideration of the theoretical line of research developed by Ellen Bialystok where she has made qualitative distinctions within the general notions of *proficiency* (see for example Bialystok, 1981) has led to the adoption of the competence/control model of acquisition. This framework combined the knowledge/control distinction of Bialystok's (see Bialystok & Sharwood Smith, 1985) and the competence/performance distinction familiar from generative grammar. We find the reworking of knowledge and control into a form that is compatible with a particular school of theoretical linguistic research a fruitful basis for refining quite a number of well-worn concepts such as *acquisition* and *transfer*. This may be effected in such a way as to draw on the precise tools developed over the years by linguists in that particular tradition. It also has the effect of facilitating much more linguistically sophisticated accounts of the structures investigated as will be illustrated in a moment. More generally, qualitative distinctions within such general concepts as *acquisition* allow for the creation of specific measurement techniques so that certain elicitation devices can focus on the intuitions and assumptions a given learner has about the target language; while others can test to the limit the control which that learner has over that (interlanguage) *knowledge* both in reception and production, that is, by increasing task stress. Clearly there are a number of objections that one might have to any particular set of theoretical assumptions and claims but it seems that, at a practical level, research can proceed much more systematically and fruitfully if more time is taken from data gathering and devoted instead to enriching the theoretical base so that 'facts' gleaned from corpora can be incorporated into a reasoned account of processes that are going on. If that particular theoretical base can interface with a substantial and coherent body of research from a related discipline then it has a headstart on theoretical bases that are developed in relative isolation from other disciplines. The Chomskyan framework does allow such an interface and this is why we find it attractive.

To turn now specifically to the notion of *cross-linguistic influence* (CLI), which embodies various, frequently loosely employed concepts such as *transfer* and *interference* (see Kellerman & Sharwood Smith, 1988), several distinctions can now be made within the competence/control model. For example, we may ask ourselves to what degree apparent interference from L1 on L2 (or vice versa in cases of language attrition) may be attributed to a genuine divergence of the learner competence from native-speaker norms rather than to immature control over competence.

Crudely put, is it the case that the learner 'knows it but can't show it' or is it the case that the learner simply does not 'know it' (knowledge here being used in the more commonly employed sense of native speaker or *target* competence)? Where the language learner does have the relevant type of competence but still has insufficient control over it, it is then hypothesised that he or she recruits native language (or other) competence to achieve whatever communicative goal he or she had in mind. CLI here would be the result of a control strategy. On the other hand, learners in this model may actually construct mental representations of the target language (that is, interim or interlanguage competence) on the basis of their own native language system. In this case, we would talk of CLI at the level of competence, and we would expect that elicitation devices designed to tap intuitions and assumptions would bear this out. CLI at the competence level may be seen as *input from within* since the developing L2 grammar is constructed on the basis of an interaction between input and inbuilt acquisitional mechanisms that we all possess. These mechanisms feed not only on information from *outside*, that is, exposure to primary language data, but also on information from what the learner already possesses, for example, L1 competence. This reflects an enduring adherence to a cognitive view of language transfer characteristics of European thinking especially. More specifically, the generative (Chomskyan) dimension of the notion of competence used here allows a more subtle analysis of how a learner might exploit familiar linguistic knowledge in building up target language knowledge. For example, the surface structure of a Dutch declarative main clause may be SVO (Subject–Verb–Object) as is the surface structure of an equivalent English clause. The production of (and acceptance of) SVO order by the learner in this instance may suggest conformity to English native speaker norms. However, if we accept that Dutch main clause order is actually derived from a different underlying order — SOV — as is accepted by most generative linguists, whereas English surface SVO order conforms to the underlying order, then we cannot assume that the Dutch learner's performance is a guarantee of attainment of native speaker norm competence (see van Berkel, 1987, for investigations into word order acquisition). The adoption of the competence/control model therefore requires a more sensitive examination of the learner's current state to establish with any degree of certainty whether he or she has properly reset what in Chomskyan terms could be called the word order parameter for English as underlying SVO. Thus it is that apparent (superficial) conformity with the native speaker norms as well as explicit deviance from the norms can both be relevant to the study of CLI at the level of competence.

Some people might object to the competence/control distinction by saying that it is a minor one and suggesting that what is 'known but not fully controlled' is simply a precursor of what is known *and* controlled. The implication is then that looking at spontaneous (well-controlled) behaviour is sufficient. This objection to looking at control separately can be countered by pointing to the phenomenon of U-shaped behaviour (see Kellerman, 1985; Kellerman & Sharwood Smith, 1988, for fuller discussion). Here, forms may appear in early learner performance and then give way to non-native forms at a later date. Hence the appropriate and apparently facile use of target forms is no guarantee that acquisition has come to a halt: future development might bring about divergence from the target in performance. U-shaped behaviour shows that forms may be only superficially target-like and have underlying them an analysis that is different from that of a native speaker using the same forms. Also, looking only at well-controlled structures might obscure certain acquisitional processes that remain at the level of competence and never really come to light in the learner's spontaneous language behaviour. In this way we would miss out on valuable information about the changing assumptions and intuitions learners have about the target system.

Some Utrecht studies

Adverbial placement

Since 1977 there have been a number of studies on adverbial placement ranging from minor pilot studies to a fairly large scale project involving research into the acquisition of this particular aspect of English by Finnish, Polish, French, German, as well as Dutch learners. The aim of this last project (see Bourgonje, Groot, & Sharwood Smith, 1985) was to test for common 'universal' patterns of development in the adverbial placement of learners of English coming from strikingly different language backgrounds. The stimulus for this was the work done by researchers following the Dulay, Burt, and Krashen approach which had focused mostly if not exclusively on fairly low-level morphological phenomena (following work in child language by Roger Brown, and others), on beginners and on learners acquiring the language in an English-speaking environment. The idea was that adverbial placement was such an 'unruly' area (cf. Jackendoff, 1972) that even learners in a formal environment receiving traditional instruction in the form of rules and other metalinguistic devices would have in this case to rely mainly upon exposure to the target language for their intuitions about adverbs, and in particular about the normal, canonical positions in English. This might manifest itself, it was hypothesised, in the form of some common patterns of development. However, research findings using acceptability judgement tasks and tasks involving actual positioning of given adverbs in various contexts showed that learners did seem to recruit native language knowledge even at a very advanced level. For example, Finnish learners tended to prefer post-verb positions where Polish learners preferred pre-verb positions. This agreed with native speaker informant information about the equivalent (canonical) placement behaviour in their own languages. This allowed us to conclude that where Poles (for example) correctly placed a particular adverb in a preverbal position it might still be regarded (potentially at least) as reflecting interlanguage competence and not as an indication of a full attainment of native speaker norms. It also allowed us to conclude that, although there was some evidence for a hierarchy of difficulty for given types of placement, for all learners, that is, irrespective of language background, there were quite striking differences in the interlanguage of the various language groups.

Not all language-specific trends could be easily explained. Of particular interest was a tendency shown in the Dutch and German data to place adverbs before the auxiliary as in '*I always must see him', a tendency that was also noticed in the Utrecht corpus of learner English. This tendency to place adverbs in what in English is either a marked or an unacceptable position suggests CLI since it was particularly noticeable in the Dutch and German learners, and Dutch and German are typologically related languages. The curious thing was that equivalent sentences in the L1 (in both cases) were also unacceptable so that direct 'transfer' could be ruled out. Some tentative explanations have been put forward (see Sharwood Smith, 1985), for example:

1. That the auxiliary/main verb distinction being less clear-cut in Dutch and German encouraged a simple pre-'verb' placement strategy with no distinction made for the type of verb involved.
2. That broad typological processes are at work whereby English is being treated as an SVO language, like Dutch and German.

In fact, English used to be SOV and Sven Jacobson has shown how, as English moved from SOV to SVO, the canonical position of the preverbal adverb moved from pre-auxiliary position to pre-main verb (post-auxiliary) position (see Jacobson, 1981). This more complex explanation would encourage the view that deviant adverbial placement might be an epiphenomenon, that is, an indication of some more basic distinction between the current learner grammar and that of a native speaker of the target language. Only a reasonably sophisticated examination of the theoretical linguistic implications of this (for example, implications concerning adjacent words and abstract case assignment) would allow light to be shed on this particular paradoxical example of CLI. What is quite evident at any rate is that adverbial placement is an area of fossilisation at a very advanced stage of acquisition. It is also an area which is highly sensitive to language attrition as another project carried out at Utrecht has shown (see Galbraith, 1982; Van Vlerken, 1980; Sharwood Smith, 1983). British and American children living in the Netherlands show a destabilisation of native speaker norms after a period of two years and this in a country where English is a prestige foreign language used by the population either receptively or productively to a much greater degree than is characteristic of a *foreign* as opposed to *second* language. Clearly, this area of grammar merits a great deal of further investigation.

Sentential complementation

There have also been a number of pilot studies into sentential complementation which have shown similar kinds of trends as were manifest in the adverbial projects, namely evidence of conformity to common patterns of development reported in other areas but also interesting language-specific trends suggesting CLI. The original impetus to this research was Janet Anderson's work on Spanish acquirers of English (Anderson, 1978) in which she claimed to have discovered a hierarchy of difficulty which suggested a universal pattern rather than one dictated by the structure of Spanish. For example, there was an overall tendency to prefer the *to*-infinitive over other constructions such as gerund or *that*-clauses. She had no overarching explanation for her findings except the speculation that structural complexity may have something to do with it since learners seem to prefer the short simple structures to the more complex one (she based her analysis of complexity on Lakoff, 1968). Studies by, for example, Bakker (1983), Polomska (1982) and Van Vugt & Van Helmond (1984) showed that Dutch learners also have an overall preference for the *to*-infinitive but that Anderson's economy principle did not seem to work as the short gerund proved typically to be acquired late, as opposed to the longer *that*-construction. Since Dutch has the equivalent of the latter but not the former, it would seem that CLI is the most likely explanation here. This area, like adverbials also proves to be partially inaccessible to many advanced learners and many tend to overextend the use of the *to*-infinitive more than other constructions beyond the limits imposed by the target norms. Van Vugt & Van Helmond (1984) using a competence/control-based design for their study (like Bakker, 1983) found that third year students at the Department (that is, after two or three years of instruction and intensive exposure to written and spoken English) showed no real advance over first year students in their control of sentential complementation. There was, however, some advance in the Acceptability Judgement Test, which was designed to tap competence more directly. In other words, within the theoretical framework sketched above, some acquisition had taken place at the level of competence but was not evident at the level of fluent control.

Preposition stranding

The most recent project started at Utrecht involves a direct application of Chomsky's *government-binding* theory to the acquisition of the phenomenon known as *preposition-stranding*, that is to say, the failure to move a preposition with its complement NP to initial position in question and relative constructions. Linguists generally argue that if a language is prepositional it is more likely not to require that prepositions should be moved with the NP. This would make, for example, a sentence like '*On* what am I sitting?' more 'normal', that is, unmarked, than what is actually more common within English itself, 'What am I sitting *on?*'. In fact, a normal prepositional language would rule out the second version. In Chomsky's terms this has to be translated into learnability terms in the following way: children exposed to data from a language containing prepositions will assume that, unless there is violation of this assumption in the data (and they perceive it), prepositions should move and not be left stranded at the end of the sentence/clause. In other words, when learning languages like French and Polish, where stranding is ruled out, they will not need to have positive confirmation that this is what they should do. Ignoring the way this inbuilt preference is explained in the theory (in terms of principles of grammar like *subjacency* and the *empty category principle*, cf. Van Buren & Sharwood Smith, 1985), it is interesting to speculate whether this notion of markedness has any effect on the rate and order of acquisition. Is it easier, for example, for Spanish learners of English to acquire the marked structure or is it more difficult? And what happens with English learners of Spanish? There have been claims in the literature on either side. Mazurkewich (1984) maintains that markedness equals acquisitional difficulty whereas White (1983) claims that the L1 will dictate the preference, that is, she favours a CLI-based approach. The Dutch–English case is interesting because both are in some sense marked languages. Both strand prepositions but whereas English strands more generally, Dutch only strands where the relevant NP is an *R-pronoun* (cf. Van Riemsdijk, 1978) for example, *waar, daar, er*. Will the initial assumption of the Dutch learner of English be influenced by markedness considerations in that he or she will start by refusing to strand; or will that learner impose (marked) Dutch structure on English and accordingly strand selectively, identifying some equivalent of R-pronouns in English, that is, *what . . . on (waar . . . . op)*; or thirdly, will the learner treat English as a less complicated language and readily strand 'promiscuously' so to speak and thus chance on something like the target norms at an early stage of development? These and many other questions spring from a consideration of the linguistic and learnability issues as applied to second language learning and the project is in too early a state itself to provide anything more than intriguing puzzles. But findings to date certainly suggest, at least in some learners, an attempt to impose Dutch structure on English. Since the processes dictating stranding are fairly subtle we may suspect that formal instruction can have little to do with their behaviour and that, again, mainly subconscious and theoretically interesting processes are at work (for further discussion see Van Buren & Sharwood Smith, 1985).

Conclusion

To conclude, there have been three main general truths that have become clear to us in Utrecht as a result of our investigations so far. The first is that cross-linguistic influence is a highly complex phenomenon and not at all as presented in simple accounts of interference or transfer familiar from work in the seventies. Second, a richer theoretical basis for examining CLI (amongst other aspects of acquisition) is not a luxury but an absolute necessity, and thirdly, that the enrichment must certainly involve the more direct application of the work carried out recently in the area of theoretical linguistics. In the process of discovering or confirming these truths, we have, like our colleagues in some of the other European centres, gathered some interesting data on the acquisition of English by advanced learners. We have also seen how a language department can function to serve the ends of research so that educational concerns are not neglected. At the same time, we have also come to the certain knowledge that if second language studies are ever going to properly serve applied ends, they will need to develop separately and not be required at every step to justify themselves in practical terms.

Note to Chapter 12

1. Language Acquisition Research Symposium (in the University of Utrecht)

References

ANDERSON, J., 1978, Order of difficulty in adult second language acquisition. In W.C. RITCHIE (ed.), *Second Language Acquisition Research: Issues and Implications*. New York: Academic Press, 91–108.
BAKKER, C., 1983, *The Economy Principle in the Production of Sentential Verb*

Complements. Unpublished master's dissertation, University of Utrecht.

BIALYSTOK, E., 1981, The role of linguistic knowledge in second language use. *Studies in Second Language Acquisition 4*, 31–45.

BIALYSTOK, E. & SHARWOOD SMITH, M., 1985, Interlanguage is not a state of mind: an evaluation of the construct for second language acquisition. *Applied Linguistics 6* (2), 101–117.

BOURGONJE, B., GROOT, P. & SHARWOOD SMITH, M., 1985, The acquisition of adverbial placement in English as a foreign language: a crosslinguistic study. *Interlanguage Studies Bulletin 8* (2), 93–103.

DULAY, H., BURT, M. & KRASHEN, S., 1982, *Language Two*. Oxford: Oxford University Press.

GALBRAITH, N., 1982, *A Study of Language Transfer in Language Loss*. Unpublished master's dissertation, University of Utrecht.

JACKENDOFF, R., 1972, *Semantic Interpretation in Generative Grammar*. Cambridge, MA: MIT Press.

JACOBSON, S., 1981, *Preverbal Adverbs and Auxiliaries*. Stockholm: Almquist & Wiksell.

KELLERMAN, E. 1985, The empirical evidence for the existence of L1 in interlanguage. In A. DAVIES, C. CRIPER & A. HOWATT (eds), *Interlanguage*. Edinburgh: Edinburgh University Press, 98–129.

KELLERMAN, E. & SHARWOOD SMITH, M., 1988, The interpretation of second language output. In H.W. DECHERT & M. RAUPACH (eds), *Transfer in Language Production*. Norwood, NJ: Ablex, 217–235.

LAKOFF, R., 1968, *Abstract Syntax and Latin Complementation*. Cambridge, MA: MIT Press.

MAZURKEWICH, I., 1984, The acquisition of dative alternation by second language learners and linguistic theory. *Language Learning 34*, 91–109.

POLOMSKA, M., 1982, *Preference and Deviance in the Choice of Sentential Complements by Dutch Speakers of English*. M.A. Working Paper. University of Utrecht.

SHARWOOD SMITH, M., 1983, On first language loss in the second language acquirer: problems of transfer. In S. GASS & L. SELINKER (eds), *Language Transfer in Language Learning*. Rowley, MA: Newbury House, 222–231.

—— 1985, From input to intake: On argumentation in second language acquisition. In S. GASS & C. MADDEN (eds), *Input in Second Language Acquisition*. Rowley, MA: Newbury House, 394–403.

VAN BUREN, P. & SHARWOOD SMITH, M., 1985, The acquisition of preposition-stranding by second language learners and parametric variation. *Second Language Research 1* (1), 18–46.

VAN RIEMSDIJK, H., 1978, *A Case Study in Syntactic Markedness*. Lisse: Peter de Ridder Press.

VAN VLERKEN, M., 1980, *Adverbial Placement in English: a Study of First Language Loss*. Unpublished master's dissertation, University of Utrecht.

VAN VUGT, M. & VAN HELMOND, K., 1984, *An Investigation into the Production of Sentential Verb Complements by Advanced Learners of English in an EFL Situation*. Unpublished M.A. Working Paper, University of Utrecht.

WHITE, L., 1983, Markedness and parameter setting: Some implications for a theory of adult second language acquisition. *McGill Journal of Linguistics 11*, 1–21.

13 Language Contact and Culture Contact: Towards an Integrative Approach in Second Language Acquisition Research

ELS OKSAAR

Introduction

The development of second language acquisition (SLA) research in the last decades has led to a change of paradigm. Whereas in the past the research interest in SLA was more focused on the language itself and on the teacher, there has been a shift of attention to a more learner-centred view. This results in an increasing concern in the learner's interlanguage and in his communicative competence.

How the second language is acquired is the subject of a number of hypotheses: the Contrastive Hypothesis, the Identity Hypothesis, the Input Hypothesis, the Pidginisation Hypothesis, and so forth.

However, untested hypotheses are not infrequently raised to the level of a fact as, for example, Krashen's Monitor Model (see Bausch & Kasper, 1979; Van Els et al., 1984; Lightbown, 1985). This is a methodological error that handicaps both research and practice.

On the other hand it should not be forgotten that galvanisation of the research scene is useful as it may stipulate a discussion on second language acquisition in which not the model but the human being is central. An individual-centred approach to language acquisition and language teaching is indeed difficult, but it is more realistic than a theoretical model approach (Oksaar, 1984; Hüllen, 1984).

An interesting parallel can be found in the development of contact linguistics, a not unimportant field in second language research. We find in recent decades a series of important recognitions and attempts at typologisations. However, construction of models, which is relevant for theoretical as well as for applied linguistics, does not show the same progress in discovery. More attention is paid to the transfer of linguistic forms and meanings than to other communicative constituents modifying or replacing them. The important issue of the transfer of sociocultural norms and patterns of interaction, too, belongs to an area which is still in its infancy, though the necessity of including these aspects has already been stressed in the seventies (Oksaar, 1975b).

The aim of this article is to widen the communication-oriented perspective to SLA research through the integrative approach of verbal and other elements of which a learner has to have command when interacting in SL. This brings us to the cultureme theory and the central role of *culturemes* and *behavioremes* in SLA research, which we are going to discuss on the background of *interactional competence* and two new congruences: pragmatic and semiotic.

The empirical foundation of my analysis derives from our Hamburg long term project: the Bilingual Language Behaviour Project (twelve years) in Australia, USA, Canada, and Sweden, completed in 1980 and the current, ten-year Multilingual Language Acquisition Project, involving children growing up with two, three or four languages.

The following facts should be emphasised as premises for our analysis. Language use in face-to-face interaction takes place in the ecological near milieu of people, in which not only linguistic, but also culturally conditioned behavioural rules are valid, which call forth and regulate situationally conditioned behavioural patterns — both for the learner and for the teacher. Traditional linguistic models and analysis instruments are not sufficient to describe a person's code switching, situational interference, his violations of pragmatic and semiotic congruence, or to understand their functions and signal values.

As language is part of a culture and at the same time a medium to describe culture, there are language as well as culture contacts. But the medium of these contacts is the acting individual, who not only takes part in languages and cultures, but is also creative in both of them. Which factors influence his or her interactional competence? How do communicative misunderstandings arise?

The problem of integration

An *integrative approach* to language contact has to pay attention to the fact that language as a means of expression and communication is more complex in its spoken than its written form, because it involves and is connected with more information carriers than the verbal ones.

First: spoken language is never existent without paralinguistic elements. Their role, however, in colouring the message in certain ways is often differently conditioned by different cultural systems (Hayes, 1972).

Second: spoken language is connected with nonverbal and extraverbal signals. Hayes (1972: 145) turns our attention to the fact: 'If these signals, differently conditioned by every cultural system, with different effects on the linguistic system, are not properly received and sent, communication is impeded'.

The necessity of an integrative approach is obvious when we are interested in language use. An integrative approach starts from the principle of the part–whole relationship in language and culture and does not isolate the verbal means of expression from other semiotic ones such as paralinguistic, nonverbal and extraverbal means of communication. Its basic unit is the *communicative act* (Oksaar, 1975a), in which the interactional competence of a speaker/hearer is realised. The communicative act, which is the whole frame of action in which the speech activity takes place, includes interactions with all communicative elements. The communicative act is embedded in situations and creates situations itself, changes the original ones and so forth. Among the most important elements of communicative acts are:

1. Partner/audience. (Here, of course, distinctions must be made according to the age and other social variables of the partner)
2. Theme/themes.
3. Verbal elements.
4. Paralinguistic elements: intonation, stress, and voice inflection.
5. Nonverbal (kinesic) elements: gaze, gesture, and other body language signs.
6. Extraverbal elements: proxemic elements, temporal signals.
7. The totality of emotional and affective elements of behaviour.

As to nonverbal elements, though their meaning must be viewed contextually, they do have stereotyped aspects, for example, hand-wave, bow, headshake, nod in various culture contexts. Malinowski (1935: 26) points to the integral role of gesture in speech as 'quite important for our understanding of an utterance as the one or two significant movements or indications which actually replace an uttered word'.

Contrary to the speech act of Austin and Searle, the communicative act has the advantage of retaining both sender and receiver relatedness in communication and the communicative elements. The speech act theory is too one-sidedly sender-related, the verbal units dominate and other components of the communicative act have not been taken into consideration.

What we actually observe in face-to-face interaction are elements of the communicative act that belong to the interactional competence of a person. The parameter *interactional competence* (Oksaar, 1977) can be defined as the ability of a person, in interactional situations, to perform and interpret verbal, paralinguistic, nonverbal and extraverbal communicative actions, according to the sociocultural and sociopsychological rules of the group. It has been necessary to differentiate the concept of *communicative competence* of Hymes (1967), in order to get a parameter for face-to-face interaction only.[1] Interactional competence, thus, is part of the communicative competence. It stresses the fact that communicative abilities can be divided not only into verbal, nonverbal and extraverbal components, but also into actional and nonactional, as one can also communicate by silence. This parameter is more differentiated than other concepts which followed later, for example Schmidt & Richards' (1980) *pragmatic competence*, used as a synonym for communicative competence in Hymes's sense. The term pragmatic competence is also used by Thomas (1983: 92) for 'the ability to use language effectively in order to achieve a specific purpose and to understand language in context'. The concept *social competence* (Bell, 1976), too, is not concrete enough. It refers to a competence housing social functions of linguistic forms. Also the descriptive model of communicative competence by Canale & Swain (1980) is not sufficient to cover the interactional components of the communicative act.

Gumperz (1984: 280) suggests redefining the notion of communicative competence as: 'The knowledge of discourse processing conventions and related communicative norms that participants must control as a precondition to being able to enlist and sustain conversational cooperation'. However, neither he nor the other authors mentioned refer to the concept of the more concrete interactional competence, which, together with the communicative act, enables us to analyse interaction in a wider semiotic context and more realistically than the models of communicative competence referred to. It not only combines verbal elements with kinesic and other communicative components but also makes it possible to focus on the reasons which favour interactional understanding or cause misunderstandings. The focus is on the components of the communicative act. In this sociocultural behaviour patterns in respect to another person are realised. They form a central area in the interactional competence, because they may send information before the verbal channel is activated or together with it.

The cultureme model

Sociocultural behaviour patterns can be systematised by the *cultureme model* (Oksaar, 1979, 1983). Its units are the culturemes: that people greet each other, that somebody addresses a person, thanks him or her, asks for something, chooses appropriate topics, and so forth, according to situational demands. Culturemes are realised through behavioremes, which may be verbal, paralinguistic and/or nonverbal, and/or extraverbal.[2] This means that in a given society we can empirically determine certain of the behaviour patterns of our fellows and the way these patterns convey messages. However, there are differences in the realisation of the culturemes already in one language community, which affects the contact situation even more.

Let us consider the realisation of the politeness cultureme *greeting* in German and some other languages. What behavioremes are important?

Verbal behavioremes

As has been shown in Oksaar (1983), the choice of the verbal behavioreme depends on time and social variables.

1. *Time variables*: There are two types of time to consider: time as part of the day and time as part of the contact period. In the initial phase of contact *guten Tag (good day)* is used, or, corresponding to the time of day *guten Morgen (good morning)* or *guten Abend (good evening)*. There is no equivalent for the English *good afternoon. Gute Nacht (good night)*, however, is used only in the concluding phase of the contact, as well as *auf Wiedersehen (hoping to see you again)*. The expressions of the initial phase, then, are more time-bound than phase-bound. That means that their usage allows deviations from the rule of fixed position; however, they are not generally common as greetings for leave-taking. In English one has to observe other aspects of the contact. Raith (1985: 174) points out that 'in English one distinguishes whether a contact takes place for the first time or not ("How do you do?" vs. "How are you?"); in English one differentiates between a shorter and longer separation ("Bye, bye" vs. "good bye")'.

2. *Social variables*: age, gender, social relationship, status, and role. Depending on the degree of formality, there is in German a scale from informal *Tag*, or *hallo* between friends to the more formal *guten Tag, Frau Müller* and still more formal *guten Tag, Frau Professor* or *Frau Professor + name*. That the more formal

behavioreme is filled also by the title and name bears witness to the sensibility to social relations. In English, the addressee of the greeting is also verbalised by social status and name: *good morning, Mrs Smith*, in French, by her status only: *bonjour, Madame*, in Swedish without any social signals: *goddag*. In Hungarian the situation is more complicated. Balazs (1985: 171) points to the fact that despite all efforts at democratisation 'Hungarian men still greet women with *kezét csókolom* [. . . (I) kiss (your) hand], while *csókolom* represents a shorter and more intimate form. A respected housewife would still consider a simple *jó nopot* [. . . good day] as an insult . . . since today only cleaning women or similar persons are greeted this way. The expanded form *jó napot kivánok* [. . . I wish you a good day], especially when the appropriate form of address is added, sounds much better, or still fairly reserved'.

Different social relationships can be marked by various behavioremes in the same greeting situation. The age of the actor plays an important role in the example that Balazs (1985) gives for the Hungarian behavioremes:

It can happen . . . that an elderly man encounters several people on the stairs at the same time. To the wife of his neighbour he says *kezét csókolom* [. . . (I) kiss (your) hand], to the concièrge *jo napot (kivánok)*, [. . . good day], to his neighbour *szervusz* or *szevasz* and to the son of his neighbour *szia*.

Szervusz is the simplified form of the Latin greeting formula *servus humillimus (your humble/devoted servant)* and is used 'only by equals who use the T-form or by older persons when greeting younger ones' (p. 171).

Paralinguistic behavioremes

In British English *good day, good morning, good afternoon, good evening* are often used with a falling intonation when meeting somebody, and with a raising intonation as farewell greeting. In German, too, paralinguistic factors may signal the beginning or the end of contact; however, as a rule, a falling intonation signals farewell. Raising intonation in *guten Tag* usually signals more than just fulfilment of a politeness norm — a wish to start a conversation, positive feelings, and so forth.

Nonverbal behavioremes

In German, interactional competence includes, with respect to nonverbal behaviour, the observance of variables of actions: handshake, bow, nod, hat-tipping, and so forth. Should every greeting be accompanied by a handshake, or not? If the partner is not in a hurry, a handshake is an expected part of the act of greeting. In English culture and in Sweden a handshake is obligatory only when meeting for the first time. In Eastern and Arabic countries, embracing and kisses on cheeks are customary, in South-East Asia various types of bowing. According to Dodd (1982: 219) Americans, when saying *hello*, use 'a greeting gesture such as the palm . . . extended outward with the fingers pointing upward, in the manner of waving, moving the palm from side to side'. And: 'as they say goodbye, North Americans place the palm of the right hand down, extend the fingers, and move the fingers up and down. In India, West Africa, and Central America such a gesture would imply beckoning, as if you were calling a cab or asking someone to move toward you'.

Extraverbal behavioremes

In German, interactional competence includes with respect to extraverbal behaviour, observance of variables in time and space, as well as social variables, their combinations and actions.

1. The combination of time and social variables in the initial phase demands an answer to the question: Who should greet first? The younger person or the older one? The man or the woman? In the hierarchy, the lower or the more elevated? Whereas in Germany and in Sweden the younger and the lower in hierarchy is supposed to greet first, this rule is broken in case of gender: the man has to greet first, the place having no significance. In England, however, the case may be that the woman greets a man first, when meeting him in the street and in public places: the place is an important factor.
2. The combination of time and space variables include who must always greet first, when and where. In Germany, one is supposed to greet when entering a room, even a doctor's waiting room; the latter would not be done in Sweden.

Situational interference

Already on the basis of these considerations it is obvious that deviations from behavioremes conditioned by the situation can lead to misunderstandings in intra- as well as interlinguistic contact situations. These can be due to the influence from L1 and C1. The notion of *interference* has been used for deviations from the norms of one language — concerning verbal means — through the influence of another. However, it cannot count for deviations caused by the influence of the pragmatic norms of the situation. When a Swede in Germany is using German *Du* addressing somebody when the politeness pronoun *Sie* is prescribed by the pragmatic norms, it is not simply a deviation from the linguistic norms of L2, but from the sociocultural norms of C2, caused by C1, the Swedish norms. It has, therefore, been necessary to differentiate the concept of interference and distinguish between *linguistic* and *situational interferences* (Oksaar, 1975b).

Situational interferences are deviations from the pragmatic conventions of the situations in which the communicative act takes place, arising through the influence of the behaviour patterns of another group or community in corresponding situations. There are different situational norms on which speakers/listeners base their expectations of how others should behave. Situational interferences cover production and interpretation of messages.

In using the cultureme model with its various kinds of behavioremes, we are able to analyse situational interferences on a rather concrete level. By doing so, we may explain culturally patterned behaviour in a considerably wider area than has been done, because behavioremes may be found in any channel and not only in the verbal one.

Some examples

In the following I shall discuss a number of culturemes, the behavioremes of which may easily lead to situational interferences, because there are great differences in various cultures. Language learners have to learn what signals to look for, contact linguists may show which communicative results situational interferences may lead to. Thus, the question is not only why, from the point of the native speaker, a non-appropriate communicative act takes place, but also what effect it can have on the act and on the relation between the interactants.

We shall first look at the cultural signals which may be important *before* the verbal and kinesic messages are sent.

There is, first, the question of the amount of coded information, according to various situations. Hall (1977: 91–92) speaks of high-context (HC) messages and low-context (LC) ones seeing the first at one end and the other at the other end of the continuum: 'A high-context communication or message is one in which most of the information is either in the physical context or internalised in the person, while very little is in the coded, explicit, transmitted part of the message'. For Hall a low-context communication is just the opposite: 'The mass of the information is vested in the explicit code' (pp. 105–106). It is true that no culture is totally HC or LC, but while the Chinese, Japanese, people of the Middle East, the French, Spanish, and Italians belong to the high context people, Americans and Europeans like the Germans, Swiss, and Scandinavians belong to the low context group (Hall & Hall, 1983). Of course, there are great individual differences in every culture concerning the context, but as a rule, there may be conflicts, when high context people meet with low context people. 'High context people are apt to become impatient and irritated when low context people give them information they don't need' (Hall & Hall, 1983: 28). On the other side, they assume that the listener knows what their real matter is in a communicative act, and therefore they very often only give hints.

If one looks at the behavioremes through an extended version of the classic formula of Lasswell, asking: who signals/interprets what, how, when, where, why, and with what effect, one finds a great variety of possibilities also in the area of one common language.

Before one starts speaking, the partner may have expectations about the structure of the conversation. Their existence becomes evident when they are not fulfilled, as the following American–French contact situation illustrates. The former Secretary of State Henry Kissinger writes about his meeting with de Gaulle: 'At the end of the dinner at the Elisée . . . an aide told me that the General wished to see me. Without the slightest attempt to small talk de Gaulle greeted me with the query: "Why don't you get out of Vietnam?"' (1979:109–110). Kissinger must have awaited small talk, which would have been the case in a corresponding situation in the USA. He must have had a lot of nonverbal and extraverbal signals that made him conclude: 'The General considered Presidential Assistants as functionaries whose views should be solicited only to enable the principals to establish some technical point; he did not treat them as autonomous entities' (p. 109).

The handling of time and the attitudes towards time are important extralinguistic factors in interactional competence. Let us look at the norms of punctuality. In Sweden, absolute punctuality is expected, in private as well as in official circumstances; it is in many situations even welcome if one comes a few minutes before the time. In Germany, when one is invited to dinner at 7 p.m., the norms of politeness do not demand absolute punctuality; however, as is customary in other circumstances, for example at universities, the *academic quarter* (arriving a quarter past the hour) is expected. In Latin America, what is called punctuality in many situations implies a much later arrival than even that expected in Germany. Differences in this area can influence a communicative act before it really starts.

The communication process itself can be influenced by differences using the time in common. Here, three factors are important: to know the time when to talk, how much to talk, and how much time to allot to pauses. There are great individual and cultural differences. These differences can be noticed already in Europe, between Scandinavians and Germans, for instance. Scandinavians, especially Finns, make longer pauses than Germans and do not verbalise everything at once during communication. Like Turks and Japanese, they are aware of the fact that the listener knows that their silence is active, a thinking silence. Germans, however, have many more signals, including verbal ones, while listening. This can be irritating for a Finn or Swede. Germans, on the other hand, characterise them as slow and not easy to talk to. As a matter of fact, Scandinavians are not bound to small talk. This may complicate their conversation especially with Americans for whom small talk has an important function in a communicative act.

An instructive approach to systematise the time factor has been made by Hall (1959) and Hall & Hall (1983). They differentiate between monochronic and polychronic time. 'Monochronic time (M-time) means doing one thing a time. Polychronic time (P-time) means doing many things at once' (1983: 22). It is evident that there must be great differences in the degree of these systems. M-time people have time scheduled, they have to learn to concentrate on one thing at a time. In P-time culture many things are occurring simultaneously, 'appointments are apt to mean very little and may be shifted around at the last minute. . . . Since promptness means little to the polychronic person, their failure to be punctual can be stressful for someone from a monochronic culture. And if the polychronic person does not telephone to explain his tardiness, monochronic people may take offence' (1983: 23).

To sum up so far: based on which sociocultural group the speaker/ hearer belongs to, there are different situational norms, on which he bases his expectations of how the other should behave, of what is expected of him and of how he himself should behave. We shall now consider a few cases of situational interference from the verbal and nonverbal area.

Verbal area. In Estonian, Finnish, and Swedish, one finds the cultureme *compliment*, just as in all other European languages and in American English. It is realised in approximately the same sort of situations. Compliments are used in the phatic function. From the point of view of the speaker they have social value establishing a positive relation to the hearer. They serve as a contact and dialogue initiation strategy. However, the reaction to a compliment is connected to various behaviour patterns. In the three language communities mentioned above compliments should be either declined, or at least very much weakened. For an object, this is accomplished by presenting the age, price, or origin of the object in such a way that the compliment appears not to be justified.

If Mrs X is told that she has a beautiful dress on, she can respond in three possible ways to express that this is not so: usually by emphasising, (a) its age (*Oh no, it's just an old thing!*), (b) its low price (*Oh no, it was very cheap!*), or (c) its origin of low prestige (*Oh no, it's just something I picked up in a sale* or *Oh no, it's just something I made myself!*). However, according to the norms in English speaking countries, it is expected that the receiver in such a situation thanks the speaker for the compliment. A situational interference arises when multilingual Estonians, Finns or Swedes in their corresponding native language thank someone for a compliment. These interferences may, however, also become parts of new conventions. It can be traced to the Anglo-Saxon influence, when a German thanks someone, in German, for a compliment. During this process of change in such behaviour patterns, misunderstandings may occur.

The result of a communicative misunderstanding or conflict is not always immediately evident. If, in a situation where the verbal realisation of the cultureme *thanking* is obligatory, a person does not behave according to this norm, the following consequences must be expected: his behaviour will be interpreted as a sign of impoliteness or arrogance or indifference, and this can have consequences for the communication which follows. Grammatical correctness need not correlate with communicative correctness and adequacy.

Choice of topic and manner of representation can also be mentioned in this context. In Europe, if a stranger asks personal questions, such as: 'Are you married?', 'How old are you?', 'How much do you earn?', or, referring to an object: 'How much did it cost?', he violates many norms of the communicative act, whereas in many Asian countries these questions are acceptable. The paralinguistic repertoire of representation is also subject to various norms: an interference arises, for example, when a Japanese in Germany gives someone a sad message with a smile.

Here, there is an interesting correlation between knowledge of a language and of the culture, from the standpoint of the receiver. The more competent a speaker is in a language, the better the hearer expects his cultural competence to be. Consequently, lack of control of cultureme realisation in a linguistically competent speaker will not be excused easily.

Nonverbal area. In German *danke* can be interpreted as *yes* as well as *no*, *thanks*, according to the situation. If a Greek means *no* and emphasises what he is saying by repeatedly moving his head up and down, this kineme may lead to a misunderstanding, since it can be interpreted as *nodding*, an expression of agreement, and therefore as *yes*. Here we see situational interference from a nonverbal part of the behavioreme, which means *no* for a Greek.

In a situation in which a visitor is offered something, for example a piece of cake, Estonian and Hungarian culturemes prescribe that, instead of accepting at once, the visitor declines. The offer is expected to be repeated at least once. German norms, on the other hand, prescribe a prompt decision. A deviation from this prompt decision, caused by interference from Estonian or Hungarian behavioremes, can have unfavourable results.

We can now establish a person-centred behavioural model of face-to-face interaction. This model represents a complex interactive process. It is, first of all, a nonverbal process in which the hearer receives signals from the speaker through various channels, such as the visual or auditive, before he or she is even spoken to. The speaker's way of looking, his or her facial expression, gestures, and clothing, for instance, are all factors which influence the hearer's attitude. This pre-phase forms part of the interpretation structure which may, however, change in the course of the actual conversation.

During such a conversation other factors may additionally influence the hearer. Deviations from the norms of prosody, such as pitch or volume, may already leave an impression on the hearer that the speaker is impolite, rude, or wily, or is accusing him of something. The other's tone of voice is generally interpreted according to one's own norms, even if one is patient with possible linguistic interference of foreigners. In this manner, prejudices may be deepened and stereotypes intensified. The meta-level of contact should be explored more carefully; however, this presupposes recognition of the problem.

The interaction of the elements of a communicative act can be represented by a congruence model. Understanding and misunderstanding depend on at least four congruences. Apart from the usual congruences, semantic and grammatical congruence, we must deal with *pragmatic* and *semiotic* congruence. I consider pragmatic congruence to be agreement between the contents of the verbal, paralinguistic, and nonverbal information carriers. Semiotic congruence points to agreement of behaviour patterns in time, space, and action. The entire communicative act must correspond to the norms of the situation.

Conclusion

In learning a new language you learn more about your mother tongue, too. Through studying foreign cultures one understands one's own. A language must be considered and taught as part of a larger entity — a culture. I would like to close this article with the following statement: the self-evident or obvious proves to be much less so if one proceeds from the individual and not from the language, because each learner brings his own creative characteristics to the learning and interacting process. We need a human linguistic approach for linguistic and culture-contact investigations and for effective SLA research.

Notes to Chapter 13

1. For discussion see Els Oksaar (1977: 138–141).
2. A different use of *cultureme* and *behavioreme* is found in Pike (1967).

References

BALAZS, J., 1985, Disturbances and misunderstanding in the use of address forms in Hungarian. In R.J. BRUNT & W. ENNINGER (eds), *Interdisciplinary Perspectives at Cross-cultural Communication*. Aachen: Rader, 163–172.
BAUSCH, K.-R. & KASPER, G., 1979, Der Zweitspracherwerb: Möglichkeiten und Grenzen der 'großen' Hypothesen. *Linguistische Berichte 64*, 3–35.
BELL, R.T., 1976, *Sociolinguistics*. London: Batsford.
BRUNT, R.J. & ENNINGER, W. (eds), 1985, *Interdisciplinary Perspectives at Cross-cultural Communication*. Aachen: Rader.
CANALE, M. & SWAIN, M., 1980, Theoretical bases of communicative approaches to second language teaching and testing. *Applied Linguistics 1*, 1–47.
DODD, C.H., 1982, *Dynamics of Intercultural Communication*. Dubuque, IA: William C. Brown.

GUMPERZ, J.J., 1984, Communicative competence revisited. In D. SCHIFFRIN (ed.), *Meaning, Form and Use of Context: Linguistic Applications*. Washington, DC: Georgetown University Press, 278–302.

HALL, E.T., 1959, *The Silent Language*. Garden City, NY: Anchor Press.

—— 1977, *Beyond Culture*. Garden City, NY: Anchor Press.

HALL, E.T. & HALL, M. REED, 1983, *Hidden Differences*. Hamburg: Stern.

HAYES, A.S., 1972, Paralinguistics and kinesics: Pedagogical perspectives. In T.A. SEBOEK, A.S. HAYES & M.C. BATESON (eds), *Approaches to Semiotics*. The Hague: Mouton, 145–172.

HÜLLEN, W., 1984, Text and tense. *LAUT-paper: Pedagogical English Grammar 14* (Series B 100/14). Trier: University of Trier, Linguistic Agency.

HYMES, D., 1967, Models of the interaction of language and social setting. *Journal of Social Issues 23* (2), 8–28.

KISSINGER, H., 1979, *White House Years*. Boston: Little, Brown & Company.

LIGHTBOWN, P.M., 1985, Great expectations: Second-language acquisition research and classroom teaching. *Applied Linguistics 6*, 173–189.

MALINOWSKI, B., 1935, *Coral Gardens and Their Magic*. London: Allen & Unwin.

OKSAAR, E., 1975a, Spracherwerb und Kindersprache: Pädolinguistische Perspektiven. *Zeitschrift für Pädagogik 21*, 719–743.

—— 1975b, A sociolinguistic analysis of bilingual behaviour in Sweden. In K.-H. DAHLSTEDT (ed.), *The Nordic Languages and Modern Linguistics 2*. Stockholm: Almqvist & Wiksell, 609–620.

—— 1977, *Spracherwerb im Vorschulalter: Einführung in die Pädolinguistik*. Stuttgart: Kohlhammer.

—— 1979, Zur Analyse der kommunikativen Akte. *Wirkendes Wort 29*, 391–404.

—— 1983, Multilingualism and multiculturalism from the linguist's point of view. In T. HUSÉN & S. OPPER (eds), *Multicultural and Multilingual Education in Immigrant Countries*. Oxford: Pergamon Press, 17–36.

—— 1984, Spracherwerb – Sprachkontakt – Sprachkonflikt im Lichte individuumzentrierter Forschung. In E. OKSAAR (ed.), *Spracherwerb – Sprachkontakt – Sprachkonflikt*. New York: De Gruyter, 243–266.

PIKE, K.L., 1967, *Language in Relation to a Unified Theory of the Structure of Human Behaviour*. The Hague: Mouton.

RAITH, J., 1985, Intercultural (mis-, non-) understanding, ethnography of communication, language teaching. In R.J. BRUNT & W. ENNINGER (eds), *Interdisciplinary Perspectives at Cross-cultural Communication*. Aachen: Rader, 173–188.

SCHMIDT, R.E. & RICHARDS, J.C., 1980, Speech acts and second language learning. *Applied Linguistics 1*, 129–157.

THOMAS, J., 1983, Cross-cultural pragmatic failure. *Applied Linguistics 4*, 91–112.

VAN ELS, T., BONGAERTS, T., EXTRA, G., VAN OS, C. & JANSSEN-VAN DIETEN, A.M. (eds), 1984, *Applied Linguistics and the Learning and Teaching of Foreign Languages*. London: Edward Arnold.

Biographical Data on Contributors

Danielle Bailly currently is Professor of Linguistics and Applied Linguistics at the Department of Linguistics, University of Lille III, France. She received her PhD from the Université Sorbonne in Paris. From 1959 to 1968 D. Bailly worked as Professeur agrégée d'enseignement secondaire in Toulouse and Paris, France. Between 1966 and 1968 she was Assistant Professor at the Sorbonne and from 1968 to 1985 Maître Assistant at the University of Paris VII. In 1985 she accepted to call to the University of Lille, France, Professor Bailly during her career has been associated with three national SLA research groups, the Commission Nationale d'Établissement des Programmes d'Enseignement des Langues Pour le Secondaire (= National Commission on Language Acquisition in Secondary Schools), the Commission des Grandes Ecoles, Groupe Langues Vivantes, and the Groupe de Recherches en Psycholinguistique, Université Paris (= the Psycholinguistic Research Group in the University of Paris VII).

Hans W. Dechert has been Professor in the Department of English and Romance Languages and Literatures in the University of Kassel, Federal Republic of Germany since 1972. In 1954 he received his PhD from the Johann-Wolfgang-Goethe-University in Frankfurt. He taught at Rutgers University, USA and the Justus-Liebig-University in Giessen. He was Chairman of his Department in the academic year 1978/79. Professor Dechert was in charge of the following international symposia at Kassel: Kassel Workshop on the Theory of Second-Language Acquisition (1976), Pausological Implications of Speech Production (1978), Psycholinguistic Models of Production (1980), Transfer in Production: A Psycholinguistic Approach (1982) and The Second International Congress of Applied Psycholinguistics (1987). At present H. Dechert is a Vice-President of the International Society of Applied Psycholinguistics. He has focused his research on temporal variables in speech and the psycholinguistics of second language speech production of advanced speakers of English and German within the Kassel Psycho- and Pragmalinguistic Research Group (KAPPA).

Rainer Dietrich is Professor in the Department of German as a Foreign Language in the Ruprecht-Karls-University Heidelberg, Federal Republic of Germany. As a graduate student he attended the University of Heidelberg and the University of Saarbrücken, where he obtained his PhD with a thesis on computational linguistics. In 1974 he received the *venia legendi* for Germanic and Applied Linguistics in the University of Heidelberg (Habilitation). From 1979 to 1981 he was chairman of the Department of Modern Languages in Heidelberg, between 1983 and 1985 Vice-President of the University. Professor Dietrich is on the editorial board of the journal *Linguistische Berichte*. He is especially known for his contributions to the European Science Foundation project on 'Second Language Acquisition of Adult Immigrants'. He was the chief co-ordinator of the German team in this project.

Werner Hüllen, at present Professor of Linguistics in the Department of Literature and Linguistics at the University of Essen, Federal Republic of Germany, received his PhD in the University of Cologne in 1951. In 1952/53 he was given a one-year appointment as lecturer at the University of Birmingham, England. In 1963 he accepted the position of Professor of Didactics of English Language and Literature in the Pädagogische Hochschule Rheinland (= Teachers' Training College Rheinland), which later became part of the University of Düsseldorf. From 1973 to 1977 he was Professor of Applied Linguistics/English and Didactics of the English Language at the University of Trier. In 1977 he was given a call as Professor of English Philology/Linguistics and Theory of Modern Language Teaching in the University of Essen. In the academic years 1970–72 and 1980–81 W. Hüllen acted as Chairman of his Department. During the summer term 1985 he lectured at the University of Vienna, Austria, as a Visiting Professor. In the late 70s and early 80s he was closely associated with a nationwide research project on the acquisition and teaching of foreign languages, initiated and sponsored by the German Research Council (Deutsche Forschungsgemeinschaft). Professor Hüllen has edited various readers and published numerous articles in dictionaries and professional journals.

Kenneth Hyltenstam is Associate Professor in the Department of Research on Bilingualism, Institute of Linguistics, University of Stockholm, Sweden. As a graduate student he attended the University of Lund, Sweden, and the University of Edinburgh, Scotland. He received his PhD from the University of Lund with a dissertation on 'Progress in immigrant Swedish syntax: a variability analysis' (1978). From 1978 to 1981 K. Hyltenstam was Assistant Professor of Linguistics at Lund. Professor Hyltenstam acted as President of ASLA, the Swedish Association of Applied Linguistics from 1979 to 1983. He has been the editor of the journal *Scandinavian Working Papers on Bilingualism* since 1982 and has published various articles in congress volumes and several papers in the journal, *Language Learning*, among others. At present, Professor Hyltenstam works on a larger project in the area of bilingualism in dementia.

Jaakko Lehtonen is Professor of Applied Linguistics and Speech at the University of Jyväskylä, Finland. He had his graduate training in the University of Jyväskylä and the University of Helsinki, and received his PhD from the University of Jyväskylä in 1970. From 1972 to 1984 he was Associate Professor of Phonetics at the University of Jyväskylä. Thereafter he was appointed Head of his Department. From 1975 to 1981 he also taught as a Docent of Phonetics at the University of Turku, Finland, and as a Docent of Applied Linguistics and Phonetics at the University of Tampere, Finland. In co-operation with K. Sajavaara he has been engaged in the Jyväskylä Cross-Language Research Project since 1975. Both of them are the co-editors of the Jyväskylä Cross-Language Studies.

Colette Noyau at present is a Maître de conférences (= Associate Professor) at the Institut d'Études Hispaniques (= Institute for Spanish Studies) of the University of Paris VIII, France. During her graduate studies she attended the Université Sorbonne, Paris, and received her PhD from the Université Paris IV. From 1966–1969 she participated in a research project of the Bureau pour l'Enseignement de la Langue et de la Civilisation Française à l'Étranger (= Office for the Teaching of French as a Second Language) in the Institut Pédagogique National, the French National Educational Institute in Paris.

Els Oksaar, Professor of General and Comparative Linguistics at the University of Hamburg, Federal Republic of Germany, received her PhD from the University of Stockholm in 1953 after graduate studies in Stockholm, Bonn and Hamburg. From 1958 to 1967 she was Associate Professor in the Germanic Department of the University of Stockholm, after having received the *venia legendi* in 1958 (Habilitation). She worked as a visiting scholar at the University of Hamburg as well as at the Australian National University at Canberra. Since 1967 E. Oksaar has been full Professor and Director of the Institute of General and Comparative Linguistics at the University of Hamburg and Head of the Research Center for Language Contact and Multilingualism. In 1979 she was Research Fellow of the Japan Society for the Promotion of Science in Tokyo. In 1987 she was appointed member of the Wissenschaftsrat of the Federal Republic of Germany. During the academic year 1987/88 she was a Fellow at the Institute for Advanced Study Berlin (Wissenschaftskolleg zu Berlin). Since 1979 she has been a member of the Finnish Academy of Sciences. In 1986 she was awarded an honorary PhD degree by the University of Helsinki, and in 1987 by the University of Linköping, Sweden. Professor Oksaar has been active in various national and international professional organisations. She was a founding member of the International Association for the Study of Child Language and held the office of President between 1975 and 1978. She is now a member of the Executive Committee. Between 1982 and 1985 she was a Vice-President of the International Society of Applied Psycholinguistics. From 1975 she has served as the President of the AILA Commission on Child Language. Professor Oksaar is co-editor of the journals *Zeitschrift für germanistische Linguistik, First Language, Indian Journal of Linguistics,* and *Semantische Hefte.* She has also been a member of the reading commission of the *Journal of Child Language.* From 1967 to 1979 Professor Oksaar was in charge of 'The Bilingual Language Behavior Project', assessing the language development of Estonians in Sweden, Australia, USA, and Canada, and of Germans in Sweden and Australia. She is the Director of the 'Hamburg Language Acquisition Project' and the comparative research project 'Identity and Language'.

Håkan Ringbom is Associate Professor in the Department of English at Åbo Akademi, the Swedish language university of Finland, Turku (Åbo). He received his PhD from Åbo Akademi with a dissertation on Old and Middle English poetry in 1968. In 1973 he published a monograph on the style of George Orwell's essays. H. Ringbom's main concern in applied linguistics and contrastive psycholinguistics in recent years has increasingly focused on the role of L1 in SLA. For about a decade he has led a research project, supported by the Academy of Finland, on the difference between Finns (the speakers of a non-Indo-European Finno-Ugrian language) and Swedish-speaking Finns (a Germanic language) acquiring English (another Germanic language). The results of this long-term study project have been published in the volume *The Role of the First Language in Foreign Language Learning* (Clevedon: Multilingual Matters, 1987).

Michael Sharwood Smith is currently Associate Professor in the Department of English, University of Utrecht, The Netherlands. After graduating at St. Andrews he worked in the British Centre in Sweden and, after graduate studies at the University of Edinburgh, at the Department of English, Adam Mickiewicz University, Poznań, Poland, from which he received his PhD.

He has participated in the Dutch project on 'Developmental Processes in Foreign Language Acquisition' in the Language Analysis and Language Education Programme and supervised the Dutch Pure Research Foundation project on 'Adverbial Placement in English as a Foreign Language'. He is the organiser of the LARS (Language Acquisition Research Symposia) at Utrecht. Professor Sharwood Smith is co-editor of the journal *Second Language Research*, the successor to the *Interlanguage Studies Bulletin*. His publications include various theoretical studies of second language acquisition.

Peter Skehan has been a Lecturer in Education, with special reference to English for speakers of other languages, at the Institute of Education, London University, Department of English for Speakers of Other Languages (ESOL) since 1982. As a graduate student he attended the University of Western Ontario, London, Ontario, Canada, where he received an MA degree in Psychology, and the University of Paris III, which he finished with a Maitrise in EFL. He received his PhD from London University, Birkbeck College in 1982 with a dissertation with the title *Memory and Motivation in Language Aptitude Testing*. From 1977 to 1982 he worked in the English Department, Birmingham University, England. Dr. Skehan is Director of the 'First and Foreign Language Learning Ability Comparison' research project which has been following up the children from the famous Gordon Wells' Bristol Language Study now that they are learning foreign languages in schools. Together with P. Meara, P. Skehan is general editor of the series 'Second Language Acquisition' published by Edward Arnold, London. His research has mainly dealt with language aptitude testing.

Renzo Titone is Professor of Educational Psycholinguistics and Head of the Department of Developmental Psychology at the University of Rome 'La Sapienza', Italy. He received his graduate training in Psychology at the Salesian University of Rome, Italy, and Fordham University, New York, USA. In 1947 he received his PhD from the Salesian University of Rome. From 1947 to 1950 he taught at Newton College, USA, from 1954 to 1969 at the Salesian University in Rome, from 1961 to 1969 at Georgetown University, Washington, DC, USA and from 1971 to 1972 at the Universities of Catania and Venice, Italy. From 1960 to 1966 he was Head of the Department of Didactics at the Salesian University, in 1972 Head of the Department of Language Didactics at the University of Venice, and since 1985 he has been Head of the Department of Developmental Psychology at the University of Rome. Professor Titone is the Director of the 'Early Bilingual Literacy Project', the 'Research on Metalinguistic Development Project', and the 'Intercultural and Interuniversity Programme' of the University of Rome. He is also the first President of TESOL Italy, the

President of the International Society of Applied Psycholinguistics, the Founder and Director of the Italian Centre for Applied Linguistics and the President of the Scientific Committee for the co-ordination of the FLES Project of the Italian Ministry of Education. Professor Titone is the founder and Editor-in-chief of the journals *Studies of Educational Psychology*, and *Rassegna Italiana di Linguistica Applicata* (= Italian Review of Applied Linguistics). He is the author of 77 books and 350 articles (written in or translated into Italian, English, French, Portuguese, Serbo-Croatian, and Russian) in numerous national and international journals.

Daniel Véronique at present is Assistant Professor at the Department of General and Applied Linguistics, Université de Provence, Aix-en-Provence, France. He attended the same university during his graduate studies, before he received his PhD with a dissertation on 'Analyse contrastive, analyse d'erreurs, une application de la linguistique à la didactique des langues II' (= Contrastive and error analysis: Linguistics applied to the didactics of second language acquisition) in 1983. From 1975 to 1986 Dr. Véronique worked as an assistant in the General and Applied Linguistics Department of his university. He is the Aix-en-Provence co-ordinator of the Groupe de Recherche sur l'Acquisition des Langues (GRAL) (= SLA Research Group) and has been associated with the ESF (European Science Foundation) research project in migrant workers' SLA. He is also a member of the Institut d'Etudes Creoles (= Institute of Creole Studies of the University of Provence). In addition to his various studies in SLA of adult immigrants in Europe, mainly from North Africa, his research has especially focused on pidginisation and creolisation. He has also studied the semantics and syntax of Mauritian creole.

List of Research Projects

Index